MW00780121

THE
KILLING
FIELDS
OF EAST
NEW YORK

STACY HORN

THE KILLING FIELDS OF EAST NEW YORK

The First Subprime Mortgage Scandal,
a White-Collar Crime Spree,
and the Collapse of an American Neighborhood

GILLIAN FLYNN BOOKS

A zando IMPRINT

NEW YORK

zando

Gillian Flynn Books is an imprint of Zando.
zandoprojects.com

First Edition: January 2025

Design by Neuwirth & Associates, Inc.
Cover design by Pete Garceau

The publisher does not have control over and is not responsible for author or other third-party websites (or their content).

Library of Congress Control Number: 2024941540

978-1-63893-122-5 (Hardcover)
978-1-63893-123-2 (ebook)

10 9 8 7 6 5 4 3 2 1
Manufactured in the United States of America

To our better angels:
Let's fix this.

The only genuine, long-range solution for what has happened lies in an attack—mounted at every level—upon the conditions that breed despair and violence. All of us know what those conditions are: ignorance, discrimination, slums, poverty, disease, not enough jobs. We should attack these conditions—not because we are frightened by conflict, but because we are fired by conscience. We should attack them because there is simply no other way to achieve a decent and orderly society in America.

—President Lyndon Johnson, July 27, 1967

Poverty is the only crime society cannot forgive.

—Journalist Junius Henri Browne, 1869

There are other types of crimes of rapidly growing prevalence that are not only menacing to society in and of themselves, but which can fan the flames of violent crimes by the poor and are, to an ever increasing degree, responsible for them.

—Robert M. Morgenthau, on white-collar crime, 1969

Mortgage fraud is bank robbery without a gun.

—Ann Fulmer, 2010

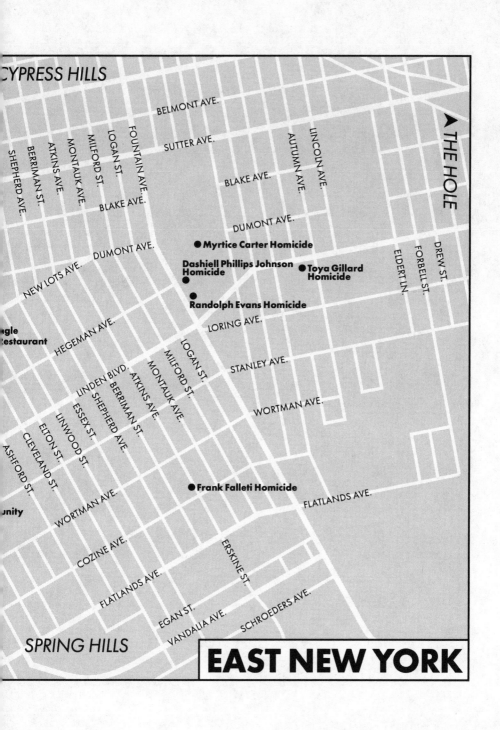

CYPRESS HILLS

THE HOLE

BELMONT AVE.

SUTTER AVE.

SHEPHERD AVE.
BERRIMAN ST.
ATKINS AVE.
MONTAUK AVE.
MILFORD ST.
LOGAN ST.
FOUNTAIN AVE.

BLAKE AVE.

AUTUMN AVE.
LINCOLN AVE.

BLAKE AVE.

DUMONT AVE.

● **Myrtice Carter Homicide**

DUMONT AVE.

NEW LOTS AVE.

Dashiell Phillips Johnson Homicide
●

● **Toya Gillard Homicide**

ELDERT LN.
FORBELL ST.
DREW ST.

● **Randolph Evans Homicide**

gle
Restaurant

HEGEMAN AVE.

LORING AVE.

LINDEN BLVD.
ESSEX ST.
SHEPHERD AVE.
BERRIMAN ST.
ATKINS AVE.
MONTAUK AVE.
MILFORD ST.
LOGAN ST.

STANLEY AVE.

WORTMAN AVE.

ASHFORD ST.
CLEVELAND ST.
ELTON ST.
LINWOOD ST.

● **Frank Falleti Homicide**

FLATLANDS AVE.

unity

WORTMAN AVE.

COZINE AVE.

FLATLANDS AVE.

ERSKINE ST.

EGAN ST.

VANDALIA AVE.

SCHROEDERS AVE.

SPRING HILLS

EAST NEW YORK

CAST OF CHARACTERS

The Destruction of East New York

ASHMAT ALI, East New York resident, friend of Julia Parker.

JULIA ARLEQUIN, grandmother of murder victim, Julia Parker.

NANCY ARLEQUIN, mother of Julia Parker.

PHILIP BROWNSTEIN, the assistant secretary of Housing and Urban Development and commissioner of the Federal Housing Administration.

LUCILLE CLARK, administrative organizer, East Brooklyn Congregations.

SARITA DAFTARY-STEEL, director of the East New York Farms!

ERIC DEAN, 1966 murder victim.

MICHAEL DOWD, police officer, 75th precinct, NYPD.

MICHAEL GECAN, senior advisor, East Brooklyn Congregations, Industrial Areas Foundation.

MEL GRIZER, director, United Community Centers.

DARRYL JENKINS, murder victim.

JOHN LINDSAY, mayor of New York City, 1966–1973.

MILAGROS MARTINEZ, sister of Julia Parker.

REVEREND EDWARD MASON, St. John Cantius Church.

MAJOR ROBERT OWENS, congressman, state senator.

JULIA PARKER, 1991 murder victim.

SARAH PLOWDEN, member of East Brooklyn Congregations.

MICHAEL RACE, detective sergeant, 75th precinct, NYPD.

FRANK RIVERA, early East New York activist.

CAREY SHEA, program director of the Local Development Corporation of East New York, executive director of the East New York Urban Youth Corps.

WILLIAM SIMON, detective, Cold Case Squad, NYPD.

SISTER MARGARET SMYTH, St. John Cantius Church.

WALTER THABIT, city planner.

VSB AND MR. FAYETTEVILLE, pseudonyms for two drug dealers, the former in East New York, the latter of North Carolina.

MARLENE WILKS, teacher, gardener.

DR. JOHNNY RAY YOUNGBLOOD, pastor, St. Paul Community Baptist Church.

The FHA Scandal

ANTHONY ACCETTA, assistant United States attorney, Eastern District of New York.

MILTON BERLIN, realtor.

HARRY BERNSTEIN, owner of Eastern Service Corporation.

ROSE BERNSTEIN, wife of Harry Bernstein.

LOUIS BERNSTEIN, son of Harry Bernstein.

FLORENCE BEHAR, assistant VP, credit analyst, Eastern Service.

JACK BLUM, assistant counsel to the Senate Subcommittee on Antitrust and Monopoly.

ABRAHAM BRODSKY, attorney for Harry Bernstein.

MELVIN S. CARDONA, realtor, salesman, and solicitor, Eastern Service.

DONALD C. CARROLL, FHA director, Hempstead, New York.

ROSE COHEN, FHA clerk.

HERBERT K. CRONIN, FHA chief underwriter.

JOHN DALY, FHA assistant chief underwriter.

FRANCIS J. DREIS, FHA appraiser.

GALE DREXLER, legal assistant, Eastern District of New York.

ALFRED FAYER, lawyer for the Bernsteins.

BERNHARD FEIN, FHA chief mortgage credit officer.

FRANK A. FEY, VP, Eastern Service.

EDWARD JOSEPH GOODWIN, FHA appraiser.

GREVILLE J. HARVEY, FHA appraiser.

PHILIP HART, senator, chairman of the Subcommittee on Antitrust and Monopoly.

PATRICK IANNUCCILLI, FHA deputy chief.

MICHAEL S. JANCOVIC, FHA deputy director.

JOSEPH H. JANKOWITZ, FHA appraiser.

CHARLES JOSHUA, FHA appraiser.

ORTRUD KAPRAKI, realtor.

EDWIN KATZ, chairman of the board, United Institutional Servicing Corporation

LAWRENCE KATZ, FHA director, Wisconsin.

ROBERT KATZ, VP, United Institutional Servicing Corporation

JEFFREY KAY, special agent, FBI.

JOHN KENNEDY, attorney advisor, HUD.

DENNIS LACINA, special agent, FBI.

PATRICK J. LAMA, FHA assistant chief of mortgage credit.

JOHN P. LOMENZO, secretary of state of New York.

ROBERT MORSE, United States attorney, Eastern District of New York.

EDWARD R. NEAHER, United States attorney, later judge, Eastern District of New York.

OTTO OBERMAIER, attorney for Dun & Bradstreet.

RUBIN ORINGER, realtor.

WRIGHT PATMAN, congressman, chairman of the House Banking and Currency Committee.

ARTHUR PRESCOTT, Dun & Bradstreet, manager.

GEORGE ROMNEY, secretary of Housing and Urban Development.

STEPHEN ROSENBAUM, president, Springfield Equities.

BERNARD ROTH, president, United Institutional Servicing Corporation.

STANLEY SIROTE, president Inter-Island Mortgage Corporation.

JIM SNIEGOCKI, special agent, FBI.

DAVID TRAGER, United States attorney, Eastern District of New York.

ANTHONY J. TRAVIA, judge, Eastern District of New York.

ROBERT C. WEAVER, first secretary of Housing and Urban Development.

Prologue

1991

In the early evening on July 17, seventeen-year-old Julia Parker was sitting on the hood of a car at the corner of Pennsylvania and Dumont in East New York when a gunman walked up, crouched behind her, and fired a shot into her head. She was taken to Brookdale Hospital, the same hospital where she was born, and pronounced dead.

Everyone was sure Julia was killed because she'd talked to the police about a friend of hers who was killed four days before. A detective said if he was her friend's killer, "I would probably do the same thing. It's very effective."

"My daughter didn't say a thing to police," said Julia's mother, Nancy Arlequin, believing, as everyone else did, that this is why her daughter was dead. She was defending her daughter's street-honor to the unknown killer, and doing what she could to protect her remaining family.

That year, 116 people were murdered in East New York. More than three decades later, forty-three of the murders, including Julia's, remained unsolved.

1

The Destruction of East New York

1966–1969

The night was clear and warm when ten young men, all white, gathered in the East New York section of Brooklyn on July 21, 1966. They were members of a loosely knit group calling themselves SPONGE. They were the Proud Boys of their day. The name stood for Society for the Prevention of Negroes Getting Everything (or "n*****s," depending on who was listening), a racist witticism currently making the rounds. Led by the red-haired James McMenemon, known as Sandy, and his younger brother John, a.k.a. Johnny Reb, SPONGE members converged on Frank's Restaurant, located just before the apex of the triangle formed by Livonia and New Lots Avenues, to make what would become their last stand.

It was a fitting location. The triangle was a famous location in East New York, and a favorite hangout of a local neighborhood gang, the New Lots Boys, who counted a number of SPONGE guys among their ranks. Frank's was their place, and one of the few remaining white holdouts in what had increasingly become a Black neighborhood over the last ten years. The SPONGE guys were there to heckle Mayor John Lindsay, who was meeting with local leaders about growing racial unrest. While Lindsay was inside discussing how they could ease the tension, SPONGE members carrying signs surrounded the place shouting, "Two, four, six, eight, we don't want to integrate." The number of picketers soon grew to thirty-five. Although the police hadn't been alerted to Lindsay's visit, word got out and a police detail of twenty-five cops were sent to keep order. Lindsay left without incident, but the boys didn't come to chant slogans and go home. They wanted something to happen. The crowd continued to grow.

When a group of Black young men and boys came up from Warwick Street and made their way down New Lots Avenue the SPONGE mob charged. The patrolmen were able to stop them, but this was a more organized protest than they'd realized. Shots were fired. As kids ran in all directions, the police were pelted with rocks from above. They'd later find caches of bricks, bottles, and Molotov cocktails stashed on the roofs.

The crowd now numbered more than one hundred. A code 10-13 was sent for Dumont and Ashford Streets. Officer needs help. The cops who rushed to the scene found an eleven-year-old Black boy named Eric Dean lying in the street. His aunt, who'd heard shots, had seen her nephew clutch his stomach and collapse. He was just there to see the mayor, she said. Eric Dean was pronounced dead at Brookdale Hospital a few hours later.

Three more 10-13s were called in that night as the fighting spread and continued. Over one thousand officers eventually swarmed the neighborhood. Days later the NYPD would send out a memo titled "Unusual Disorder: 75th Precinct."

Frank Fauci, the owner of Frank's Restaurant, told reporters there hadn't been any "real trouble" with the Black people who'd moved into the neighborhood, "until last week when they bombed a cab service where the white kids used to hang out." From his point of view the trouble only began when Black residents fought back against ongoing resistance to their presence in Brooklyn. "The SPONGE kids?" Frank continued. "Oh, they're just boys. There are about twenty of 'em and there's no real harm in them. They're just kids." According to one SPONGE member, "The Negroes are breaking us up, and trying to throw us out of the neighborhood. We're standing our ground and we're not leaving." The police report would say the crowd had grown to two hundred.

Two days after Eric Dean was murdered, Mayor Lindsay brought together twenty-four-year old SPONGE leader James McMenemon, thirty-five-year-old Vincent Jones, who was Black, and Robert Benjamin, a twenty-nine-year-old, who was Puerto Rican. Lindsay got the three men to shake hands and agree to a truce. "I understand Mr. Jones has a lot of friends," McMenemon said, "and he seems to be a nice fellow. I'll talk to my friends and he's going to talk to his friends."

Although Lindsay's gathering was credited with calming things down, another meeting entirely was responsible. After learning what had happened, a few of Lindsay's aides gathered to discuss how to respond. It was the first year of the Lindsay administration, and "We were still novices in a lot of ways," Sid Davidoff, administrative assistant to the mayor, remembered. Dr. Frank C. Arricale, director of New York City's Youth Board, had told them that morning that he knew a guy who knew Albert and Larry Gallo, mobsters who had ties to the Genovese crime family. Let me see if the Gallos would be willing to have a word with the SPONGE kids, he said. They might not care what the police say, but they weren't going to ignore the Gallo brothers. It was an outrageous idea, but everyone agreed. Lindsay, however, was not consulted.

East New York was essentially under martial law, but the police issued Albert Gallo a pass. We don't need the heat, Gallo told McMenemon. This is going to stop, right? When a member of SPONGE replied with a racial slur he was slapped to the ground. What choice did McMenemon have? SPONGE, who'd always been considered attention-craving posers in the neighborhood, was no longer a problem for the Lindsay administration.

The next day, when Lindsay gathered them in City Hall to meet with Black and Puerto Rican representatives, "We had a very different meeting than we would have had." Lindsay would later defend Arricale from fierce criticism when word got out about how he'd addressed the situation. "You can't always deal with people who are leaders in the Boy Scout movement. Sometimes you must call upon individuals with fairly rough backgrounds."

"I would have sent the devil in if I thought it would have worked," Davidoff says of their decision. "We were in unchartered territory, but one thing we knew was the police were not going to solve it. They always say the police are your first line of resistance. It's actually your last line."

Seventeen-year-old Ernest Gallashaw, a Black boy, was later arrested for Dean's murder. Fauci was relieved. "Just think if it had been a white boy," who had pulled the trigger. But Ernest Gallashaw hadn't killed Eric Dean. Dean's case was added to the growing list of unsolved murders in East New York, and it remains a cold case to this day.

Reverend Joseph Judge, of Our Lady of Mercy Church, said, "The whites in East New York have to get over the idea that this place is theirs." It's our home too. Another big problem, he said, was a lack of community organization. But East New York was brimming with community groups. Within weeks of the brawl, Frank Rivera and William Wright formed the United Negro and Puerto Rican Front (which was quietly investigated by the NYPD, who had a tendency to see community activists as a possible threat). SPONGE and those who shared their views not only objected to the influx of Black residents, but also to the many Puerto Rican families who were moving in.

East New York would simmer for the rest of the summer as helicopters hovered over the neighborhood during the day and a beefed-up police presence roamed the streets at night.

It hadn't always been like this. East New York wasn't perfect. Like every other neighborhood in New York, there were bad parts of town. The mob was in East New York. But they were more of a danger to each other than to their neighbors. For the most part.

Just a few years before racists had converged on Frank's Restaurant, East New York had been a thriving community of working-class and middle-class Jewish, German, and Italian immigrant families and their descendants. It was the kind of place where all the moms in the neighborhood banded together to make sure you had dinner every night when your father lost his job. In 1948, Frederick Heidenreich, the son of German immigrants, published a memoir called *Old Days and Old Ways in East New York*. He described how the neighborhood grew from a "small cluster of farms to a community of modern homes, churches, and schools," which still preserved "the best elements of suburban character."

It was also a neighborhood on the way up. When actor Danny Kaye's family moved to East New York from Williamsburg, they were surrounded by a lively and prosperous group of doctors, lawyers, dentists, and musicians. As far as the Kaye family were concerned, they'd arrived. For Jan Goldberg, who came to East New York in 1957 from Brownsville, the move to the Linden Houses was a step up. "It was like we moved to Heaven." It was a feeling shared by many of his neighbors. When Jeff Eisenberg's parents heard about the new middle-income housing in East New York (built by the New York City Housing Authority), they packed up their basement apartment in East Flatbush, also in 1957, and moved into the same projects, where Jeff began "a wonderful, wonderful childhood. It couldn't have been much better. It was a great upbringing in great surroundings."

"Those projects were a city unto themselves," said Steven Lang, who also grew up in the Linden Houses. And every building was "a neighborhood within a city," Goldberg added. Ira Cutler, whose grandmother bought a home across the street, made many friends in the projects. "There were hundreds and hundreds of kids in each building and on each block," he said. When school was out kids ran through the halls, knocking on doors to ask if their friends could come out to play. From morning until night in the summertime, and after school the rest of the year, if they weren't playing in the fields at George Gershwin Junior High, dozens of kids were always hanging out in front of the buildings, playing football, softball, or a street game called Ringolevio. "Everyone knew tons of people," Ira said, and many remain friends to this day.

Then, in the 1960s, everything changed. It happened so quickly. It felt as if "the neighborhood was ruined overnight," Ira recalled. Jeff's mother was mugged. Ira was mugged. Eric Dean was murdered. On the day of Martin Luther King Jr.'s assassination, before they sent the kids home from Thomas Jefferson High School, administrators asked the football team to patrol the halls, protecting the students from possible protesters. "By 1970, you couldn't walk down the street," said Barry Kestenberg, who grew up in the projects. By that time, the families of Jan, Jeff, Ira, Steven, and Barry were gone. Like many others in the neighborhood, they fled the place that had once been a blissful and protected paradise.

How did East New York transition from a thriving neighborhood of German, Italian, and Jewish immigrants to a declining and neglected African American and Hispanic neighborhood where children were shot and killed? Many factors contributed. "We all knew somebody who went off to Vietnam and either didn't come back or came back a shell," said Steven Lang. Then heroin and other drugs started to appear. The lives of people "who were shining stars . . . were ruined by drugs," Steven continued. For some, their "lives ended because of drugs," adding, "Friends of mine robbed my house." But two racist financial practices that had ramped up in the fifties and sixties, blockbusting and redlining, were the ultimate triggers. Brokers would convince white homeowners that if Black families moved into their neighborhood schools would go downhill, crime would rise, and property values would fall. They'd parade a Black family down the street to scare white homeowners into selling cheap, then sell the homes to struggling African Americans at inflated prices and pocket the difference. Blockbusting leveraged racial prejudice for profit. Once a neighborhood became predominately Black (or Puerto Rican), banks would literally draw red lines around the neighborhood boundaries, term everyone living within high credit risks, and automatically disqualify them for mortgages, credit, and other financial services.

Still, in the late sixties, East New York was not yet wholly lost, and two historic pieces of legislation passed in 1968 promised to be as important as the 1965 Voting Rights Act and the answer to the decline.

Together they would put an end to housing discrimination, redlining, and blockbusting, and make it easier for low-income families to find a decent home. In the same year that African American sanitation workers held up signs declaring "I am a man," because it was something that still needed to be said, it looked as if the arc of the moral universe might actually be bending toward justice.

Black and Puerto Rican families who moved into well-cared-for homes left behind when white families fled began building safe, family-oriented enclaves. Walter Thabit, a city planner who'd been hired in 1966 to revitalize the area, wrote, "It would be incorrect to suggest that East New York must be raised from the dead. Much of the area is attractive; thousands of families live in the community with a certain amount of harmony, grace, and satisfaction." East New York needed help, certainly, but it was also full of opportunity. "The two-family homes are modest in size, but structurally sound. They provide Negro and Puerto Rican families of modest means with the chance to own their own home and establish a middle-class life for themselves and their children."

East New York was still a lovely neighborhood, and not everyone wanted to take up arms against the new neighbors. When long-time East New York activist and community leader Vivian Bright moved to Pennsylvania Avenue in the 1960s, she and her husband were the first Black family on her block and their white neighbors brought casseroles to welcome them. There was still a chance to turn it all around, and reason to believe they could.

The next year, Julia Arlequin brought her twenty-year-old daughter Nancy back to East New York; she had sent her to Puerto Rico a few years earlier for hanging out with the wrong crowd and getting into trouble. Things had quieted down. The danger was passing. In the small corner of East New York, where'd she'd made their new home, Julia's other daughter was about to have a baby. It was time for Nancy to rejoin the family and help with the new arrival.

The FHA Scandal

1967–1968

Across America, greed was igniting. When an idea's time has come, it usually comes to more than one person. All over the nation, the pieces of an immoral scheme were firing up in the minds of a particular kind of predator, one who now couldn't wait to begin. They were going to get rich. And they couldn't lose.

A long history of horrific events had lined up just right to allow the design for the perfect financial crime to arise. In the 1960s, after more than three centuries of racism, riots convulsed the nation as Black citizens fought back against discrimination, police brutality, racial profiling, redlining, unemployment, poverty, assassinations, and countless other injustices that invaded almost every corner of their lives. Riots in Los Angels in 1965 led to thirty-four deaths, more than a thousand injured, and over a thousand buildings damaged or destroyed. Despite the toll, the riots continued. During the summer of 1967, more than 150 uprisings erupted across the United States, leading to at least eighty-three deaths.

The very word "riot" was part of the problem, a misdirection. It not only shifted the focus away from the underlying causes—racial injustice and the violence routinely inflicted upon people of color in America—it sidestepped responsibility for doing anything about them, and justified the continued use of violent measures in those communities. The uprisings were not senseless eruptions, but rebellions in the truest sense of the word.

"We want freedom," the Black Panthers demanded in their Ten-Point Program. We want the basic civil rights accorded to every other American, including "decent housing fit for the shelter of human beings." How can you set out in life from a vermin-infested home without heat or hot water, and a roof coming down on your head?

All around the country that summer, civil disobedience spread. In response, President Lyndon Johnson, who aspired to a Great Society without poverty and racial injustice, established what came to be known as the Kerner Commission to study the uprisings. "What happened?" Johnson asked. "Why did it happen? What can be done to prevent it from happening again and again?" "Find the truth," he demanded. Why are people "rioting"?

That fall, the assistant secretary of the Department of Housing and Urban Development (HUD) and commissioner of the Federal Housing Administration (FHA), Philip Brownstein, gave a speech to a large group of FHA employees. He was sure the FHA could play a unique and crucial role in addressing the needs that drove what they all saw happening across the country. In the bureaucratic world of housing and mortgages, it was the come-to-Jesus speech of a lifetime.

Like all Americans, Black Americans just wanted to participate in the country's dazzling and "unparalleled abundance," he told them. They just "want a chance."

"I am asking you and every employee of FHA to enter into a new crusade," he beseeched them. We're going to improve housing conditions for the poor and resurrect the inner city. It was going to be their "greatest and most urgent responsibility," their "principle reason for existence in 1967."

"We have got to recognize that stimulating a flow of mortgage funds into the inner city, yes, even the slums . . . is an FHA mission of the highest priority." Oh and by the way, "You should work at this task as though your job depended on it—because it may." Up until then, like the banks, the FHA was redlining the inner cities and they would not insure mortgage loans there. This would end, or else.

The push was on. President Johnson would soon give Brownstein almost everything he needed to accomplish this new mission.

The Kerner Commission presented their report to Johnson in February. Why are Black people rebelling? Their conclusion was breathtakingly simple. America is a racist country. "Segregation and poverty have created in the racial ghetto a destructive environment totally unknown to most white Americans . . . White institutions created it, white institutions maintain it, and white society condones it."

According to Johnson's committee, among the most serious problems, in a long list of them, were the police, unemployment, and housing discrimination. Racism in America was so bad and so systemic, that only a "compassionate, massive, and sustained" effort could even begin to address it.

Looking back at the decade of Alabama governor George Wallace's refrain, "segregation now, segregation tomorrow, segregation forever," it's hard to imagine that anyone would quibble with the commission's conclusion. But Johnson balked. Fred Harris, a member of the Kerner Commission, would later tell an NPR reporter, "It hurt his feelings. He had done more against poverty and racism than any president in history." But Johnson had asked them to find the truth, and "That's what we did," Harris said. Johnson thought the uprisings were the work of outside agitators, and he tried to prevent the report from being released. But the concept of "outside agitators" would become yet another way to delegitimize the rebellions. These were not civil rights activists from the neighborhoods where the uprisings occurred, many claimed, but bad actors from elsewhere who came to stir up trouble. When the *Washington Post* published a leaked draft, most of the country balked too. The Voting Rights Act had been passed. Segregation had been made illegal. There were white people marching with Martin

Luther King Jr. America had fixed the problem. The "riots" are not our fault, white America thought.

Martin Luther King Jr. called the report a "physician's warning of approaching death, with a prescription for life." He was assassinated one month later. Another one hundred uprisings followed. Within a week, Johnson signed a bill that he'd been trying to get passed for two years: the Civil Rights Act of 1968, also known as the Fair Housing Act. It addressed housing discrimination, redlining, blockbusting, and other civil rights issues raised in the Kerner Commission's report, and what many felt was the more immediate problem, riots (as they were referred to historically). But the takeaway was fair housing. To this day, no one calls it the Civil Rights Act of 1968. It's the Fair Housing Act. With it there would be no more discrimination. Everyone would have a decent place to live, and everyone would live where they chose.

The *New York Amsterdam News*, the most widely read Black newspaper in New York City, took it all with a grain of salt. "It is meaningful and shows progress, although we always wonder why we must cheer for rights that should be ours at the outset by virtue of our birth." Warning also that it would be "both cruel and dangerous to raise the expectations of Americans who are trapped . . . to believe that the new legislation will have any immediate impact on housing conditions or restrictive housing practices."

Of all the problems cited by the commission's report, housing discrimination must have seemed like the one there was some hope of rectifying. It could be solved with money, with infrastructure. Providing fair housing would be a walk in the park compared to police reform, particularly since most people in America didn't believe the police were really a problem. And if housing was taken care of, if we remove this justified grievance, it would calm things down and other reforms would naturally flow from there. At the signing ceremony, Johnson declared "that fair housing for all—all human beings who live in this country—is now a part of the American way of life." Meanwhile, federal troops brought in to put down uprisings continued to occupy Black neighborhoods.

Fifteen days after signing the Fair Housing Act into law, President Johnson nominated Anthony J. Travia to a seat on the U.S. District Court for the Eastern District of New York. Travia was a longtime resident of East New York, which was exactly the sort of inner-city neighborhood Brownstein and Johnson hoped to turn around. He was confirmed by the Senate two months later.

On a hot summer morning in August, Johnson put his signature on the bill that laid out exactly how he would bring decent homes to the poor, the Housing and Urban Development Act of 1968 (usually referred to as the HUD Act). For Johnson, who had announced he would not be running for reelection, the two pieces of legislation would be the last major acts of his presidency, and his final shot at giving rise to his Great Society. Of the two acts, this one was the most important to him. "Today, we are going to put on the books of American law what I genuinely believe is the most farsighted, the most comprehensive, the most massive housing program in all American history."

It could have been. The timing seemed so right. Democrats and Republicans were relatively united about the need to help low-income families buy a decent home, but they didn't agree about what the housing programs should look like. Until the uprisings they had no real impetus to come to an agreement quickly. But now the country was in outright, inescapable racial turmoil and the Black community was no longer taking it lying down. A substantial number of voters appeared to favor fair housing, and they certainly didn't want more rebellion. Senators on both sides of the aisle recognized they had to do something. The HUD Act passed the Senate 67–4, and without debate.

Then, just as many had come together for a brief moment to try to address centuries of racial injustice, violence, and despair, bankers and other white-collar workers immediately saw the incredible gift Johnson and Congress had just dropped in their laps.

Harry and Rose Bernstein, the owners of the Eastern Service Corporation, one of the largest mortgage banks in New York, invited Federal Housing Administration (FHA) appraiser Edward Goodwin up to their office to pick up keys for a couple of buildings they wanted him to look over. Goodwin didn't know how to respond. This was not how appraisals were done. There were procedures in place, forms to fill out. But Herbert Cronin, his boss and the chief underwriter, had okayed it. The FHA underwriter evaluates mortgage applications and decides whose loan is going to be insured. The underwriter's word was law and the chief underwriter had just said to Goodwin, it's fine. Go talk to them. Goodwin didn't have far to travel. The FHA and Eastern Service offices were in the same building in Hempstead, Long Island.

"I hear you're going into Brooklyn," Harry announced when Goodwin walked in. That was unexpected. Cronin had only just told Goodwin the week before that he was being assigned to Brooklyn. We've got plans for Brooklyn, Harry told him before sitting down for a long talk. The following Monday Cronin asked how it went with the business of the keys. "No problem," Goodwin answered.

Harry and Rose Bernstein, well aware of the FHA's new crusade, took one look at the details of the recent legislation and immediately grasped the criminal possibilities. Brooklyn's East New York, and neighborhoods like it, was the perfect target. It had high numbers of just the kind of victims they were looking for.

The Bernsteins knew they couldn't lose because the government, a dependably racist nation, and those who were trying to do something about it had inadvertently united to help them. Exploiting hope, it turns out, was going to be very good business.

2

The Destruction of East New York

1969–1970

Shoe merchant John Pitkin was a master of reinvention. In 1835 he imagined he could turn the quaint Brooklyn town he'd just bought into a glittering metropolis, one that would rival the mighty Manhattan. To begin, he changed the name of his town from New Lots to East New York, as if to announce that there was now another New York, just across the river. He built a shoe and boot factory, established his town's first newspaper, and had maps made to help families and businesses find their way to paradise. Two years into his efforts the financial Panic of 1837 ended his fantastic dreams.

Pitkin did just fine. Three months after the banks had run out of gold and silver, he had a plan B. In a letter printed in a local newspaper and addressed to "Mechanics, Artisans, and Manufacturers," he now pronounced East New York economical. "Extravagance and luxury have had their day." But these days the "humble and industrious man will seek to accommodate himself to the times." Land was cheap here. So were building materials. For the kind of outlay that wouldn't have gotten you anything the year before, one could now build a home and a business, "almost within hail of the greatest market in America." Become a proprietor in East New York, he wrote. We have already

built what "may be justly called" a "beautiful manufacturing district."
Everything is ready and waiting for you to set up shop.

After announcing the many businesses that would prosper in East
New York, he put out an appeal to the workers, an appeal that would
be heard for the next one hundred years. Here, "a poor man may purchase in a healthy country, with delightful water, and ocean air, a lot of
ground," and for a great deal less than what they'd pay for "a miserable
hovel" in Manhattan, "crowded also under the same roof with so many
as to endanger life." There "is nothing more certain," than that the
labor of the honest, hardworking poor would always be welcome in
East New York.

The first to be intrigued were the Germans. They came, they bought,
they built homes, churches, factories, and stores. From then on, as wave
after wave of immigrants came to America—Italians, Polish, Irish,
Jewish, and others—some would find their way to East New York and
thrive. Pitkin had not oversold his dream. Surrounded by green hills to
the north and the lush Jamaica Bay to the south, East New York became an almost enchanted place where you could arrive with nothing
and work to build something. Everyone had a chance. Pitkin eventually
sold most of the lots he once owned, but he kept a few for himself,
including a large parcel along a block now called Wyona Street. He
died in 1874.

By the time Nancy Arlequin came home, East New York had expanded to 5.6 square miles. The rolling hills to the north now included
some of the largest cemeteries in New York, and to get to Jamaica Bay
you had to pass through landfills piled with garbage and the buried
bodies from decades of mob hits. Far away enough from Manhattan,
where the people with money lived, East New York was seen as just the
right spot for a city dump. By 1970, over 160,000 people were living
in East New York. Roughly two thirds of the residents were white, and
the remaining third were Black and Hispanic. Tension between the
races would rise and fall, but just as the immigrants had in Pitkin's day,
each minority group managed to build a safe space in East New York.

It didn't mean life was easy outside their community, but for Nancy and her neighbors, life in their corner was magical.

Mayor John Lindsay and others had recognized the growing housing problem in East New York, where redlining and blockbusting, now illegal due to the Fair Housing Act, had taken a toll, and they'd begun to take steps to do something about it. Among those steps was an affordable housing plan called the Vest Pocket and Rehabilitation Program. Congress had approved President Johnson's Model Cities program, which would distribute funds to improve conditions in inner cities, but they hadn't yet come up with the money. Lindsay hoped to get some of those federal funds. The Vest Pocket program was his way of giving New York a "head start" toward fixing the housing situation.

To come up with a plan for East New York, Lindsay hired city planner Walter Thabit. Thabit had a history as an activist. The founder of Planners for Equal Opportunity, an organization that strove to steer city planning toward social justice, Thabit was already working with Lower East Side residents to block the city's plans to demolish a huge swath of their neighborhood. He was a perfect, if daring, choice.

At the first planning meeting of what would ultimately be called the East New York Housing and Urban Planning Committee, twenty-seven-year-old Black activist Leo Lillard was elected chairman. Thabit would meet with the committee and wider community members every Wednesday night for over four months. He would later write, "They need help but are not helpless." In the beginning, as far as the community was concerned, Thabit was just like anyone else. "It takes a riot to get you down here, and after the fuss dies down you disappear and leave things as they were." Before he could raise the topic of housing they hit him with a barrage of demands. "We need a health center or a hospital." "When are we going to get the swimming pool we were promised?" There aren't enough recreation centers for our children, or schools. They didn't just have a housing problem, they tried to explain, they had a services problem. The list of what they called out for was long, and the need was desperate. Hundreds of people attended, Frank Rivera among them, and over thirty community groups joined them for at least four meetings, while many others were approached and interviewed for their input. Thabit needed to earn their trust, but he was up to the challenge. He would do whatever he could to address all their issues, but it would be housing first.

To begin to identify which areas had the greatest housing need, Thabit hired people to walk around surveying East New York. They were asked to count the abandoned buildings and empty lots and write down their thoughts. "Parts of East New York suggest death," was one man's contribution.

"I felt a heavy mood of deterioration," wrote another. "It was as if you could actually see the motion of decay."

And still another survey read, "I was very disturbed by this area, which at this stage of my planning career, I imagine I should be cal-loused enough to work in an area such as this and remain a bit more objective . . . I am still depressed by this exposure."

Many of the surveyors said, remove the abandoned buildings, and the area could recover. They are "used as junkyards," the surveyors said, and "are centers for garbage." In 1966, they counted a total of 350 of them, and wherever there were abandoned buildings, there was danger. During the year of Thabit's survey the body of a nineteen-year-old girl was found in a vacant building on Barbey Street, in an area that had an average of two abandoned buildings on each block. Her murder was never solved.

The parts the surveyor referred to as suggesting death were largely confined to an area west of Pennsylvania Avenue they called the "Industrial Quadrant," and the "Tenement Area" directly below it. This was John Pitkin's once beautiful manufacturing district, which, like other pockets of East New York, had been feeling the effects of redlin-ing and blockbusting.

Seven potential areas for rehabilitation were considered. After much heated debate, the community and Thabit reached an agreement. They chose the Tenement Area. Bounded by Sutter, Pennsylvania, Livonia, and Van Sinderen Avenues, encompassing twenty-one blocks, the Tenement Area was the worst residential section in East New York. Almost one hundred of the 450 buildings left standing had been abandoned. Practically every block had at least one burned-out, boarded-up building, and some had as many as three or four. But housing was never going to be enough to build a thriving community and Thabit didn't forget the community leaders' cry for services. In addition to the new housing, the plan called for a health center, day care and community centers, a park, and a swimming pool.

The committee's plan was approved by the city in the fall of 1968. A year later, the first round of building rehabilitations was complete, and construction of new housing had begun.

When the federal government came up with funds for the Model Cities program, Thabit was once again hired to work with the committee members to come up with a plan. Although final approval was still months away, Lindsay came to East New York in 1969 to break ground on one of the future Model Cities sites, at the corner of Miller and Pitkin Avenues. "This is the first living proof," Lindsay announced to a crowd of around 250 people, "that a community, by planning, designing, and arranging all of the work, can create housing in record time." The project they would build was "supported by the community—instead of resented by it—because it has been planned by the community." The community was well aware of the role it played in finally getting attention for East New York.

This particular corner lay within the area Thabit had designated the "Family Area." It ran north of New Lots Avenue, and east of Pennsylvania Avenue. Despite the fact that the Family Area was right next to the Tenement Area, Thabit described it as a nice neighborhood. It had many family-friendly amenities like Linton Park, the Thomas Jefferson High School field, and the New Lots Library branch. It also had fewer abandoned buildings, and a good number of active block and community organizations working to make things better. One of Thabit's surveyors wrote, "There is no doubt what ever that this can be a really lovely area for families." The neighborhood was also home to Nancy Arlequin and her growing family.

In the spring of 1969, while everyone was hard at work on the Vest Pocket program, Thabit became aware of a new kind of housing problem. Andrea Malester, who'd come aboard to help with the Model Cities program, had just returned from a disturbing interview with government officials at the FHA's office in Hempstead. The FHA's Hempstead office was one of their largest. 130 employees in a fifteen-thousand-square-foot office processed nearly all the one-to-four family homes in eleven counties in New York State, including all five boroughs of New York City.

Just a few years earlier, the FHA had taken possession of fewer than twenty buildings in Brooklyn through foreclosures. Andrea learned that not only did they now own 132 buildings, but they were acquiring more, at a rate of ten to fifteen a month. Most concerning was the fact that a growing number of the foreclosed buildings were in the Family Area. Thabit had been told by brokers that you couldn't get FHA insurance in this area, but that had clearly changed, and for some reason, this was not the positive development it should have been.

Something was going on, but no one could say what was causing the rise in foreclosures. Unlike street crimes, which tend to leave many obvious signs of a crime, like shell casings and a body, when a financial crime has been committed, somebody has to do a lot of work to find the evidence. Unfortunately, it is not unusual for victims of white-collar crimes to be unaware someone has taken advantage of them. Without obvious evidence or a victim filing a complaint, investigators usually don't even know a crime has been committed and that they should start looking for proof. Foreclosing a building was unfortunate, but it was not against the law.

In the meantime, unrecognized evidence was growing rapidly. A year after Andrea had interviewed administrators at the FHA they went from owning 20 percent of the vacant buildings in East New York to 40 percent. East New York had been declining, but now, just when they were on the eve of turning everything around, the decline accelerated so suddenly and so precipitously it looked like East New York would collapse before anyone discovered what was happening.

The FHA Scandal

1968

Real estate broker Ortrud Kapraki had recently been accused of using a phony mortgage scheme to fleece senior citizens in Queens. When word got out, she quickly closed down her office and fled to Brooklyn to set up a new shop, where no one knew her. It was meant to be her clean slate, but things were not going so well. The FHA refused to insure mortgages for any of her clients. Over and over she'd line up eager buyers for her buildings, but the FHA kept turning them down. After repeatedly broadcasting their willingness to insure the mortgages of lower income families in the inner cities, all the applications she submitted were denied. What was the problem? Kapraki, the daughter of German immigrants, was now forty years old, and struggling to make a living was becoming increasingly harder to endure. But there was something not quite right about Kapraki. In Queens, she'd hunted for victims at church social gatherings and she was completely without remorse about swindling the elderly. "It's not my fault," she would say whenever she got into trouble. "But it was," a lawyer who knew her would later say.

Florence Behar was an assistant vice president at the Eastern Service Corporation. Unlike conventional banks, all mortgage banks like Eastern Service do is process, fund, and service loans. They don't take deposits, they don't have checking or savings accounts, and for many years mortgage banks were almost entirely unregulated. While Kapraki was trying to figure out what she was doing wrong, Behar was sizing up Kapraki. If Kapraki was okay with stealing the life savings of senior citizens, perhaps she'd be okay with what they were planning. Together with realtor Melvin Cardona, who also had a job soliciting real estate brokers for Eastern, they sat Kapraki down to explain why the FHA was turning her down and what they all could do about it. Bring your business to Eastern, they encouraged her. We accept any kind of houses, and we know how to makes things happen.

Meanwhile, when FHA appraiser Edward Goodwin returned from his meeting at Eastern, his superiors pulled him aside to explain exactly how he would fit in with their plan.

■

The FHA had been helping hardworking Americans buy homes by insuring mortgages since they were created in 1934. For over thirty years they'd had two complementary goals: help honest people buy decent homes, and thwart scammers. Systems to regulate and enforce these goals had been put in place, and they'd been tinkering, refining, and improving those procedures ever since. The mortgagor had to qualify. They had to demonstrate that they could make their mortgage payments. The FHA also had to determine if the house being sold was worth the price the seller was asking. If sellers were told they had to fix something to qualify for insurance, they fixed it. Through the FHA's efforts, millions of working-class and low-income families became homeowners, the foundation for the nationwide middle class to come. It's safe to say that without the FHA, for most Americans, there would be no American dream.

In 1965, when the Department of Housing and Urban Development (HUD) was established, the FHA was folded into HUD. There were growing pains. "As a conglomerate of formerly independent agencies (some of which had promoted segregation) with numerous missions and complex measures of success, HUD was in a relatively weak position to fulfill these multiple missions," writes Christopher Bonastia, author of *Knocking on the Door: The Federal Government's Attempt to Desegregate the Suburbs*. Still, more procedures and people were now available to help all citizens realize the American dream and to stop grifters.

The headquarters in Washington and seven regional HUD offices were staffed with directors and administrators who managed the operations of appraisers and credit analysts, who were supported and overseen by teams of underwriters, clerks, and supervisors, and the people who gave them their assignments. A chief in each section had the authority to overrule applications that had been denied, or to request changes to appraisals. Between all these people, they would ensure that mortgage insurance applications were in order, that potential buyers could make their mortgage payments, and that the homes were sound.

The FHA had evolved into a bureaucratic gem of efficiency, helping Americans gain the one thing from which almost all good things spring: a decent home. But the middle class that had arisen through FHA-aided homeownership did not, for the most part, include people of color. Only 2 percent of all the mortgages the FHA had insured until 1950 were for homes owned by people of color.

The Civil Rights Act of 1968 and the Housing and Urban Development Act of 1968 aimed to ensure that everyone had a fair shot at homeownership. The first act outlawed discrimination. The second act put programs and procedures into place to help minorities and low-income families buy homes. HUD was now required to affirmatively further fair housing.

Just like that, people all over the country who'd never thought they would be able to buy a home now could. Low-income individuals and families could buy a home for only $200 down, and their monthly mortgage payments would not exceed 20 percent of their household income. The new homeowners had more years to pay off the mortgage, and some of the new programs provided subsidies, like help with interest payments. Others were closer to a conventional mortgage, but with some key differences: the customer, the location of the homes, many of which were in formerly redlined neighborhoods, and how the FHA assessed risk.

Of all the programs to help low-income families afford a home, the one that attracted Eastern Service was Section 223(e) of the HUD Act. Section 223(e) was created to allow for mortgage insurance to be provided in "older, declining urban areas," areas where low-income people of color lived and where it was previously almost impossible to get a mortgage. Like East New York. To do this, the FHA had to continue to relax their standards for determining which loans were insured. Previously, they had to calculate the "economic soundness" of the loan. Often, the criteria for determining economic soundness, like where the building was located, "was certainly tied deeply to race," said Christopher Bonastia, professor of sociology at Lehman College and the CUNY Graduate Center. In 1968, older buildings in formerly redlined areas where buyers of color lived were included under the umbrella of acceptable risk, technically removing at least some of the racial bias from the FHA underwriters' practices. Buyers still had to demonstrate that they could make the mortgage payments, and the houses still had to meet all the previous criteria. They couldn't be deteriorating or substandard. If repairs were needed, they had to be made before a loan was insured. "The FHA employees took pride in it being a 'conservative business operation,' that became self-sustaining by 1940," Bonastia noted. "Avoiding 'risky' neighborhoods was part of its DNA, so the changes to its policies in the late '60s were pretty dramatic." Accordingly, a Special Risk Insurance Fund was created to cover the foreclosures that would inevitably come with increased risk.

To make these new, and riskier, mortgage loans attractive to lenders, the FHA would insure qualified loans, as they'd been doing for decades. As long as the homes passed inspection by FHA appraisers, and the buyers demonstrated they could make the minimum payments, lenders were protected. If the new homeowners defaulted, the FHA would repay the loan.

It was the opposite of redlining. The United States government was doing everything possible to encourage lending to people of color and low-income families. They brought into being a market that until then did not exist. They had essentially just created the subprime mortgage business. Loans that were previously deemed risky—that is, not "prime"—were now a hot commodity.

There were a number of other programs in addition to 223(e) to help the poor, such as Section 235 (which provided subsidies for interest payments), or the earlier 221(d)(2), but those put a cap on the price of the home the poor could buy. There was no cap on 223(e) homes. Eastern Service also bought and sold homes in addition to granting mortgages, and they were happy to sell a Section 235 home or two, but why stop there? They made more money on 223(e) homes. As long as they had FHA insurance, the government would always pay. They couldn't lose.

Harry and Rose Bernstein wanted to do better than not lose. The new programs gave them an idea for a new take on an old crime, and they were going to get rich. One of the keys to their plan's success was volume, and they needed an area with a large number of potential buyers whose mortgages the FHA was eager to insure. East New York was perfect. But they couldn't do it alone. They needed help. Ortrud Kapraki and Edward Goodwin were among their first recruits.

Robert C. Weaver, a Black man who was the very first secretary of Housing and Urban Development, and the first Black cabinet member, had a different reaction to the new programs. To him the world was now filled with "a new sense of excitement and optimism that we can solve the massive urban problems that have plagued us for so long."

As the keynote speaker at their annual convention, he presented the National Bar Association with an enormous challenge. "There is a unique opportunity now to establish a spirit of cooperation, to achieve a climate of widespread voluntary compliance . . . Fair housing must become a primary consideration in the actions of every government agency—Federal, State, and Local. It must be understood by every element of the housing industry—builder, broker, banker, owner, and manager . . . tenant and landlord, every home buyer and seller." But some of those on that list had other plans. And there were other problems that legislation alone could not fix.

Because of its long history of redlining and segregation, the FHA did not have a great deal of experience insuring mortgages for poor people of color, nor with appraising buildings in the neighborhoods where they lived. Their operations were also informed by the same institutional racism found in virtually every other major organization in 1968. Bringing them up to speed would be like getting a small country to make an enormous cultural change overnight. That the new acts had been created in service of LBJ's Great Society and a Democratic vision of change reaching back to the New Deal of the 1930s complicated matters. Just months after the laws to implement fair housing had been enacted, the Democrats no longer had the power to protect that vision. Richard M. Nixon had been elected and the Democrats were no longer in charge. It was in the hands of the Republican party now, and they had been resisting that vision for just as long. Whether or not America would have fair housing was all up to them.

3

The Destruction of East New York

1970–1971

East New York is policed by the 75th precinct—but cops never say the "75th precinct," they'd say the "Seven-Five." According to the Seven-Five, the number of abandoned buildings in East New York was now up to one thousand. Walter Thabit's latest tally was 850, but he accepted the NYPD's numbers. Perhaps because the NYPD counted all buildings and Thabit was mostly counting residential homes, and primarily those on blocks being considered for new and rehabilitated housing. Because empty buildings attracted crime, the NYPD established the vacant-house team in 1968 when they became aware of the rising numbers.

Two patrolmen, Thaddeus Hall and Arthur Molinelli, were assigned to walk the abandoned-building-beat, evicting anyone they found living there, people involved in drug activity, and potential vandals. The job sometimes brought them to 383 Milford Street, where Molinelli's family had lived for fifty-five years. Molinelli described to a *New York Times* reporter how they'd sold the family building to a real estate agency in 1967, who then resold to a Puerto Rican family. Just one year later, in 1968, the Molinelli family home, where his grandmother had peacefully tended forty rose bushes, was abandoned, a refuge for blowing leaves, discarded refuse, and squatters.

Newcomers like the Arlequin family over in Thabit's Family Area were largely insulated from what was happening around them. Most of the abandoned buildings were west of Pennsylvania Avenue, which, while only three blocks away, was largely industrial and so different in character it felt worlds away. Nancy's family simply avoided that part of town. Their neighborhood was a Puerto Rican oasis of music, food, and family, where everyone looked out for each other. They were safe.

Many of the newcomers to the Family Area didn't pick up on the initially small, almost imperceptible indications that things were changing. They noticed white families had started moving out; that's what allowed them to live there. But soon more and more families took flight. As the number of people leaving started to grow, the city began to retreat as well. It was little things, like the trash not being picked up as often. It was more annoying than frightening. They knew the danger was out there, but it was far enough away to allow them to feel sheltered on their quiet, tree-lined slice of Heaven.

Julia Arlequin and her daughters didn't know the East New York Frederick Heidenreich described in his memoir. They were just happy there now. They could overlook little things, like the man who sold ice cream from a Good Humor truck but wouldn't come to their block after the sun went down. They were living a few subways stops away from the big city, after all. There was bound to be a little trouble. The Good Humor man was just being cautious.

Meanwhile, the whites-only neighborhoods kept moving north. First it was above Linden Boulevard, then New Lots, until they were finally all the way up to Atlantic Avenue, which cops jokingly referred to as the "Mason-Dixon Line" of East New York. The white families also clustered south, leaving the families of color in the middle.

Community leaders like Frank Rivera, who'd started the United Negro and Puerto Rican Front, were more alarmed by the rapidly growing numbers of vacant buildings and the subsequent problems that arose. Before the FHA would pay out a mortgage and take possession of a foreclosed home they insisted that the building had to be vacant. It was referred to as the FHA's "vacancy-rule." Once everyone had been evicted the banks put tin over the windows and collected their money. But one thousand empty buildings was an irresistible temptation. It wasn't long before the tin was torn off the windows, the glass was broken, and everything that could be stolen from the abandoned buildings, such as copper pipes and wiring, was taken. Teenagers would party inside and trash the place. Sometimes water was left running, and floors would bow or worse, collapse. Drug users and the homeless moved in next, while rats as big as cats scampered in and out. Once happy homes were now places children crossed the street to avoid.

Vacant buildings were also in danger of graduating to vacant lots. Walter Thabit described how FDNY "sirens were a constant accompaniment" to their Tuesday night meetings. "The engine company keeps its trucks in the street," he was told, and "as soon as it comes back from one call, it goes out on another." Engine 225 and Ladder 107 went out on a combined total of 10,500 runs in 1971, more than double the number from five years before. It was like a constant flame was burning at all times somewhere in East New York, and the FDNY had to race from block to block, playing a deadly game of whack-a-mole to put it out. Neighbors complained that over time the fire department became slower and slower to respond, and buildings were allowed to burn until they were beyond repair and torn down.

Fearing that water leaks and running water from severed pipes in the abandoned buildings might be contributing to reduced water pressure in East New York, hampering the fire department's efforts and also sewage treatment, the Department of Water Resources hired teenagers to help explore 937 vacant buildings to identify leaks. But they couldn't get into 306 of the buildings due to vandalism.

That May, the *New York Amsterdam News* ran an articled titled "East New York could be the next to blow up." Instead of stepping up aid to East New York, the city responded to the decline with an increased withdrawal of city services. Although the Department of Sanitation said they picked up garbage six days a week, East New Yorkers said it was more like once or twice a week and sometimes worse. Mounds of debris would sometimes lie untouched for weeks.

To make matters worse, East New York was one of a small handful of truly affordable neighborhoods in New York City. As the area declined, many families there had no better place to go to. Despite recent legislation, the suburbs were fighting fair housing with all the political might they possessed and their influence was considerable. Black families who managed to buy a home in the suburbs were in danger of losing it when they were bombed by their not-so-welcoming white neighbors. Anyone who wasn't lucky enough to have settled in sections of East New York like where the Arlequins lived found themselves trapped in what one community worker described as a "corridor of despair," forced to make the best of an increasingly dangerous situation. Recent city budget cuts only exacerbated the problem.

In East New York, everyone agreed that the problem began with the abandoned buildings. A group of community leaders, including Rivera, met on May 4, 1971, to come up with a plan to fix the problem themselves. Starting small, they selected a few vacant houses for renovation. They christened their new effort the Repair and Reoccupy Our Homes program, and left the meeting elated, convinced it was within their power to halt the downward spiral of their neighborhood.

They knew they needed publicity, though. Unless someone lived in an adjacent neighborhood, their fellow New Yorkers were largely unaware of East New York and its problems. After the 1966 uprisings, an aide to Mayor Lindsay admitted that previously, City Hall "hardly knew of its existence." It must have been that much easier to make cuts in a place they hardly knew of, and whose citizens did not comprise a terribly influential tax base.

A press conference was planned for June 17. Members of the new program went back and forth for weeks on the wording of a press release sent to seventy newspapers, radio stations, and TV shows.

While they didn't know for sure that crimes had been committed, they knew something was up and it seemed to be connected to the FHA and the banks. In their press release they listed four mortgage banks who were linked to the greatest number of foreclosed and abandoned buildings, Eastern Service Corporation, United Institutional Servicing Corporation, Inter-Island Mortgage, Springfield Equities Ltd., and one commercial bank, Chase Manhattan. They added that they would be happy to give tours of East New York and arrange interviews with homeowners, tenants, and businessmen to any member of the press who desired it. "We are not going to be satisfied with press coverage alone. Our committee is going to take the fight for action to city offices, federal agencies, and to Mayor Lindsay if necessary . . . More is happening even as this is being written."

On the morning of June 17, volunteers were already hard at work clearing out trash from the buildings they had chosen for renovation, while a group of East New York leaders headed to the pleasant offices of a nonprofit in Manhattan to answer questions and build support for their cause. "We waited till 2:00 p.m.," wrote city planner Walter Thabit. "Not a single media person showed up."

What that first press conference made abundantly clear, and what the Bernsteins and others were counting on, was the fact that it was particularly easy to commit financial crimes in the neighborhoods of people of color. Fewer people were looking and when anyone complained even fewer people were listening.

"Frustration, bitterness, and despair were on everyone's lips." The absolute indifference was almost too much to bear, and soon after some community leaders left the neighborhood. "It was one of the most disappointing days of my life," Thabit said. The growing danger to some of the most vulnerable residents of New York City was beneath notice. "Outrage was everywhere."

But someone had detected the danger, and while the press was ignoring their plight, investigators had begun quietly gathering evidence.

The FHA Scandal

1969–1970

To Nixon, HUD was just "a meaningless department." When he picked George Romney, his opponent in the Republican primaries, as the new secretary of Housing and Urban Development (HUD), it wasn't because he'd hoped Romney would actually accomplish anything. He meant to bury him, "never to be noticed again." But for Romney, the man reporters were said to have nicknamed "Saint George," bringing fair housing to the country would become a mission. He took to the assignment with all the heart Nixon lacked.

Romney's support of civil rights went back decades. He'd been fighting segregation since WWII. As Michigan's governor, he passed the state's first fair housing law, and he refused to back Barry Goldwater, his party's candidate, when Goldwater would not support an antidiscrimination bill. Romney viewed housing discrimination as "the most crucial and pressing" civil rights problem of his time. After the uprisings broke out in 1967, Romney went on a twenty-day, ten-thousand-mile tour of the most troubled neighborhoods in the country. "America must see riots do not develop out of thin air," Martin Luther King Jr. said. "Certain conditions continue to exist in our society which must be condemned as vigorously as we condemn riots. But in the final analysis,

a riot is the language of the unheard." Romney may not have understood the full extent of the structural racism that undergirded society,
but he grasped King's message and he listened to the people he met on
his tour. The nation would only see more of the same if our "response
is punitive, instead of positive and curative." There were real problems
we needed to fix, and we were missing the point if we focused on the
fact that people rebelled and the form the rebellions took and not the
reasons why.

It was a mission that defied his church. In 1964, Delbert Stapley, one
of the Twelve Apostles of the Mormon church, wrote Romney, "After
listening to your talk on Civil Rights, I am very much concerned." He
then referred Romney to a section of the teachings of Joseph Smith
titled "The Status of the Negro," in which Smith referred to Black
people as a separate species. Romney was not deterred.

The same year Romney assumed his new position, evidence of a
financial crime spree began to emerge.

People in East New York already had their suspicions. City planner
Walter Thabit got one of his first hints from Reverend Jose Gonzales.
"Do you know that a Hispanic or a Black broker cannot get an FHA-
insured mortgage? But if you go to Inter-Island or Eastern Service,
you can get it?" Thabit was well aware of all the recent foreclosures and
the growing number of abandoned buildings. Gonzales was suspicious
that something more than a few bad credit decisions was going on at
the new mortgage banks. They certainly weren't acting out of a sudden
concern for people of color.

But the first to glean more specific details of the crime was Secretary
of State John Lomenzo and his investigators. It happened while they
were conducting what they thought was a routine blockbusting probe.

Lomenzo was proud of his department's track record fighting
blockbusting. It was a particularly ugly crime, and it destroyed lives.
When Richard Rabinowitz's parents were finally able to buy a home
on Bradford Street in East New York they'd thought they'd reached
the end of a long battle, that they could finally rest. "These people

had survived immigration, and the Depression, and the Holocaust, and they had landed in East New York." It was a struggle, but they'd "gotten this foothold . . . It was a sanctuary, it was a refuge for them, and I think they expected to live there forever." Then the blockbusters came. "My parents remember the phone calls coming all the time . . . and post-cards, 'Don't be the last person on the block, you're going to lose everything.'" When they finally did sell, "they lost their whole world." No more neighbors they "could see every day." No more mahjong games. Richard's parents would never find community like they'd had there again. "The rug was pulled out from that whole generation of people."

Ira Cutler's grandmother had also been successfully hounded, bullied, and blockbusted out of her home on Vermont Street. "My grand-mother was heartbroken that she had to do that," Ira said. For the first few months, while she looked for a place to live, she moved from one of her children's homes to another, until she had a stroke and died. The mortgagee for the new buyers of her former home was the Eastern Service Corporation.

After frightening families like the Rabinowitzes and Ira's grand-mother out of their homes, the blockbusters would look for a middle-income minority family willing to pay anything to get a house, and then charge them a super-inflated price for the property they'd essentially just stolen.

But this time Lomenzo's blockbusting investigation had taken them to a family who, without any source of income or collateral, had some-how managed to secure a mortgage for a house that cost $28,000. Estimates for the average cost of a house at the time range from $17,000 to $23,000, already a challenge for middle-income families, and far out of range for a low-income household. How did a family with no income manage it?

The team had already started hearing about the growing number of foreclosures in lower income neighborhoods in New York. "We called in all of the homeowners," Lomenzo remembered. They spoke to Black homeowners, and Spanish-speaking homeowners, and at a certain point they noticed one thing all the homeowners had in common. The brokers weren't just primarily targeting minorities, they were going after poor minorities. They'd never seen this before. They knew there were federal programs to help lower income Americans buy homes, but how were families without any resources whatsoever getting mortgages in the first place? It was a recognizable sign that some sort of crime may have been committed and they began to investigate.

They found a broker who was willing to explain, and who didn't seem to be aware that he was, essentially, confessing. When they asked him if he wanted a lawyer, "He said he had nothing to hide, he was glad to tell the story."

After the broker finished spelling out the amount of money they were making and how, Lomenzo's investigator was stunned. "I looked at him," he said, "and I just paused for a moment, looking at him . . . I couldn't believe what I was listening to and I told him . . . 'Don't you realize that you were selling to poor people? Do you realize that some of these people have already lost their homes?'" The investigator was no stranger to ruthlessness, but to target people who had nothing? "Why didn't you help these people? They needed help and assistance." Instead, buyers were robbed of what little they had and left homeless, more desperate than before. The broker's attitude seemed to be, Everyone else was doing it. Why not me? Why shouldn't I be making this money?

Lomenzo's investigation had inadvertently led to what would become America's first subprime mortgage crisis, and the broker had unknowingly provided the first piece of evidence. The exchange between Lomenzo's investigator and the broker would be repeated in a scene from the movie *The Big Short*, about the 2007 subprime mortgage crisis. When two mortgage brokers admit to giving loans to people without money and without verifying their applications, one character, played by Steve Carell, stands aside with his colleagues and asks, "Why are they confessing?" "They're not confessing," they answer. "They're bragging." Steve Carell's character goes back to the brokers and asks, "Do people have any idea what they are buying?" One of the brokers answers, "I focus on the immigrants, you know. Once they find out they're getting a home they sign where you tell them to sign."

Lomenzo had uncovered what he called a "massive fraud condition," one that he suspected was being committed "not only in New York but throughout the country." Because federal crimes were suspected it was out of Lomenzo's jurisdiction, and he sat down with United States Attorney Edward R. Neaher of the Eastern District of New York. Neaher agreed that Lomenzo's team had uncovered something worth investigating further and contacted the FBI.

Lomenzo and his team were not the only ones to see that something new was going on. Eastern Service Vice President Frank Fey noticed some problems with the credit applications for Ortrud Kapraki's buyers. Fey did not suspect how close to home the problem was. Florence Behar, who was in charge of processing applications at Eastern, had signed off on them. When she acted like she didn't know what Fey was talking about he snapped, "Florence, let's stop the bullshit, you know as well as I that these deals are phonies." It was always the same accountant who verified the buyer's applications, so he told Behar not to use him anymore. He was off-limits. Behar told Kapraki, and Kapraki found a new accountant. Nothing else changed. Behar continued to sign off on all of Kapraki's clients, and the number of abandoned homes in East New York continued to rise.

Eastern Service and other speculators were flooding into East New York, buying up properties they could sell for five times what they'd paid for them. The impression that everyone was doing it was understandable. Eastern Service was not alone. They were just the biggest. There were other companies and banks, along with countless tiny, one-man shops, helping to take East New York down. Earlier and extensive blockbusting had fertilized the crime-field, and all Eastern Service and everyone else had to do now was seek out already depressed and/or foreclosed buildings. And as more buildings were abandoned and fell into disrepair, so too did the community. In his book *Cities Destroyed for Cash*, author Brian Boyer describes the people committing these crimes as thugs "who have eaten away at our cities with the grim tenacity of human termites." It is an accurate description. Harry and Rose Bernstein were nothing more than heartless, mindless scavengers, who didn't give any more thought to the lives they ruined than an insect would.

Meanwhile, HUD added the Office of the Assistant Secretary of Equal Housing Opportunity to its ranks to ensure that all the new housing programs were administered without discrimination. Like Fey, they did not yet know the full scope of the crimes Lomenzo had discovered and that housing discrimination would not be the only illegal obstacle to their mandate to further fair housing.

Buying up buildings was just one piece of the Bernsteins' crime scheme, and they were not working alone.

4

The Destruction of East New York

1972

Walter Thabit's involvement with Model Cities, a program he called a "sham from the word go," came to an end in 1971. His proposals to stem the destruction and save East New York were repeatedly ignored by the city; only thirty units of new housing had been built, and 210 existing units rehabilitated. The program was "just another cruel hoax played on minority and other poor communities."

East New Yorkers were being funneled into an ever-shrinking supply of available housing, and the FHA, whose mandate was to come to their rescue, were contributing to the problem. A nationwide scandal involving the agency and the housing programs for the poor had recently come to light. Thousands of FHA-insured buildings had foreclosed across the country, and although investigations had for the most part just begun, it looked like the suspicions of the East New York community leaders were justified.

HUD had responded to what would become known as the "FHA scandal" by running an audit. Unfortunately for the population they were supposed to be helping, they were also temporarily shutting down the Section 235 program and others beginning in January 1973, and suspending all pending applications. Homeless families would soon have even fewer options available to them. Romney did not support the action. While pointing out to Nixon's new head of the Office of Management and Budget that this was coming at a time when the administration was granting "massive tax subsidies for the middle income and wealthy," Romney wrote to Nixon that this "will only be taken by the American people—and especially those in the central city—as further evidence of a hardheaded, coldhearted indifference to the poor and racial minorities." On a more personal note, he added, "My frustration is at the apparent message to me that all the good we have accomplished is to be undone."

In the suburbs, the landmark legislation to end housing discrimination was being circumvented with various zoning laws. They were designed to exclude people of color, but as long as they focused on things like multifamily homes or income, and didn't explicitly refer to race, they weren't breaking the law. It has nothing to do with race, they would claim. We just don't want poor people here. Except, as Keeanga-Yamahtta Taylor points out in her book, *Race for Profit*, there is "no history or record of angry white mobs protesting housing for poor whites." Minority families like those in East New York were trapped. The neighborhood was imploding and all the exits were blocked. When things got bad, white families had plenty of places to go. But the families of color "couldn't get out," said Steven Lang, a lawyer who grew up in East New York and whose family had fled in 1970. "They're still there."

Once again, the FHA made matters worse. Before paying out on a mortgage insurance claim, the FHA demanded that banks adhere to their "vacancy rule" and empty the foreclosed buildings of people first. Mortgage banks were not just evicting owners who had defaulted, but any tenants they'd taken in to help with mortgage payments. Families who'd been dutifully paying their rent every month, unaware that the owner of their apartment wasn't making his mortgage payments, were put out on the street.

In the summer of 1972, nine Brooklyn tenants filed a lawsuit against the FHA, arguing that the vacancy requirement was "arbitrary, capricious, and contrary to law." They lost. They lost despite the article on abandoned buildings in the May issue of *HUD Challenge*, HUD's own official magazine, the theme of which was: vacant buildings are bad. "The degenerative effects on peripheral building and blocks cannot be exaggerated ... The abandoned building is not merely a symbol of the decline ... but an active factor itself in the abandonment process."

Compounding the problem, in response to the growing mortgage scandal, the FHA stopped insuring all mortgages in Brooklyn (and elsewhere).

Empty buildings were spreading through East New York like an unchecked virus, providing fuel for what researchers Deborah Wallace and Rodrick Wallace, who have written extensively about the fires in the 1970s, described as a plague of fire. During this period, fire was an "epidemic" that not only destroyed the physical infrastructure of neighborhoods like East New York, but the social and public services framework as well.

A retired member of law enforcement wrote how the "older clapboard houses ... burned like match books. If a fire started in one, the whole block would go up in flames." He remembered driving down Sutter Avenue with his partner and calling it the "ENY [East New York] National Forest. No houses standing for block after block, just trees and brick chimneys." To this day the fire department refers to the late 1960s and early 1970s as the "War Years."

The Lindsay administration had contracted The New York City—Rand Institute in 1967 to study fire services and other management issues. Rand researchers discovered that the fire department's busiest hours were 3:00 p.m. to midnight. This led to the creation of Tactical Control Units (TCU), which worked only those nine hours. East New York, which had seen a substantial increase in fires, got Tactical Control Unit 531 in 1969, along with a new engine and a new ladder company the following year.

This helped for a time, but foreclosures continued, emptying buildings and providing a steady supply of propellant for the flames. With abandoned buildings almost everywhere the threat of fire was always present, and by 1972 people in East New York felt like they were surrounded by unexploded ordnance that could go off at any time.

East New York in the 1970s was "nuts," according to retired firefighter Captain Joe Sapienza, who worked on Engine 236. There were so many fires they didn't have time to shower in between. When the alarms rang, you had to instantly stop what you were doing, jump into your gear, and get in the truck. No one was going to wait for you to dry off, and you couldn't miss a run. The simple act of going to the bathroom required a leap of faith. To give the East New York firefighters a chance to rest, they would sometimes swap shifts with guys from quieter neighborhoods in Queens. It was during this period that the city asked the Rand Institute to look at the fire department and make suggestions for reducing their budget. Two days after Thanksgiving, based on recommendations from Rand, six fire companies were disbanded. Most were located in poor, working-class, immigrant, and minority neighborhoods. East New York had already lost TCU 531 just two years after they arrived, but they were spared from further cuts in 1972.

In the 1970s, firefighters in East New York could get to the alarm boxes, or pull boxes, installed on street corners throughout the city, quickly. Unlike Manhattan or Queens, where firefighters have to deal with traffic jams involving cars, taxis, buses, bikes, horses, dogs, and pedestrians, East New York didn't get a lot of traffic. "East New York didn't even have groceries, didn't even have supermarkets," Sapienza remembers. "They had bodegas. But no traffic. There was nothing that would hinder us or slow us down."

For the guys who'd been swapped in from Queens however, getting to the alarm box, and quickly, could be a challenge. Thousands of streets signs were missing in East New York because thieves had taken them down and sold them for scrap metal, and the city never replaced them. Father Edward Mason, an East New York priest, remembered how when he first arrived, he had to continually ask, "What's the name of this street that I'm standing on?" For seasoned East New

York firefighters, finding the fire alarm box wasn't an issue. The location of every box in their assigned territory was ingrained in the memories of the fire fighters in each fire company. To help Queens firefighters get around, the East New York guys made "route cards," one for each alarm box. If the dispatcher sent them to box 1842, they'd grab the three-by-five card and, as they were racing to a fire, one of them would read aloud, "Upon leaving quarters, make a left. Go four blocks, make a left. Go two blocks, make a right. One block, make a left." If they immediately got another call to head to yet another fire, though, they'd have no idea how to get there. The Queens firefighters would have to "go back to the firehouse and get the route card and start from square one," Sapienza explained, because even if they'd taken all the cards with them, the directions always began with the firehouse as the starting point.

Finding the firebox was only the beginning. Then they had to find the actual fire. A battalion chief interviewed for the Wallaces' book, *A Plague on Your Houses*, explained. "Usually we have someone waving us in the right direction." If they're lucky they could "see the smoke or fire from the street." Next they'd have to find the hydrant, pray it was working, and lay the hose.

East New Yorkers complained that it was taking longer and longer for the fire department to arrive; the fire department said that wasn't true. Resentment toward firefighters had grown so precipitously that in the summer of 1972, when a group of around twenty-five kids threw rocks and bottles at firemen trying to put a fire out in an abandoned building, a hundred people just stood and watched.

Most people don't spend a lot of time thinking about city services. We don't think about the city when we turn on the faucet to get water for our coffee, or when we flush the toilet. The city picks up our trash, keeps the streets lit, installs signs so we know where we're going, provides subways, buses, and ferries. They are responsible for getting children from kindergarten to high school, for health care, for our police and fire departments. They also create and maintain parks, zoos, pools, libraries, and playgrounds. These services may not seem as crucial as police and fire departments, but life in New York City would quickly become miserable without places for children to play, or parks to sit in when you need a moment to relax, or somewhere to go to shoot hoops, swim, or read the book you can't afford to buy.

Our "everyday life is inextricably bound up with governmental decisions on these and numerous other local public services," city planner Michael Tietz wrote. In general, the only time we think about city services and the decisions behind them is when something goes wrong. The Rand Institute argued that disbanding fire companies would not affect the time it took for the first company responding to get to a fire. And it didn't.

Once the first responding company left the firehouse it took the same time it always did to get to the fire. That is if the closest fire company was not at another fire and unavailable to respond. Companies from neighboring firehouses like Brownsville, which may have come to help prior to the cuts, had troubles of their own. Did one less engine lead to more serious fires? "Of course, it did. It had to. You have less manpower, you're asking to make things worse, of course," said Sapienza.

It would be difficult to point to an actual policy decision. It certainly wouldn't have been written down. But the retreat from East New York, which had already begun, went from the equivalent of slowly backing out of the room to a full-on race for the door. East New York was already lacking in municipal services, from health care to recreation to education, but now it was going up in flames. The Kerner Commission had called for a "massive and sustained" effort. New York instead opted for surrender.

A 1971 book reporting on *The State of the Cities*, concluded that "the expressions of sympathy and concern that the Kerner Report elicited from a large number of those who, privately or publicly, wield the power that governs the United States, did not signify that they were willing to take the drastic action necessary to make American cities livable again." Mayor Lindsay, co-chair of the commission who produced the report and who had served as the vice-chairman of the Kerner Commission, could not claim to have successfully taken drastic action in East New York. After the Kerner Commission's findings had come out, Lindsay initially talked about the 18 billion spent on highways, the 18 billion spent on the space program, and the cost of the war on Vietnam. The United States was certainly in a position to come up with the money for the programs needed to combat racism, he argued. But Lindsay underestimated the massive resistance he and others would face to even the smallest steps to improve the lives of people of color.

The fires kept burning, and the conditions that created them were unchanged. The Department of Sanitation came less often to pick up trash, so there were more trash fires. The FHA wasn't properly inspecting the buildings they were insuring and faulty electrical systems left in disrepair became fire hazards. Every month more buildings were foreclosed and abandoned.

The presence of burned-out hulks contributed to the general decline and the continued withdrawal of services from the city. For those who lived in the hardest hit areas, where their children's health and well-being were threatened, anger in the face of continued indifference was understandable. People threw rocks at firemen because there were no mortgage bankers or government officials around to throw things at, and the police were armed.

Centuries of racism, discrimination, and segregation had led to this moment, and the people of East New York were stuck where they were. They had no choice but to stay and fight it out.

There were glimmers of hope in 1972. Almost fifty individuals and ten companies were indicted in New York for defrauding programs meant to provide housing for the poor and working class. The suspicions that community organizers had had about the mortgage bank Eastern Service were confirmed. Eastern was among the indicted, as were employees and officials at the FHA.

Perhaps it made the FHA seem less invincible. Early in 1973, community groups in Queens and Brooklyn decided to band together and take another shot at the FHA's vacancy requirement. A civil suit was filed against the FHA, who now owned 1,600 foreclosed buildings in Brooklyn. They planned to argue using expert testimony from 1970 Senate hearings that vacant buildings infected the neighborhoods, spreading blight wherever they appeared. In East New York and elsewhere, the fires were not the epidemic, but instead a symptom of a different outbreak. The damage that had already been done would need to be repaired, but if they were able to halt the destruction there would still be time to save East New York.

The neighborhood where Nancy Arlequin and her family lived was as lovely as before, and the buildings around them were intact. But every day and every night Nancy and her mother would have heard the fire engine sirens drawing closer.

The FHA Scandal

1970

There are ninety-four federal district courts in the United States where trials involving federal laws are held. Four are in New York. Two of them—the Southern District of New York, which was established in 1789, and the Eastern District of New York, which came along seventy-six years later—have been engaged in a largely unacknowledged sibling rivalry for over 150 years.

It all came down to Manhattan, which the Southern District covers, versus Brooklyn, which falls under the Eastern District's jurisdiction. Who has the best cases, the best lawyers? Who is the most powerful, Manhattan or Brooklyn? "The attorneys in the Southern District thought they were the top dogs, not just of New York but the entire country," said Otto Obermaier, a former U.S. attorney in the Southern District. "The world, too, probably," he added, "but that didn't come up." The polished Southern District lawyers thought so highly of themselves they generally didn't even acknowledge that there was a competition. Fight all you like, Brooklyn, but it's us. We'll be over here in our nice suits trying our high-profile financial cases while you roll around in the mud with the mob and the drug dealers. The Eastern District lawyers thought they were tougher, more street. But in the battle for supremacy, the Southern District always won. They got all the press, and all the glory.

But not everyone wanted to work with them. "The guys in Brooklyn were real guys," said Jeffrey Kay, an FBI agent who would later be assigned to the FHA fraud case. "Southern district? Prima donnas." When the FBI has an investigation that is bearing fruit, they take it to the U.S. Attorney. "If I have a case that can go either place," Kay continued, "I'm taking it to Brooklyn. I took everything to Brooklyn. I avoided the Southern District like a plague. There were real guys in Brooklyn. You could talk to them, you could work with them. You could go out to lunch with these guys. Okay? Southern District of New York? No."

Edward Neaher was confirmed as the U.S. attorney for the Eastern District of New York in 1969. A former FBI special agent who was born in Brooklyn, Neaher was also a partner at Chadbourne, Parke, Whiteside & Wolff, a prestigious law firm in Manhattan. Neaher made it his mission to raise the Eastern District out of its stepchild position in the federal prosecutorial system and make it every bit as sophisticated and prestigious as the Southern District.

Each district office has a staff of assistant United States attorneys (AUSAs) who prosecute cases. The AUSA is a young lawyer's job. Working as an AUSA is the best way to get a lot of trial experience prosecuting a wide variety of cases to take with you when you move on to a more financially rewarding position elsewhere. One of the first things Neaher did to elevate the Eastern District was bring in AUSAs with a white-collar background. He wanted lawyers who could take on the cases he planned for the Eastern District's future. Some of the district courts had a reputation of hiring lawyers based on their political connections; Neaher hired on merit. AUSAs who worked with Neaher loved him. "He was a class act," said a former AUSA. "It was a pleasure to work for him."

In September of 1970 Neaher hired Anthony Thomas Accetta. Tony to those who knew him. Accetta had almost become a boxer instead of a lawyer. He'd shown so much promise at age twelve that Floyd Patterson's manager approached Tony's mother, offering money and boxing equipment if he would agree to sign a contract when he was older. He might have done it, but a Boy's Club of New York scholarship to the elite Phillips Academy–Andover changed the direction of his life.

Accetta was at the high-powered Wall Street law firm Shearman & Sterling when he appeared on Neaher's radar. Accetta wasn't happy at Shearman. "I thought I was smarter than a lot of the people working there, and I realized it would be six or seven years before I got into a courtroom." If he stayed at Shearman & Sterling, he'd spend the next five years carrying the partners' briefcases. A pay cut was nothing next to the chance to get the kind of experience offered at one of the largest and most active federal district courts in the country. When the offer came to work at the Eastern District, Accetta grabbed it.

Over at the FHA George Romney was going all in on fair housing. He opened twenty-three new area offices and got to work on a program he called Open Communities. The President's Task Force on Low-Income Housing had encouraged using "eligibility to participate in federal housing assistance and community programs" as leverage for promoting fair and affordable housing. Programs like sewer and water grants could be withheld from communities that refused to accept subsidized housing for low-income families. Romney likely took that as a mandate. This went well for a while, until they came to Warren, Michigan.

Warren had been receiving funds for city housing and service problems since 1967; HUD cut their funding in May 1970. It was determined that their housing policies discriminated against Black homebuyers. For funding to resume they had to change those policies. When Romney traveled to Warren to hammer out an agreement, the government made a lot of concessions and Warren conceded little, but the modest project to introduce low-income housing in Warren would move forward. Unfortunately the *Detroit News* published a series of inflammatory articles about how Romney was using Warren to spearhead his desegregation plans.

When he returned to Warren to repair the damage, he needed a police escort back to his car. Romney insisted that this was not "forced integration," but "affirmative action." He tried again to come to an agreement. "We're not going to ask you to provide housing for anyone other than those who want to live in Warren." But the battle was already lost. Michigan voters decided they would rather lose the $10 million than take steps to integrate. Between relatively wealthy voters who could afford to turn down $10 million dollars and a government without the will to take stronger measures, low- and middle-income families who were trying to get out of neighborhoods in Detroit where crime was rising were locked in, just like the families in Brooklyn.

In New York, Mayor Lindsay met with similar resistance the following year. He'd developed plans for an 840-unit low-income housing project in the middle-class Queens neighborhood of Forest Hills. It was an important step. It would provide options for fair, affordable housing outside areas like East New York, and it had George Romney's full support. But after years of bitter community meetings, court battles, threats of impeachment, and protests with rocks and actual flaming torches, the project was scaled back to 432 units that would eventually be filled with tenants from nearby Queens locations, 70 percent of whom were white.

The Nixon administration was not happy with what had gone down in Warren, Michigan. Not the rejection of Black people as potential neighbors, but the position Romney had put the president in with white voters. John Ehrlichman, assistant to the president for Domestic Affairs, wrote Nixon in October, warning him that they had "a serious Romney problem," and they'd have it "as long as he is there." Nixon responded, "stop this one," and later suggested, "Romney will go . . . if we can find a good Black to replace him." They floated the idea of Romney leaving the cabinet to become the ambassador to Mexico, but Romney declined. "George won't leave quickly, will have to be fired,"

Nixon's Chief of Staff H. R. Haldeman wrote that November. "So we have to set him up on the integrated housing issue and fire him on that basis to be sure we get the credit."

Called into a meeting with the president in December, Romney thereafter stood behind the administration's policies. The Nixon administration would fight discrimination because of race, but not because of "economic status." It was the perfect out for communities to reject housing that might include people of color. Once again, it wasn't that the people were Black, it was because they were poor. The prospects for those trying to leave East New York kept getting dimmer and dimmer.

Erhlichman had called Romney's efforts "the result of what the secretary perceives to be both his legal and moral obligation." According to those who knew Romney, Erhlichman's assessment was completely correct. He was not a young man, he was well aware of how terrible humanity could be, and he must have known how vulnerable his support of fair housing would make him politically, but Romney had truly believed he could appeal to the better angels of our nature and make the country more fair. His public support of the administration's new position was perhaps the only practical way he could continue to try. To those who put their faith in his promise of fair housing, though, providing cover for Nixon's fair housing sleight of hand was a stinging betrayal of their confidence and hope.

In the middle of the summer, and just days after he was jeered at in Warren, Romney heard from Wright Patman, the chairman of the House Banking and Currency Committee, who wrote to say the committee had uncovered "a national scandal of the most sordid type." Buyers in the FHA's housing programs "have either been installed in slums or have been saddled with long-term mortgages in far greater amounts than the worth of their property, or both." The committee's report read, "Many of these FHA purchasers have been victimized by unconscionable real estate speculators who have made fantastic profits in short periods." After paying a relatively high price, new homeowners were moving into buildings with faulty wiring, condemned furnaces, ceilings that had just fallen in, water tanks that had to be replaced, rats, and more. "It is our understanding that where existing housing is sold, minimum FHA standards must be met . . . it is not difficult to imagine the human agony of the homeowner." The report called for the problems to be fixed, legislation to prevent it from happening again, and "the bilked, cheated, defrauded, and unsuspecting homeowner must be made whole." Patman concluded his letter with seven questions for Romney, beginning with, "How conceivably can FHA approve substandard slum housing as meeting the minimum standards of existing housing under Section 235 or any other program?"

Three days after receiving Patman's communication, the FHA sent out a circular, reiterating that property standards must be met and repairs made before granting insurance. Under no circumstances were these standards to be waived in "blighted" areas.

Romney would later say this was the summer when he first became aware of the abuses. Up until then Romney had reason to be proud. The HUD Act had set a goal of 26 million new or rehabilitated housing units by 1978, 6 million of which would be low-income housing units. In his first two years as secretary of HUD, Romney had increased the number of subsidized housing units from 162,722 to 429,800. That accomplishment would be forever overshadowed by the abuses.

Another potentially ground-breaking program Romney initiated was also in trouble. Inspired by the assembly line techniques employed by the American Motors Corporation when he was CEO, in 1969, Romney announced Operation Breakthrough. The program used new technology and mass production practices to help meet the HUD Act goal of 26 million new or rehabilitated housing units in 10 years. To ensure a cutting edge approach, Romney brought in rocket scientist and NASA administrator Harold B. Finger to become HUD's first assistant secretary for Research and Technology to oversee the program. Nine sites were chosen where prototype communities were built using prefabricated housing. Analysts disagree about why the program failed, but one key factor was racism. New homeowners in the mixed-income communities would be eligible for mortgage interest subsidies under the HUD Act's low-income home-ownership programs. To suburban residents, that meant Black people, and they opposed the program. When they tried to build in Delaware, "there was an uproar in that community," Finger told historian Kevin Rusnak. "Automatically, if it was government coming in, it had to be public housing. They didn't want public housing." Despite the problems, eight of the nine sites still provide housing, and Romney's vision of factory-produced homes is again gaining momentum.

Over the next few days the story about what had been found in Patman's investigation was reported in the *Philadelphia Inquirer* and elsewhere. But Patman's committee had only become aware of abuses in Philadelphia and Washington. "If these two cities are typical of the rest of the nation," the report read, "then the operation of the program is nothing short of scandalous."

As the news hit, Ortrud Kapraki was ramping up her closings of FHA-insured homes at Eastern Service, and Eastern Service was smoothing her way. FHA appraiser Edward Goodwin regularly left his office on the third floor to go up to the Eastern office on the fifth floor to meet with Harry and Rose Bernstein. Eastern was now responsible for 10 percent of the FHA's Hempstead office business. The Bernsteins always made sure to have Goodwin's favorite scotch, Johnnie Walker Black, on hand whenever they discussed business.

Although Romney's response to Patman did not acknowledge anything criminal on the part of the FHA, addressing only "appraisal deficiencies," the FBI had started investigating at the request of the Eastern District of New York, and a much darker picture had begun to emerge.

5

The Destruction of East New York

1973–1974

East New York could not afford to lose any more housing. At the beginning of 1973, groups from the neighborhood joined others from Brooklyn and Queens to bring a second suit against the FHA, this time charging that their vacancy requirement amplified urban blight. "Buildings formerly in good condition that were suitable for housing have been lost to the market because of vacancy and neglect." It was among the first lawsuits in the country to cite the National Environment Policy Act, which required federal agencies to determine the environmental impact of their proposed actions. The groups wanted the court to compel the FHA to conduct a study to determine the effect of their vacancy requirement on the neighborhoods where it was imposed.

Soon after, a court's injunction stopped the FHA's bulk sale of 182 vacant buildings in Brooklyn. The FHA had made it known that the homes would not be eligible for FHA mortgages. Community groups had hoped to rehabilitate the buildings, but without FHA insurance only a speculator who didn't care about the neighborhood would buy them. The buildings would then either be torn down and replaced with parking lots or warehoused until better options presented themselves.

No new homes would be made available, and more than one hundred future sites of a murder or a fire would be created.

Housing anxiety was ramping up due to the Nixon administration's moratorium on subsidized housing, which had begun in January. The suspension could mean up to twenty-three thousand units of housing lost in New York, according to the city's Housing Development administrator. "The freeze, quite simply, is a massive breach of faith." Worse, HUD found that the decision to halt the programs was based on reasoning that was "paper-thin, highly subjective, and totally unsupported by any back-up data," and only made after the moratorium had been announced, in order to justify a decision that had been made without informed research.

If you were living in East New York in 1973, whether your priority was to leave or to fix the growing problems, the wall of indifference and obliviousness could be so impenetrable it was hard not to succumb to a sense of both futility and dread.

While thousands of mortgage crimes that destroyed entire neighborhoods housing the most vulnerable were just now making their way to court, the Rockefeller drug laws were signed into law in May, giving New York the toughest drug laws in the country. Something needed to be done about the drug problem, but punishment wasn't the only tool nor was it the most effective. Something also needed to be done about rampant financial crime and yet no one was talking about passing stricter laws with minimum sentences to stop the white-collar criminals who had targeted low-income families without mercy. It did not escape notice that laws that were disproportionately applied to people of color were easy to pass, while laws that would primarily affect white criminals were not even suggested. Instead, buildings continued to be foreclosed and abandoned, and programs aimed at helping their victims were in danger of disappearing.

Homicide was up 144 percent since 1964 in the NYPD Brooklyn North Patrol Borough, which included East New York. Johnny Alite, who grew up in East New York, saw one of his first murders when he was eleven. It wasn't unusual. "We all saw murders on a regular basis, dead bodies, this was all normal in my neighborhood." In 1973 he was on his way to the YMCA when he saw some guys chasing a man toward Highland Park. "They were shooting at him, they hit him, the guy went down, screaming, and they kept on shooting him." After the shooters calmly walked away, John went up to the body, glanced at the pool of blood, then continued on to the YMCA to play basketball. His routine exposure to murder and his dispassionate response would serve him well in his future career as a hit man for the mob.

East New York was draining jobs as well as housing. That fall, after ninety years of operation, the Piels Brothers were closing down their plant on Liberty Avenue. In the last five years, East New York had lost five thousand jobs, and now another eight hundred were gone.

One small bright spot appeared in October. The Eastern District of New York announced that they were bringing a civil suit against Fred C. Trump, Donald Trump, and Trump Management, Inc. The Trumps were charged with violating the Civil Rights Act of 1968 by refusing to rent to people of color in their buildings in Brooklyn, Queens, and Staten Island. Edward Neaher, the former U.S. attorney, was now a federal judge and he would be the one to hear the case. Donald Trump immediately claimed, "I received many calls and letters of surprise from tenants and community leaders expressing their shock and disbelief that our organization should be charged with such outrageous lies." Two months later he held a press conference. The Trumps had filed a counterclaim, accusing the government of making false statements about them, and they were seeking $100 million in damages.

Cases like those against the Trumps were good news for East New York. Perhaps the Civil Rights Act was not entirely another empty promise and places to live outside East New York would soon become available to them.

The next month another bit of hope appeared. The Ideal Corporation, a transportation equipment manufacturer, had taken out a big ad in a local newspaper to proclaim their pride about being in East New York since 1913, and to announce that they were putting up a new building on Pennsylvania Avenue. It would mean five hundred more jobs.

Two new and much needed health centers were also going up; one nearing completion at the corner of Pennsylvania and Pitkin Avenues, and another that was ready and waiting at the corner of Sutter and William. In addition to homes and jobs, East New York needed hospital beds and health care.

For Nancy Arlequin and her family, the next year, 1974, brought the birth of Nancy's first child, a daughter, who was born on March 3. She was named Julia, after her grandmother, and she was given the surname of her father, George Parker. Cocooned with her new baby girl, in an area with buildings that housing community activists called "attractive and basically sound," Nancy and Julia were surrounded with relatives to help, and the kind of hope that generally accompanies a new arrival.

But hope for the future repeatedly turned into something of a trap for people in East New York. The year 1974 also brought Nixon's new budget.

At the beginning of Nixon's second year in office, Senator Daniel Patrick Moynihan had put together a memo for Nixon about the current status of Black people in America, recommending a period of what he called "benign neglect." Moynihan claimed that talking about race issues so much had "created opportunities for martyrdom, heroics, histrionics, or whatever." Less attention, he argued, would produce better results. In 1974, journalist Samuel F. Yette declared that "the new Nixon budget escalates 'benign neglect' to malignant abandonment. It tells the nation that the Black and poor are—at best—left to fend for themselves."

The activists who called Nancy's corner of East New York attractive and sound had added, "If the major action is taken now East New York can be restored to a healthy self-sufficient community." But major action was never taken. With the new budget, Nixon signaled his determination to put an end to any thoughts of a Great Society or a War on Poverty. His administration would be phasing out urban renewal (a series of initiatives developed to revitalize cities) and the Model Cities program, along with around one hundred other programs, like the Neighborhood Youth Corps, which mainly affected kids in Harlem, and Brooklyn neighborhoods like East New York. Aid for hospital construction would also end, Nixon announced. The country had enough hospital beds.

Nancy Arlequin was very lucky to have found a bed at Brookdale Hospital in neighboring Brownsville to give birth. Hospital beds in East New York were scarce. Although construction of the new health center at the corner of Pennsylvania and Pitkin Avenue had finished, the doors had yet to open due to lack of operating funds. Two of the three small hospitals operating in East New York would be closed in the next few years.

The fire department eliminated five more engine companies and three ladder companies in 1974. Once again, most were in communities of color, and this time the disbanded companies were among the busiest in the entire city. East New York's Ladder 103-2, the seventh busiest ladder company in all of New York City, was one of the eliminated.

When a fourteen-year-old girl was found hanging from the staircase, naked from the waist down, in a foreclosed and abandoned building on Wyona Street, the boys who found her pulled the nearest fire alarm box. They'd been playing outside the building and had gone inside for a game of hide-and-seek. One of the boys had run out screaming, "There's a dead girl inside!" Engine 283 from Brownsville responded, presumably because all the fire companies in East New York were already out on other calls. The girl had been dead for two days. The foreclosed building, which was owned by HUD, was located in Thabit's Family Area, where Nancy Arlequin was living with her new baby girl. It was not the only breach in their neighborhood, and it made it clear that their happy enclave was no longer immune to the dangers that surrounded them.

Nixon rescinded the moratorium on the housing programs for the poor in summer 1974, and it was a relief. Then, on August 8, he resigned, and for some that was a relief too. Later that month Congress passed the Housing and Community Development Act of 1974, which now President Gerald Ford signed into law on August 22. Section 235 and 236 resumed, although with a lot less money, and the Section 8 Program was created to help low-income families with rent. The Act also established community-development block grants (CDBG), intended to primarily aid low-income neighborhoods, but by the second year 56 percent of the grants went to higher-income communities to build things like tennis courts, swimming pools, and golf courses.

In the meantime, community groups won their suit against the FHA and HUD. The judge required HUD to assess the cumulative effects of their vacancy requirement, and HUD agreed to table the bulk sale of 182 properties, and to conduct an Environmental Impact Study first.

The year 1974 saw a number of big wins. That summer the federal trial in the Eastern District against those responsible for the largest number of abandoned buildings in East New York had concluded. The mortgage bank for the building where the girl was found hanging had also been indicted, and another trial was anticipated. It looked like some of the people responsible for the foreclosures were finally going to be held accountable.

The FHA Scandal

1970

On two occasions in the late 1960s, the FBI came this close to discovering the crimes of Eastern Service. A few days after Christmas in 1967, the Intelligence Unit of the Suffolk County Police Department contacted the New York office of the FBI to let them know about the "shylocking and gambling activities" of Eastern Service, who were buying up houses that were in rough shape in Brooklyn, making minor repairs, and somehow obtaining mortgages insured by the FHA for amounts far greater than the buildings were worth. The case went into a "0" (zero) file, the destination for case files that were never opened or investigated.

The following year the New York office was contacted by HUD to let them know that Assistant District Attorney Leon Port was heading an investigation into blockbusting involving Eastern Service. Soon after, Port got in touch with them to say that he was aware this was in the FBI's jurisdiction, and he was going to turn over any pertinent leads, but the investigation was on hold while he was busy with other things and he'd get back to them. That was the last they heard from Port.

In February 1969, Irving Seidman, the chief of the Racket Squad in the DA's office, called with an update. Port had resigned from his position, he told them. Since then they'd found that the allegations against Eastern Service did not contain evidence of false statements or fraudulent activity and since there "is no specific statute to cover blockbusting," they hadn't actually committed a crime. No crime, no investigation. Although there now was a federal statute covering block-busting, Port's tip also went into a 0 file.

One year later, United States Attorney Edward Neaher, who had been contacted by New York Secretary of State John Lomenzo about what his investigators uncovered, had come to a different conclusion about the activity involving Eastern Service. On February 3, 1970, he made a formal request to the FBI to investigate. His request was sent via Airtel from the FBI's New York office to FBI headquarters in Washington. Airtels had to be typed up and mailed that day, signaling that they should be looked at sooner rather than later. "In order of importance," special agent Jim Sniegocki explained, "a letter is routine, an Airtel means priority, and a teletype, which is sent and received immediately via a teletype machine, means give this your immediate attention." The fact that it was sent by Airtel meant the New York of-fice knew this was not a run-of-the-mill case, but they didn't want to oversell it until they had more information.

■

Jim Sniegocki felt he had two choices when he graduated from high school in Dickson City, a small coal mining town in Pennsylvania. Join his father in an anthracite coal mine, or continue working at the Golo Shoe Factory, where he spent his days on a machine pressing leather and shoe linings together for thirty dollars a week. When a friend told him the FBI was hiring clerks, he thought, "white-collar job, annual leave, sick leave, a pension," and immediately applied. He got the job, but it wasn't long before Sniegocki saw that there were more excit-ing opportunities to be had at the FBI. He could be a special agent. Toward that aim, he went to night school, got an accounting degree, and applied for a spot in the next agent's class. His supervisor told him not to get his hopes up, but he was accepted. After his first assignment he was sent to the Defense Language Institute, where he did so well he was given an assignment to work in foreign counterintelligence in New York.

The Foreign Counterintelligence Squad was a prestigious squad, but it also involved a lot of paperwork, and agents spent most of their time in the office. Jim wanted to get out of the office and solve crimes. "That's what I signed up for." The Accounting and Fraud Squad, which investigated white-collar crimes, was a criminal squad, but it was at the bottom in terms of prestige. "In the 1960s," says FBI historian Dr. John Fox, "white-collar cases were not a huge priority with the Bureau. The FBI was focused on civil unrest, the violent aspects of the protest movement, domestic security." This period of time will not go down as the FBI's finest hour, as they were fixated on things like destroying Martin Luther King Jr. and the illegal operations of COINTELPRO, an FBI program that focused on taking down the Black Panther party and a long list of left-leaning groups including animal activists, environmentalists, and feminists.

While most of his fellow agents wanted to work in the Fugitive or Bank Robbery Squads, Sniegocki knew the Accounting Squad was his best chance at getting into a criminal squad. The FBI needed agents with a background in accounting, and he had an accounting degree. In 1966 Sniegocki was transferred to the FBI's New York Accounting and Fraud Squad, a.k.a. Squad 23.

"The FBI in New York is different than any other FBI office," Sniegocki says. The New York office was big, around one thousand agents. The cases in New York were also larger, and more complicated. "That was just the nature of New York." And FBI agents assigned there quite naturally developed a "New York attitude." From another former agent in the squad: "The New York office runs the world. New York always got it done."

At the time, the FBI's New York headquarters were on the Upper East Side, on the corner of Sixty-ninth Street and Third Avenue, just blocks from some of the toniest addresses in Manhattan. The Criminal Division was on the seventh floor, with squads in bullpens all the way across the floor. The Squad 23 supervisor had a corner office, while anywhere from 225 to 260 agents sat in rows of desks around ten feet deep.

The Accounting Squad sat in the back. Although the squad was made up of close to twenty special agents, they'd been assigned only two cars. Often when they had a lead they had to go down into the subway and do their best to squeeze into the packed cars along with everyone else. The agents in the Accounting Squad worked on bank embezzlement cases, fraud involving government contracts, bankruptcy, investments, and the FHA. Typically an agent worked on one type of case at a time; one agent might be taking the bank cases, while another took the mortgage fraud cases.

When United States Attorney Edward Neaher asked the FBI to look into Eastern Service, Sniegocki was working on around twenty fraud cases. One case in particular had taken a trajectory similar to the one that originally got Secretary of State Lomenzo's attention. Was it blockbusting? Mortgage fraud? The FBI would call the Eastern Service case a blockbusting case in the beginning, although they wouldn't for long. Like Lomenzo before him, Sniegocki quickly figured out something else was going on, something that looked like blockbusting, and sometimes did involve blockbusting, but was much worse.

The first thing Sniegocki did was go back over the 0 files on Eastern. Their initial focus was on Ortrud Kapraki, who was still being investigated by the New York secretary of state for blockbusting. The secretary of state had turned over to the Eastern District twenty-four files that they believed indicated additional crimes that were federal crimes and not under their jurisdiction, and Kapraki's name was on a lot of them. For some reason, the AUSA who had the cases did not share those files with the FBI and Sniegocki for months.

Sniegocki had seen his fair share of mortgage fraud, and a typical case involved one mortgage. Once they had the files from the Eastern District, the FBI's New York office immediately realized something more substantial was going on. They were up to twenty-six related cases and they'd only just started investigating. News about similar crimes had already appeared in newspapers in other cities. It looked like New York had joined the party.

On August 3, they got an Airtel from the Bureau in Washington asking for an update. Everyone, including the Bureau, knew that something unusual was going on and that it was big. Sniegocki's supervisor, Vince Cunningham, immediately answered with another Airtel. Still calling it a blockbusting case, he explained that it had taken two months for the Eastern District to give them the original twenty-four files. The leads had been divided between a number of agents, and Cunningham promised they'd have an interim report ready by mid-August and a completed investigation by the end of September 1970.

Sniegocki and his supervisor knew it was going to take a lot longer than a month and a half to conclude their investigation, but they had to provide a date. We'll have a better idea of what was going on by September, they thought, and we can give the Bureau a better picture of the case then.

6

The Destruction of East New York

1975–1976

In 1975, three months after the defendants in the case brought to the Eastern District by Secretary of State Lomenzo were convicted and sentenced, and two months before Julia Parker turned one, a thirty-five-year-old commercial photographer was thrown out of a fourth-story window at 490 Alabama Avenue in East New York. He had just finished taking pictures of a family who lived in the building when he was grabbed in the hallway and dragged into an abandoned apartment. There he was stripped, bound with wire, mutilated with knives, and finally tossed from a fourth-story window to the street.

This was not far from where Julia Parker was growing up, and her mother, Nancy, could no longer ignore the fact that conditions in East New York were deteriorating. She would have passed by all the abandoned buildings on her way home to a neighborhood that was still relatively protected. She was aware of the fires, increasing crime, and the eruptions of violence due to racial unrest. But the whole country had been in turmoil for a decade. Uprising after uprising followed assassination after assassination, and crime had gone up everywhere. Things had settled down for a while, though. Local newspapers were running a steady stream of articles about the city's plans to address East New

York's decline. Nancy had every reason to believe that, like the rest of the country, things would get back to normal in East New York.

In any case, there weren't a lot of housing options in New York for a young family from Puerto Rico without a lot of money. Despite her limited choices, Thabit's Family Area, where Nancy and her family were living, was still relatively nice. If she had any misgivings, she put them aside. If she had even read about the photographer who'd been tortured and thrown out a window, perhaps what she remembered was that he'd survived. Besides, his attack had taken place in what Thabit called the Tenement Area South, one of the worst sections in East New York. If they just continued to stay away from this and other pockets of crime, they'd be okay.

The friends of Dr. Johnny Ray Youngblood, who had been assigned to the East Brooklyn St. Paul Community Baptist Church the previous summer, were not as optimistic. "You are being sent to one of God's Alcatrazes!" they told him. They weren't exaggerating. "The image of a brutal island prison," the National Research Council would later write, "captures a piece of the isolation that characterized East New York."

The city's rosy plans for East New York began to fade in 1975 as the area drifted further into decline. The ongoing cascade of deterioration bred increasing indifference, and over the years city hall grew deaf to the calls for more and better schools, health centers, regular sanitation pickups, and a swifter response from the police and fire departments.

Linden General, a local hospital, was still in operation in March 1975 but had lost accreditation that month after being deemed dangerous and obsolete. Although Linden was surrounded by abandoned buildings and vacant lots, those seventy-nine beds were too precious to lose. Despite "serious fire safety violations, inadequate toilet facilities, and poor sanitation," patients continued to be admitted.

In June, fourteen-year-old Valerie Whitely was found laying face down in a bathtub in an abandoned building on Fulton Street. She'd been strangled with her own scarf. Valerie, a ninth grader at nearby Franklin K. Lane High School, had been missing for several days.

When news that a body had been found reached her parents, they rushed to the building. They waited outside until her father was finally allowed to go upstairs, extinguishing any hope that it was not his daughter. Her case was never solved. People in the neighborhood were still pleading with the city a year later to do something about the abandoned building where she was found.

New York's financial troubles mounted. At midnight on July 1, thousands of police, firefighters, sanitation, correction, and park workers were laid off. And yet articles about how they were going to save East New York still appeared. Two days after the layoff, the city announced a pilot program that would initially rehabilitate eighty one-to-four-family houses and eighteen vacant lots.

By the fall New York was near bankruptcy. This was the year the *New York Daily News* ran the now famous headline, FORD TO CITY: DROP DEAD, when then president Ford declined to come to New York's rescue. Budget cuts were imperative.

Four years before Moynihan's benign neglect memo, Roger Starr, the executive director of the nonprofit Citizens Housing and Planning Council, had started kicking around an idea about how to address urban blight. He fully supported urban renewal, "in the course of which we may displace poor people to make room for middle-class people." Urban renewal included "slum clearance," the process of clearing residents out of slums, demolishing their homes, and rebuilding new ones. Starr didn't think relocating poor people would affect them too much. "Provided only that a certain homogeneity of social class and income can be maintained, American communities can be disassembled and reconstituted about as readily as freight trains."

Poor people who complained were overstating their problems, Starr insisted, milking their poverty for all it was worth. "Since they have no property, their only marketable asset is hardship," he wrote, and that we've all been duped to the point that it was now "immoral" to suggest "that some of the people displaced by urban renewal might just possibly be exaggerating the sense of deprivation that they feel over their 'lost homes.'" He even urged "taking an indeterminate number of children away from the homes of their natural parents or parent, to raise them in new, small, pioneering institutions."

Starr had fought Lindsay's efforts to build low-income housing in Forest Hills. "The government cannot force housing to be built in middle-class areas through policy.

However, he didn't support Nixon's 1973 moratorium on programs for the poor. In a *New York Times* editorial Starr addressed the new housing goals that had been set by Congress. "In 1971 and 1972 the housing industries surpassed their annual targets. A remarkably large 25 percent of the housing units that were started in 1972 were subsidized by the federal government so that families with relatively low incomes were able to move into them. Is anyone ashamed of this achievement?"

Later that year, perhaps forgetting Starr's position about disassembling and reconstituting low-income communities and taking the children of low-income families away from their parents, Mayor Abraham Beame appointed Roger Starr to be the city's new Housing and Development administrator.

In early 1976, as New York teetered on the verge of bankruptcy, Starr's contribution to the effort to address the city's financial problems was a program he called "planned shrinkage." If they thinned out essential services in places like East New York, such as the police, firefighters, subways, health care, and schools, this would not only help them trim the budget, the neighborhood would become so unlivable it would prompt even more people to leave, freeing them to withdraw still more of the city's limited funds.

Once empty of all the poor people, they could use the land for other things, like industry. "Better a thriving city of five million," Starr would later write, "than a Calcutta of seven, destroyed by its internal wrangling."

Public outrage prevented the open adoption of their plan, and yet when thousands of firefighters, police, and sanitation workers had been laid off the year before, their absence was felt more in communities of color. "They were still picking up garbage in Canarsie," a former East New Yorker remembered, referring to the white neighborhood bordering East New York to the southwest. East New Yorkers took their complaints to city hall. "We are entitled to the city services we pay our hard-earned tax dollars to get." They picketed outside a Department of Sanitation office about the poor collection and lack of enforcement. Starr resigned that summer.

It was one battle after another. When the city considered giving the Linden General Hospital building over to the Department of Correction to use for a Work Release Program, five hundred people showed up to a Community Planning Board #5 meeting to oppose the idea. It was the second time the Department of Correction tried to locate their program in the neighborhood. East New York was already the site of many social reform programs, they argued, like the Alpha School, a drug treatment program for teens, a methadone center, and P.I.N.S (Persons in Need of Supervision). They were tired of being used as a bureaucratic toxic waste dump. The attendees wanted the building to be used as a senior citizen's center or a youth or community center. But federal funds were about to be cut off due to fire hazards within the building.

In an eighty-nine-page report, a federal task force found that "New York City is not fulfilling its primary responsibility to the people of New York when it reduces emergency service manpower and equipment." They understood the city's fiscal problems, but it "is unrealistic, however, to expect police, fire and emergency medical service personnel to adequately respond to serious emergencies or disasters if any further reductions in operating manpower are made." Still more fire companies were disbanded in November. While a "Rally for Crime Prevention" took place in East New York, two men were shot to death ten blocks away. Twelve-year-old Chuck Harrison (now a retired NYPD detective) walked into St. Michael's church one day just after Pastor Pancratius Krieg was murdered. "Everybody was frantic . . . Just go home. Go home," they told him. Chuck saw the body, "then I turned around and left. It was crazy. But growing up in East New York, your journey as a kid, seeing bodies was something you experienced."

That fall, despite all the community's efforts to stop it, city cutbacks led to the closure of two day care centers in the area.

The FHA Scandal

1971

In the beginning of 1971, the House Banking and Currency Committee released a report showing widespread abuse of Section 235 of the Housing Act. Ten cities were investigated, but New York was not among them. Wright Patman, the chair of the committee, told reporters, "Instead of buying a home, people purchasing these houses are buying a disaster." Mike Wallace broadcast a piece about HUD and the FHA on *60 Minutes*. "The Department of Housing and Urban Development and its Federal Housing Administration may be well on the way toward insuring itself into a national scandal." The jig was up. In March, Anthony Accetta was assigned to what would become the Eastern Service case.

Before being handed off to Accetta, the case had languished on a couple of desks while the AUSAs who initially had it worked on other crimes. Mortgage fraud isn't sexy. It's complicated and difficult to prove. It takes time and a lot of work to put it all together and lay it out in a way that a jury can understand. So it fell to the rookie. But even if all the AUSAs in the office had wanted it, it was always going to end up with Accetta.

Tony Accetta grew up in a part of New York City that is now called

Alphabet City. At the time it had a large Puerto Rican community. "I lived *West Side Story*," Accetta would say. Accetta didn't like to see people who could have been his former neighbors targeted, fleeced, and destroyed. He was the only guy in the U.S. Attorney's office who could have taken what would ultimately turn into a twenty-five-thousand-page monster of a trial and develop it into a coherent case that anyone could follow. George Bashion, who would join him at the prosecutor's table, said he was "the only guy who had the motivation and the desire, and the feeling of 'this isn't right.'"

Accetta was a smart, dark-haired, good-looking guy, who also had a healthy ego. He wasn't afraid to try something that was going to be hard to prove. "On the other hand you could say he was an overzealous prosecutor, that he overreached." But he was going to right this wrong. "Accetta was the driving force for the case." Had his fellow AUSAs known what Accetta would ultimately uncover, they would never have let him anywhere near those files.

Accetta met with Lomenzo's guy, Patrick Cea, who told them what they'd found and what they knew so far. This wasn't simple mortgage fraud. It was something far uglier, and he hadn't yet discovered the worst of it. When Accetta got the Eastern Service case he'd been working on bank robberies, hijackings, and drug cases. After he started investigating the crimes of Eastern Service he uncovered so much evidence of similar crimes committed by so many others that these kinds of cases would be all he'd work on until the end of his time at the Eastern District.

When the House Banking and Currency Committee released their report showing extensive abuse in January, Romney would initially call the report "misleading and very incomplete." Eight days later he conceded that "abuses are more prevalent and widespread than had previously been evident," and immediately froze Section 235, in order to conduct an audit of the program.

But the House Banking and Currency Committee had looked at only ten cities. "This is not a national scandal," Romney said. At this point there was no evidence of fraud, and the worst cases involved inexperienced, even incompetent, FHA appraisers who were appraising the houses for more than they were worth. This was as bad as it got, and it seemed like an easy problem to solve. Fire the bad appraisers, tighten up appraisal procedures, retrain everyone who remained, and everything would be okay.

By March 1971, Romney's audit found that 42.7 percent of the homes that were found eligible for an FHA mortgage threatened the health, safety, and livability of those who bought them. The smell from backed-up sewers pervaded the homes and daylight could be seen through rotting walls. The audit also uncovered a more disturbing problem. FHA personnel expressed the opinion that "as long as the people were getting better housing than they were accustomed to the goals of the program were being met." This attitude had never been adopted when insuring the mortgages of white homeowners. Romney's own people were not furthering fair housing, and were, in fact, perpetuating discrimination.

The next month, a two-hundred-page report from the U.S. Civil Rights Commission was leaked. Among other things, the report charged the FHA with "abdicating its responsibility" to further fair housing and were instead practicing segregation themselves. White homebuyers were shown new 235 homes in the suburbs while Black homebuyers were shown rehabilitated housing in neighborhoods of color in the cities. Romney knew by now that those rehabilitated homes were little more than slum housing. The report also pointed out that HUD had promised to promote "open communities" by using the withdrawal of federal funds to insure compliance, but later retreated from this position, and was now opposed to the "use of federal leverage to promote economic integration." This must have been particularly galling for Romney since this was Nixon's decision, and if it were up to Romney they would still be withholding federal funds. But of course the committee would have no way of knowing that. Publicly, Romney supported the new stance. A couple of months after the report came out he mocked the idea that the government should "assume the role of omnipotent hero righting all wrongs, knocking down all barriers with a flourish and redrawing the crazy-quilt map of our metropolitan areas." But if Romney was mocking anyone, it was himself, because that is exactly what he himself had once believed. Although he called the report "largely unfounded," he knew there was some truth to it, and he would soon learn just how terribly true it all was.

That spring, AUSA Anthony Accetta met with the lead FBI agent Jim Sniegocki and other members of the team of special agents, including Dennis Lacina and Ron Hodges, who, together with a team of prosecutors and lawyers, would help him ultimately uncover the full extent of the crimes in New York. They reviewed what they had and devised an initial plan.

Bribing appraisers was nothing new, but until now it had always been one case here, one case there. They now had more than twenty-six. It was no longer just some guy lying on his mortgage application. Something bigger and more coordinated was going on.

While Sniegocki and Lacina started talking to the buyers to learn more, Accetta went to his boss, Ed Neaher, about convening a grand jury. FBI Agent Jeffrey Kay called the federal grand jury "the greatest vehicle in the world to do a white-collar crime investigation." Accetta needed subpoena power, he needed to get documents, he needed to be able to question people "and scare the shit out of them" if necessary. With a grand jury, he could do all this and more. Neaher had been convinced this was a good case when Lomenzo first brought it to him. He sent a request to the federal judge, and the impaneling process commenced.

Accetta went to Washington in the summer to speak to a HUD lawyer about their suspicions concerning the FHA's involvement in the crimes. The case was turning out to be more complicated than the possible bribing of a few appraisers, he told the attorney, and to prove it he needed their full cooperation. He needed a HUD lawyer, and HUD personnel who could provide documents and explain what all these procedures and forms meant. An agreement for this kind of cooperation had to come from Romney.

A meeting was arranged. Romney was a commanding presence, but he was also down to earth and Accetta could tell him frankly: "Sir, I need you to keep your mouth shut. No one knows what we're doing and the minute this gets out we'll be compromised. People will smarten up and doors will close."

Accetta was very nervous going into that meeting, but he came out elated. Romney "was cordial, concerned, and cooperative." He felt respected. "I walked into his office, this young obnoxious lawyer, and he gave me all the logistical support I could possibly need. I trusted him. He was a terrific guy."

Romney never did say a word to anyone who might expose Accetta's investigation. Instead, he had the General Council set Accetta up with John Kennedy (no relation to the president), an attorney advisor with HUD. After this meeting, Romney could have no more illusions about what was going on in offices he'd established across the country. He'd already experienced deep disappointment with those above him, and now he was disillusioned with those below. But if Romney felt surrounded by people who'd let him down, it was, of course, nothing compared to what the people of color in East New York and the rest of the country were enduring.

In the course of the FBI's investigations and Accetta's grand jury examination, one realtor's name and one mortgage bank kept reappearing: Ortrud Kapraki and Eastern Service.

When going after a criminal organization, you don't start with the people at the top. "You start at the bottom," Accetta explained, "and work your way up." Anxious underlings who played a part could be frightened into giving up those above them. At the bottom of the criminal ladder they hoped to climb was Ortrud Kapraki. As the FBI case agent, Jim Sniegocki would reach out first. Kapraki returned his call and said she would be happy to cooperate. But when they called her lawyer to set it up, they were told that under no circumstances would he allow her to be interviewed without a "complete discussion of this matter with the assistant United States attorney who is handling this case." Accetta.

While all this was going on, articles about the growing scandal were popping up. The *Philadelphia Inquirer* were already publishing an on-going series of investigative reports about a possible mortgage scandal involving the FHA. In New York, in an article about the vacant building issue, the *Daily News* was reporting that "the FHA, the banks and insurance companies, and the city are all at fault. Exploitive practices are at the root of the problem," and nothing was being done about it.

Community groups in East New York suspected that the banks were a large part of the problem. They'd spent months carefully planning a press conference about the connection between banks like Eastern Services and the abandoned buildings, but not a single member of the press attended. They were left surrounded by hundreds and hundreds of empty buildings wondering, What the hell is happening? No one cares, they concluded. But no one yet knew what Accetta and Sniegocki were up to.

After being turned down for a meeting with Kapraki, Agent Sniegocki and his partner Ron Hodges went after a different realtor associated with Eastern Service, Melvin Cardona. On a hunch, they went out to Cardona's Long Island home to see if they could get some information out of him. Their hunch led to the first big turning point in the investigation.

7

The Destruction of East New York

1976–1977

Danger was coming at East New Yorkers from every direction. On Thanksgiving Day, 1976, Police Officer Robert Torsney was standing in front of the Cypress Hills projects after responding to a domestic violence call. City planner Walter Thabit would later say that housing projects like the Linden Houses and Cypress Hills, once sanctuaries, were among the most dangerous spots on earth.

Randolph Evans, an African American ninth grader, had just returned to Cypress Hills after walking his grandmother to the bus.

"Did you just come from apartment 7-D?" he asked Officer Torsney.

"You're damned right I did," Torsney said, then shot Randolph in the head. Point blank, without provocation. Ignoring calls from his fellow officers to stop and explain what was going on, he walked back to his squad car and sat beside his partner, Matthew Williams. Another officer yelled to Williams to get his partner out of there. "What did you do?" Williams asked Torsney.

"I don't know, Matty," Torsney answered, while replacing the spent cartridge in his gun with a new bullet. "What did I do?"

In *The Link*, a local newspaper published by the United Community Centers, they wrote, "In poor communities policemen don't see human beings, only potential danger. Frightened, poorly trained, and prejudiced policemen are as dangerous to us as inadequate police protection. We do need more police, but we need police who are concerned about the people they are supposed to protect." Journalists writing about the Randolph Evans killing had a grim number of cases of Black children killed by police to compare it to.

Major Owens, a local librarian who was Black and who had recently been elected to the state Senate, wrote an op-ed about the police shooting of another Black child, Clifford Glover. If he had been white, the officer "would have hesitated those extra few seconds needed to see that he was pointing his gun at a harmless child."

"We're backing him all the way on this one," the patrolmen's union responded, defending Torsney. "In the dark shadows of a high crime area, he did what he had to do to protect himself." Rising crime was definitely a problem, but it's hard to see Torsney as the valiant officer defending his life when the threat was an unarmed child with an innocuous question. Torsney was charged with second-degree murder, and none of the officers who were there would corroborate his story of self-defense. Two had testified that he shot the child without provocation from only two feet away and had seemed completely calm while doing so. Torsney was later found not guilty by reason of insanity, though he'd never shown any signs of mental illness before the shooting or after. The all-white jury accepted this explanation. Torsney was admitted to the Mid-Hudson Psychiatric Center and was later transferred to the Creedmoor Psychiatric Center, where doctors concluded that he did not suffer from any mental illness and did not require patient care. The state appealed the decision to release him and lost. Torsney was freed on July 9, 1979.

On December 11, 1976, the mayor and other officials met with members of the community at the Seven-Five precinct. Among the problems discussed were the abandoned buildings, which were seen as contributing to the soaring crime rates. Assemblyman Edward Griffith called East New York "a disaster area" and demanded action. The only thing

Mayor Abe Beame had to offer was the hope that Washington might do something once Jimmy Carter took office the following month.

Carter was inaugurated on January 20, 1977. Three days later, eight-year-old Miriam Malave was raped and thrown from the roof of a six-story building in a housing project called Unity Plaza. Miriam was taken to Brookdale Hospital where she was pronounced dead. Posters offering a $5,000 reward for information went up soon after. That was never a good sign. It meant the police had exhausted all leads, if they'd ever had any, and had reached a dead end. In February, a seventeen-year-old girl was raped and thrown from a roof a few blocks away on Sheffield Avenue, but she survived. She'd hit two clotheslines on the way down, which was just enough to break her fall. Five days later three-year-old Jimmy Bivins either jumped, fell, or was thrown from the roof at 85 Wortman Avenue. The grim tally of East New York deaths kept rising. NYPD's clearance rates for murder, which weren't great to begin with, were falling. They aimed for clearing at least 60 percent of all murders, but they'd gone from solving 55.4 percent of homicides in 1975 to 51.4 percent a year later. If you killed someone in New York City in 1976, odds were almost even you'd get away with it.

Until now, most of the attacks in East New York were outside the Family Area. Randolph Evans was killed on the east side, not in the part of town where Nancy Arlequin and her family lived. But on March 4, a sixteen-year-old girl was raped and murdered on Vermont Street, right in the middle of their haven. Retired grade 1 Detective Thomas Maher, who worked in the Seven-Five from the '70s to the '90s, said on an NYPD podcast, "You were lucky back then in the 75th precinct if you were able to both leave your house, walk to the subway without getting mugged, get to work without getting mugged, come home, not get mugged on the way back home, get home and find out your house wasn't burglarized." The danger in the Family Area was increasing.

Once again, community leaders gathered at the Seven-Five precinct, and another rally for crime prevention was planned for March 24, four months after the last rally. Five months later, after the murder of a local Black activist, flyers went back up around the neighborhood, and a third rally against crime was scheduled for October.

The community demanded more police protection, especially in the streets surrounding the Van Siclen Avenue subway station, which had become "a virtual combat zone between muggers and passengers," according to a local newspaper, the *East New Yorker*. They also called for repeat offenders of lesser crimes to actually serve their sentences, and to serve them working at something useful, like sealing abandoned buildings and cleaning out empty lots.

On November 17, a twenty-three-year-old man, Bill Berryman, was convicted of the rape and attempted murder of the girl who was thrown off the roof on Sheffield Avenue. After extensive and painful reconstructive surgery, she was able to take the stand and identify the man who tried to kill her. Berryman was sentenced to twenty-five years to life.

The district attorney believed Berryman was also guilty of murdering eight-year-old Miriam Malave and three-year-old Jimmy Bivins. He was living in Miriam's building at the time of her death and living with Jimmy's sister at the time of his, but they didn't have enough evidence to get further convictions. For years afterward, East New York girls were warned against going up to the roof, and supers locked roof doors to prevent anyone from being dragged there.

The year 1977 was an abysmal year. The same month Berryman was convicted, a subway porter was killed at the Van Siclen Avenue subway station, where East New Yorkers had begged for more police. The next month a reporter and columnist for the *New York Times* wrote that "East New York, where the buildings are withering fast as a life-sick forest" was being "put to fast death by fire and abandonment."

Early the following year Walter Thabit wrote, "Every year of inaction, means another one hundred buildings and three or four blocks destroyed." Church leaders had been watching for years as the destruction of East New York spread. It was as if some building-necrotizing disease had infected the neighborhood and was steadily consuming it.

The number of funeral masses for their slaughtered congregants also steadily increased. The city was still in retreat, and the federal programs made everything worse. Every solution proposed had failed. What was left? What hadn't been tried? The following spring, a group of religious and lay leaders began to meet regularly to answer these questions.

The FHA Scandal

1971

A picture of the crime was beginning to emerge. In many ways it had all the elements of a Racketeer Influenced and Corrupt Organizations (RICO) case, which was conceived as a tool to go after the mob. The RICO statute, enacted in 1970, enabled the prosecution to bring together an array of criminal acts and try them all together instead of separately, if they can demonstrate that they were committed in order to aid the criminal enterprise. It denotes a pattern of criminal activity referred to as racketeering.

To explain the thousands of foreclosures in front of them, Sniegocki and Accetta had to identify the pattern of activity. They would uncover what was essentially an organized crime syndicate so effective we've never recovered from the damages they inflicted.

Procedures and people to prevent these crimes were in place. Manuals outlined each step necessary to ensure that FHA houses were in decent shape and buyers would be able to keep up with mortgage payments. At least three separate organizations were required to confirm all procedures were being followed and everything was in order before the FHA agreed to insure a mortgage. The only way the criminals could have circumvented these deterrents was if someone in every organization, including the FHA, was in on it. Someone at every step of the way had to have committed a crime.

It began with whoever bought the properties. Mercenary speculators like Ortrud Kapraki and mortgage banks like Eastern Service, which also sold buildings, had scoured East New York, snapping up the cheapest properties they could find. They'd buy a run-down building for, say, $5,000. Then they'd spend $500 on cosmetic repairs, such as a coat of paint, but leave major problems, such as sewage pipes that were about to burst or a nonworking furnace, unaddressed.

Next, they'd find a family who never thought they'd be able to own their own home. It might be someone who'd come into their office looking for a rental. "Never mind renting a house, buy one. It won't cost you anything. What have you got to lose?" The speculators would coach the buyer through the mortgage application. If the buyer had any misgivings about the condition of the house, they'd say, "Do you think the government would approve this if the house wasn't okay?"

They targeted people of color because the FHA had a mandate to help low-income families of color buy homes by insuring their mortgages, and they were willing to bend over backward to make this happen. It was a good deed all teed up and ready for Eastern Service and others like them to exploit. Speculators would also specifically go after low-income immigrant families who didn't speak English and who were completely unaware that they hadn't just signed a rental agreement, but had instead bought a house.

If any of the buyers were aware that their job history or income was being exaggerated, they may have thought, "We've been playing by the rules all our lives and where did that get us?" Eastern Service, and others like them, were showing them how the system works. This is how it's done. This is how you get a house.

The buyer's credit application was then sent to a credit reporting agency, like Dun & Bradstreet. Their job was to verify the buyer's employment or income and supply a credit report.

The complete application would then be submitted to the FHA, using two forms, one requesting an appraisal of the building, the other reporting the buyer's credit information. The FHA would send out an appraiser while credit analysts went over the application and credit report to confirm that everything was as it should be. Within about a week the seller would get a conditional commitment, listing all the repairs the FHA required before finalizing the commitment, as well as the valuation of the property, often twice what the seller paid or more. Once the FHA confirmed the repairs had been made and that the building was structurally sound and that electrical, plumbing, and heating were in working order, the application, with the FHA guarantee, went to the mortgage bank, and the $10,000 went to the speculator, who had just doubled his money. In the case of Eastern Service, they were sometimes both the speculator or seller, as well as the lender.

For this all to work, there had to be a crooked real estate broker; someone at the credit reporting agency to rubber-stamp the phony credit history; an appraiser at the FHA willing to ignore the repairs that hadn't been made and set the price for a building that was falling apart as if it were a nice home in the suburbs; an underwriter at the FHA who not only okayed the whole thing, but would bump up the amount of the appraisal one last time before giving the final approval; and someone at the mortgage bank who would overlook every fishy piece of paper that crossed their desk and every crooked character who was a part of this deal, and lend the buyer the money.

Prior to the National Housing Act of 1934, when a bank made a mortgage loan, it assumed all the risk. If the buyer stopped making payments, the bank now had a bad loan on the books. But with an FHA-insured loan, that risk was taken on by the government. When the bank foreclosed, the FHA paid out the loan. It was an arrangement that benefited the lender, and not the homeowner, but for decades it had worked out well because, for the most part, few were committing fraud that targeted the new white homeowners.

But now, after moving in—sometimes months, sometimes sooner—new low-income buyers learned what Congressman Patman had learned: They'd bought a disaster. Sewage pipes might burst only a day after the new owners moved in. Or a furnace that had been inspected by an FHA appraiser wouldn't work. The audit Romney was conducting while Sniegocki and Accetta were investigating found that 54 percent of the 223(e) buildings had never been repaired before being granted FHA mortgage insurance. People were getting sick due to the lack of heat. They would fall through holes in the floor that had been hidden rather than repaired, some suffering serious injuries. Ceilings would collapse while children slept beneath them. The new homeowners didn't have the money to replace the furnace, or fix the pipes, or address any of the other problems that started to pile up. Foreclosure was inevitable. Families that couldn't believe they'd finally escaped the kind of apartments they'd been renting from slumlords found their disbelief was justified when they were thrown out onto the street. Any money they'd managed to save over the years was gone. And with a foreclosure on their credit history, they would likely never be able to get a mortgage again.

Eastern Service wanted them on the street. The government was going to pay out the mortgage, and with the family gone they could now sell that same building again, to someone else who wouldn't be able to afford to fix the pipes or replace the furnace. Or they could just move on to other buildings that were falling apart. Either way, poor people were money in the bank. The increased risk the government had taken on when insuring the mortgages of low-income families didn't come from the buyers, it turned out. It came from the sellers and the mortgage banks and the FHA itself.

Sniegocki and Accetta could see what must be happening, and their rage at the injustice fueled their investigation. It was without question an organized criminal operation. Now they had to identify the crooked players, come up with hard evidence of their crimes, and prove it. Gathering evidence of financial crimes is a lengthy, complicated, and tedious process and it's no surprise that no one had yet taken it on.

Now, thanks to the work of John P. Lomenzo and his investigators, and the continuing investigation of special agent Sniegocki and his fellow agents, Accetta was zeroing in on Eastern Service. But Eastern Service wasn't responsible for every foreclosure in New York. There were other mortgage banks and realtors, a whole cast of characters who had swarmed in and were now making themselves rich at the cost of building after pillaged building, life after plundered life. Eastern Service was just one among many, but they were the biggest. Eastern had 140 employees and processed 2,500 to 4,000 applications a year. Accetta was going to start with Eastern Service, but he fully intended to go after every one of the perpetrators they uncovered.

For now he turned his attention to the person he believed would lead them to the next rung of players. Ortrud Kapraki.

8

The Destruction of East New York

1978–1979

However terrible things had become, it continued to get worse. In 1978, in neighboring Brownsville, the body of a seventy-year-old woman who had died in her sleep was found practically devoured by rats. The rats were fleeing an extermination effort in the area, the city health commissioner explained, and East New Yorkers feared their grandmothers might suffer a similar fate.

Abandonment continued. The *East New Yorker* wrote how "Devastation, decay, rotting hulks, and burned out buildings is the rule—not the exception. It's there for anyone to see." But no real effort was being made to fix or contain the problem, and instead it "is permitted to spread like a cancer in our community."

The paper began publishing a series of articles written by Rose McCarthy titled "Who's Killing East New York?" It all came down to money. In an essay about fire and property insurance, she deplored how homeowners and businesses had essentially been redlined when insurance companies stopped issuing or renewing policies in East New York, even in cases in which premiums had been paid regularly for twenty years. Unlike banks, which had to publicly disclose mortgage data, insurance companies had no obligation to reveal how many policies they were issuing in a particular area.

Her essay "The Crumbs We Didn't Get" about a new federal initiative called the Neighborhood Strategy Area (NSA) program described yet another monetary insult. Funding for five years for housing rehabilitation was being granted to designated areas, which would be chosen by HUD. Criteria for selection was evidence of community involvement in the area; commitment of local government; the possibility of outside investment; and an actual chance of revitalizing the area within five years—the areas could not be "completely devastated." The HUD manual suggested this as a general rule: "not too big" and "not too bad." That left out the areas that needed the help most.

The section of East New York submitted for consideration was carefully chosen to fit within HUD's guidelines. The city selected a small part of the Family Area, which, while still in reasonably good shape, was starting to see trouble. The proposed section also extended one block into the much rougher Tenement Area beside it. This way they could stabilize the area with the most promise, while also expanding it ever-so-slightly into an area that needed the help more.

There must have been some awareness of the irony of applying for help from an agency that had contributed to the neighborhood's decline. By now, several FHA officials had been sent to prison for the very crimes that had led to so many abandoned buildings in East New York.

East New York and the South Bronx, probably the two areas in New York with the greatest need, were turned down. The city failed to show enough involvement or public action in addressing the problems, and as Rose McCarthy pointed out in her *East New Yorker* essay, the ruin was conspicuous.

But not everywhere in East New York was beyond hope. Lindsay's Vest Pocket program had completed 2,300 housing units by 1978. There were many established and grassroots organizations addressing the decline. Organizations like the United Community Centers and the Council for a Better East New York (CBENY) worked alongside the United Negro and Puerto Rican Front, and the United Block Associations of East New York.

Among them all, one very new group almost immediately stood out. The Brooklyn religious leaders who'd gotten together in the spring of 1978 to discuss solutions for the neighborhood problems took what would turn out to be a monumental first step. They'd reached out for help to Ed Chambers, the director of the Industrial Areas Foundation (IAF). Founded by Saul Alinsky, the IAF works with community organizations, religious and otherwise, to transfer power from politicians and back to the communities. "Churches are already organized—they're little pockets of power," Chambers told a *Wall Street Journal* reporter. Chambers met with the group from Brooklyn, and among his many suggestions, the most challenging was achieving financial independence. Before you do anything, you need to raise money. Money is power. But it can't come from government grants or grants from other organizations. Raise it from your neighbors and your congregants. Money you've collected among yourselves is the most powerful. Until you've raised $300,000, I won't help you.

Ask for money before we've actually accomplished anything? $300,000? That would be an astronomical amount to the people in this community. But coming on the heels of so many recent failures like Model Cities and the Neighborhood Strategy Area program, along with more abandoned buildings every month, the need to raise money themselves and not depend on the government rang true. Besides, they had nothing to lose.

In the first eighteen months, they collected $185,000, gathered more groups and members, and officially formed the organization they initially called East Brooklyn Churches (EBC). Later, when the first synagogue joined, they changed the name to East Brooklyn Congregations. In addition to fundraising, members started attending local seminars that taught organizing skills, and some were sent to Chicago for a ten-day training session offered by the IAF. Among those who attended the Chicago trainings was Johnny Ray Youngblood, the pastor of the St. Paul Community Baptist Church. Youngblood had come to Brooklyn in 1974 and was proving to be a powerful and effective

leader. Only eighty-four people were there to greet him when he came
to St. Paul's. By 1979 they'd outgrown the former social club where
they were meeting and would soon move to an abandoned synagogue
Youngblood had just put a deposit on in East New York.

EBC members were gathering regularly at what they called house
meetings, which were held in people's homes or sometimes at the
church and were usually attended by up to a dozen people. Anyone in
the EBC could hold a house meeting; you just had to get your neighbors to attend. "If you can get ten of your acquaintances to come to a
House Meeting," said Sarah Plowden, who came to the EBC in 1979,
"you had power." House meetings were used to find potential leaders and identify issues that needed to be addressed. Attendees talked
about all the problems they were experiencing, pinpointing major areas
of concern. They were helping to decide which problems would be
attended to with what they called actions. They had a lot to choose
from.

East New York was perpetually on fire. In the spring of 1978 almost
an entire block of Pine Street had gone up in flames in just two hours.
Residents said the fire department took fifteen to twenty minutes to
get there. The fire department insisted that the first engine had arrived
in under four minutes, from a firehouse only a few blocks away. The day
after the fire, one angry woman told fire officials on the scene, "I don't
call you firefighters—I call you fire spreaders."

One year later there was a block party on Pine Street to celebrate the
thirteen homes that had been rebuilt. It was a rare win. At the party,
Lena Goldstein, seventy-eight, who'd grown up in East New York,
reminisced to reporter Pete Hamill about her childhood. "In those
days it was all fields and farms and nanny goats." "Most of us came
here from the East Side and to us it was a paradise." She lived first
on Wyona Street, where "we used to walk through all those trees to
Goldberg's Farm to get buttermilk and three slices of brown bread for
five cents." Politicians talked about how they would accomplish what
they had for Pine Street for the whole area, one block at a time. Lena
Goldstein offered a different perspective. "I've been mugged five times."

At the same time, the lack of health care worsened. Although the new health care center at the corner of Pitkin and Pennsylvania finally opened in 1977, the old Linden General Hospital was still abandoned, and in the summer of 1979, after ninety-eight years of operation, Lutheran Hospital was shuttered. "It's all finished—nothing more can be done," said a former trustee. "The state didn't think we needed Lutheran, and neither did the mayor."

The EBC members were itching to do something. IAF organizer Michael Gecan, who'd been sent by Chambers to work with them, had advised them to begin with smaller, achievable goals. Lucille Clark was a young mother in 1981, and she wanted to try working from home after her son was born. She put up flyers and Gecan hired her to be a secretary for the EBC; eventually she became an administrative organizer. When the EBC first formed in the late 1970s, Clark explained, people in East New York were "beaten, battered, and bruised," from the big battles they had lost and had been losing for years. If they immediately took on yet another fight they might potentially lose, it would only dishearten them further. But when people win smaller battles, they get the "taste of victory and then they want more. They realize we can do more, we can really make this thing happen."

So they started small. They talked about food. "The quality of food in local chains stores is abysmal. Meanwhile, food prices are exorbitant," they'd written in a report. They talked about the mood of East New York. "To ride or walk down the streets of East Brooklyn is spiritually depressing and physically harrowing . . . A subway ride, a walk to the store, a stroll to church—every act is filled with tension."

One cause of the tension was the lack of street signs. Eighty-five percent of the street corners in East New York were missing signs. Even if you grew up there, it wasn't unusual to be walking for a few blocks deep in thought and unless you spotted a familiar store or landmark, you'd look up at some point and think, Wait, where am I? Which block am I up to? Gecan, now a senior advisor to Metro IAF New York, remembered a priest from St. Barnabas Episcopal telling Gecan how to find him. "When I called him, he said, 'Head west on Atlantic

Avenue; turn left at the abandoned building on Elton, drive past the lot with a pile of abandoned tires; and pull over at the next corner. My church is on the left.'"

"You lose precious time," Clark said, "when you have to find where some place is" without the benefit of something as simple as a street sign. Ambulances might arrive too late. People can't help you if they can't find you.

Over the next year and a half, 1,500 residents of East Brooklyn attended one hundred house meetings where they chose one of their first actions: replacing the missing street signs. It seemed like something they could actually make happen and they desperately needed a win.

The FHA Scandal

1971

While Sniegocki and Accetta continued their investigation, city planner Walter Thabit learned that in the past fifteen months 225 more buildings had been vacated in the designated Model Cities area alone. Like fresh blood spatter at the scene of a shooting, the newly abandoned buildings were evidence that East New York was still an active crime scene. After talking to many of the homebuyers who'd lost their homes, Sniegocki learned the names of the realtors who were selling people disasters. He'd approached the first realtor they'd learned about, Ortrud Kapraki, but Kapraki's lawyer wouldn't let her talk to him. Sniegocki decided to take a shot at realtor Melvin Cardona, who was also one of about a dozen commissioned mortgage solicitors who worked for Eastern Service. A solicitor brings mortgage borrowers and lenders together. Cardona found brokers for Eastern Service, who, like Ortrud Kapraki, would go along with their scheme. Cardona was in deep, the investigators believed. He'd be a good place to start.

Sniegocki and his partner Ron Hodges preferred to interview subjects in their homes. It was easier to get a confession out of them when their associates weren't nearby, listening and ready to jump in if necessary. On a hot summer evening in August, Sniegocki and Hodges rode up to Cardona's home in the Bronx.

They gave Cardona the same line they gave to all their subjects. "Help yourself by being honest and helping us with the investigation and we will tell the AUSA who recommends sentencing to the judge." They were hoping to flip him. They weren't successful, but Cardona turned out to be enormously helpful in another way. Accetta really wanted Kapraki. "Without her," he said, "we don't get to Eastern Service. We don't get to the FHA." Before leaving, Sniegocki and Hodges asked Cardona for his help in getting Ortrud Kapraki to talk to them.

As soon as they left, Cardona made a frantic call to Kapraki. She came over that evening, and she wasn't just perfectly calm, she was smug. In the parlor, Cardona's four-year-old daughter was sleeping on the couch, his wife, Cecilia, beside her. Kapraki sat down in a swivel chair, looked first at Cardona, then his wife, then she laughed and swiveled around in the chair, smiling at both of them.

Cardona told Kapraki she needed to talk to the FBI, and without her lawyer. She didn't say anything. She just continued to turn in the swivel chair, smiling at them at each pass. Cardona was not smiling. He repeated his request. Kapraki said she'd think about it. He reminded her that Lomenzo had taken away her real estate license; that they were on to her. For some reason she thought she had nothing to fear.

"Yes, I lost my license, but even when I lost it, neither the government or the FBI, they can do nothing, they can do nothing to me."

Cardona insisted they could and it would be better for her if she confessed to the FBI, and if she did so without her lawyer, it would seem like she was helping voluntarily and was willing to speak frankly and freely. Kapraki just kept laughing.

Don't be so proud and so vain, Cardona told her. Kapraki got off the chair now looking furious. She walked to the door and slammed it behind her on her way out.

Sniegocki, meanwhile, had other leads to follow, and one that took him to employees at the Long Island office of Dun & Bradstreet. There Sniegocki found a few women who were more than willing to talk. They'd been trying for months to get someone to listen to them. They kept finding false statements on the applications. They'd report it to their boss, who would okay the application anyway, certifying that everything was true and in order. Once, while making calls to confirm details on a credit application, two of the Dun & Bradstreet women discovered that they were on the phone with different men, both of them claiming to be the same buyer. They put the men on hold and went to their boss, Arthur Prescott. "There are two Jose Gonzalezes," they told him. "What do we do?" Pick the guy you believe the most, he answered, ignoring the obvious problem.

Josephine Santiago told Sniegocki she would contact AUSA Accetta immediately. Accetta would later say that the Dun & Bradstreet witnesses were "some of the most intelligent, brave women I ever met. They put their jobs on the line, they were absolutely essential."

At the end of August, one week after they first approached her, Ortrud Kapraki's lawyer reached out to Accetta to arrange a meeting.

People who knew Kapraki tended to describe her as a piece of work. She was of medium height, heavyset, and was a bit of a scatterbrain, but very smart. She was also merciless. "She knew that foreclosures were coming," Accetta said. She knew the families she was selling to would soon be homeless. "She was a sociopath."

An FBI agent described her as "very autocratic, disciplined, dogmatic, and not pleasant." He remembered Dennis Lacina, another FBI agent working on the case, and Kapraki going "to war a couple of times during interviews, trying to get her story straight. As corrupt as the day is long."

Accetta had her come to his office. "That's much more powerful than going out to them." Accetta's office was on the fifth floor, one side of a two-person suite, a secretary in between. As the case evolved, and the number of boxes of reports and evidence multiplied, he took over both offices. "I had a view of Cadman Plaza Park, and the giant eagle over the entrance to the federal courthouse. Potential defendants could clearly see the eagle of justice behind me," as they talked.

Taking Cardona's advice, Kapraki came in without a lawyer, and she was nervous. Flipping her was almost effortless. Accetta told her what he had. Among other things, they knew she gave buyers blank forms to sign, and she was the one who had actually filled them out. "You're going to be indicted," Accetta told her. She didn't like the sound of that. Kapraki had already been in trouble. She'd been investigated by the offices of the Secretary of State, the Queens District Attorney, and the District Attorney for Brooklyn. The worst that had happened to her was losing her real state license. That hadn't even slowed her down, but she knew her luck couldn't last forever.

She took the deal. She would plead guilty to a felony, and Accetta would seek no more than a five-year sentence. In exchange, "You cooperate fully, accurately, and no lies or withholds. You tell us everything you did, everything you know, and you testify at any trials. You're on call to us anytime we want you."

Then she started talking. The FHA in Hempstead, she told Accetta, "works for Eastern Service Corporation." She bragged as she produced names and general information about the bribes and false statements made to the FHA. "I can get any appraiser I want." Before that first meeting ended, she gave him what would turn out to be a very important name: Edward Goodwin, the forty-seven-year-old appraiser for the FHA.

On August 27, Sniegocki sent an Airtel to the Bureau. Kapraki was cooperating now, and Accetta wanted the FBI to halt their investigation of the FHA. Now that he had Kapraki, Accetta was going to work his way up. Kapraki would tell the grand jury what she'd told him, and they would soon get indictments against realty people, attorneys, employees, and executives at Eastern Service, executives at Dun & Bradstreet, and finally, federal employees and officials at the FHA.

The next month the news broke about Accetta's grand jury. By this time U.S. Attorney Edward R. Neaher was a federal judge in the Eastern District, and he'd been replaced by Robert Morse, the second-in-command to Neaher. Morse was a Brooklyn guy, and he continued the mission Ed Neaher had started, to raise the Eastern District.

Accetta liked working with the new U.S. attorney. "Morse let me go. He didn't put any obstacles in my way, he didn't interfere in any way, I reported to him on a regular basis about what evidence was turning up and what was developing in the grand jury and his attitude was go for it." Gale Drexler, a summer intern who was helping with the case, said he was "wonderful. The office ran so smoothly under Morse."

At a press conference after the grand jury had been announced, Morse told reporters they were up to six hundred corrupt sales in East New York and other Brooklyn neighborhoods, involving $15 million and at least half a dozen companies. It would grow from there.

Romney continued to lose faith in the government's ability to end housing segregation and began looking for a more modest goal. "What we should support now are policies . . . that will make maximum progress toward the day when every American is free to choose a decent home in a suitable environment."

While Sniegocki and Hodges were questioning Edward Goodwin, the Senate held hearings about corrupt mortgage practices in Boston. A group of banks had come together to help African Americans obtain FHA-insured mortgages for homes outside Roxbury, but they had actually granted mortgages only for homes within Roxbury and its immediate surroundings. The Boston investigators also uncovered signs that the crimes that Accetta and the FBI were investigating in New York were also occurring in Boston. Jack Blum, the assistant counsel to the Senate subcommittee, immediately understood what Harry and Rose Bernstein had recognized when the HUD Act had passed in 1968. Corrupt sellers, with a little bit of help, couldn't lose. This crime, Blum realized, would be found anywhere the FHA was insuring mortgages for low-income buyers. Every neighborhood in the country where you found low-income people of color was a potential target. When questioned by reporters Blum said, "We believe that the set of events in Boston illustrates what is going on all over America." The hearings, he said, would determine what role, if any, the FHA had played in what was happening.

9

The Destruction of East New York

1980–1981

The fires consuming East New York were now so bad NBC television news came to shoot a story, and the March *East New Yorker* was filled with articles about the constant conflagrations. But in a front-page story titled "East New York—The Arson Capital?" the reporter pointed out that what had really brought NBC to their neighborhood was the death of a white fire department lieutenant who'd perished fighting a fire in an abandoned building. "We, the citizens of East New York, have lost property, family members, friends, and hope." Yet that was not enough for "NBC or any other member of the media to express concern for us." The abandoned buildings, the reason for many of the fires, were a result of the FHA scandals, he wrote, and Nixon's freezing of funding for redevelopment that had already been underway was just another indication that "Planned shrinkage is evident here."

It was impossible to escape the conclusion that no one cared because the evidence was everywhere. Building after building burned. Lieutenant Robert Dolney, whose death had brought NBC to East New York, had died beneath a collapsed wall in an abandoned building after pushing a young probationary firefighter to safety. The next day the Department of Buildings placed a UB (Unsafe Building) designation on the building and the abandoned building beside it. Had this been done sooner, the building would have been demolished and Lieutenant Dolney might not have died. The Department of Buildings explained that they didn't do routine inspections due to a manpower shortage. For an inspector to come out to East New York to declare a building unsafe, an official complaint about the building must be made first.

Earlier that month Lydia Rivera died when she ran back into a burning building on Fulton Street to rescue two of her children she thought were still within. A month later another fire in the building next door sent two firefighters to Brookdale Hospital. The Department of Housing Preservation and Development's Seal Up and Demolition Office said it never got the documents it needed to secure and demolish the building after the first fire. Even if it had been a priority, reporters were told, it usually takes six months to bring a building down.

By this time, some of the people who'd gone to prison for the financial crimes that led to the abandoned buildings had completed their decidedly lenient sentences, while East New Yorkers were still dealing with the wreckage they'd left behind. Instead of focusing on preventing similar white-collar crimes, in 1964, in order to get tough on street crimes, the now infamous "stop and frisk" and "no knock warrants" bills that would destroy the lives of countless men and women of color were passed. To get still tougher on crime, in 1978 New York State passed a juvenile offenders law, also known as the Willie Bosket law. While mortgage crimes continued to destroy the homes and neighborhoods they lived in, children as young as thirteen could now be tried as adults. The whole of the criminal justice system continued to decline any suggestion of getting tough on financial crimes. They weren't stopping and frisking bankers, or breaking down the doors of their homes or offices to gather up files and ledgers as evidence. The same year NBC came to East New York to report on the fires, Louis Bernstein, Harry and Rose's son, who'd been indicted in 1972 in the Eastern Service case but whose indictment was later dismissed, bought Long Island's first Black-owned bank. In nine years federal agents would padlock the bank and seize its portfolio of federal mortgages while they investigated Louis and others for fraud.

Those who could leave East New York did, but that usually meant businesses, not residents, so East New York was also filled with empty storefronts.

The Ideal Corporation laid off 40 percent of its workers and closed its plant for two weeks while it worked to rebuild its business, which had fallen off. On the upside, after four years of trying, Mrs. Maxwell's Bakery on Atlantic Avenue was finally able to acquire space in the building behind them, vacated by the Ideal Corporation years earlier. The bakery had been in business at that site for over fifty years and needed to expand.

Homicide was up in East New York. In 1980, fifty-eight East New Yorkers were murdered. Given the NYPD's clearance rates, that meant still more murderers who had gotten away with it were added to the increasingly dangerous streets of East New York.

The night before Thanksgiving 1980, Hilton Rivera was on the corner of Belmont Avenue and Jerome Street when he heard a young girl screaming across the street. Hilton ran to help her. Her purse had been stolen and she'd been beaten by the thief, who ducked into a nearby abandoned building. Rivera followed him inside where he was shot in the head. He died on December 1 in Brookdale Hospital. Hilton, twenty-three, was a member of the Guardian Angels, and he had a wife and an infant son. But the deaths of people who die in Forgotten Land, a name for East New York that was coined by journalist Earl Caldwell, are only sporadically reported, and the *East New Yorker* was the only paper to cover his death. Several organizations wrote to the police commissioner, requesting a posthumous civilian commendation, which he was granted six months later.

With all of this going on around them, replacing street signs might seem insignificant, but the members of the East Brooklyn Congregations knew that they had to remain focused on what they hoped would be their first, small, winnable battle.

Their first step: document the missing signs. EBC members fanned out through the streets of East New York and Brownsville to make a list of every corner that was missing a sign. Sarah Plowden, an early EBC member, would wake up every morning before dawn and walk the streets from 6:00 a.m. to 8:00 a.m. writing down where signs were missing and what kind. Was it a street name, a stop sign, or a one-way sign? The EBC members identified roughly three thousand missing signs.

Next, they reached out to the Department of Transportation to request a meeting. Everyone was taken aback by how smoothly it went from there. But they'd essentially done a large part of the work. They handed over the lists they'd compiled, and within a year the signs were replaced.

Lucille Clark would never forget what it felt like when the signs went up. "It had been so many years since signs had been put up, there was a difference in the size of the signs, and the newness of it. New poles had to be erected. It felt wonderful to know you've been a part of making this happen."

"It felt like we could make a difference," Plowden said. "It felt like my children would no longer have to know a place in order to get there, to know that the firehouse was there, and when you went past the firehouse, you got to Hendrix Street. You could go by street signs."

Despite the time she'd put in early each morning, Plowden wasn't completely convinced they could make it happen. "When I saw the street signs, I said, 'Hey!' I got excited about what we did as a group, and what we did as individuals."

Plowden also remembered the impact the house meetings in her home had on her son. "My son saw me speak up and speak out for a better neighborhood and it influenced him. My son David said, 'That's my mom up there.' He knows that I made a difference. Even before I knew that I was powerful."

The city took the credit for replacing the signs of course, "but we didn't care. All we knew is that we got signs. And that was good for our people to know that we could win something."

The year the EBC began the action that would lead to their first victory, Julia Parker turned six and started school at P. S. 149, also known as Danny Kaye Elementary. Actor Danny Kaye's first appearance on a stage was at P. S. 149, where he had a small part as a seed in a slice of watermelon. East New York was very proud that one of their own had become so famous, and they were happy to name the school after him. Kaye would come back from time to time to visit the school that bore his name, and he was always kind to the staff and students when he was there. But he once told an audience, "Everywhere I go in the world I meet people from my hometown, Brooklyn. I don't know why. Some say it's so awful the constituents have to leave."

The FHA Scandal

1971–1972

The investigation continued to gather momentum. On November 18, 1971, Accetta got a four-count indictment against Milton Berlin, one of the realtors they were looking into. It was the first indictment to come out of his investigation. Berlin appeared before Judge John F. Dooling Jr. in black slacks, a canary-yellow polo shirt, and a blue and white checked jacket, an outfit that seemed to indicate that he didn't have a care in the world. He pleaded not guilty to helping people falsify their FHA loan insurance applications, and was released on a $10,000 bail bond. Berlin would turn out to be a test case for the larger cases to follow. "If I lose that case," Accetta realized, "I am going to have a hard time going forward with the others." Everyone involved, both criminals and prosecutors, was watching the Berlin case closely.

That year news broke about similar crimes in Detroit, while the investigations in Philadelphia and Boston forged ahead. Similar cases were found in Chicago in 1972. Jack Blum, the assistant counsel investigating Boston, started investigating other cities. What he uncovered in Boston was nothing next to what he found in New York. "East New York was ground zero," he said. The players there were a "vicious, rapacious bunch of thugs," who'd done nothing less than destroy an entire neighborhood without remorse. "I'll never forget getting off the subway on New Lots Avenue and being attacked by a pack of wild dogs." As the investigation went on, "the characters who started to turn up in this thing were out of a very, very dark movie." When Blum and his summer intern got to the "office" of a drug dealer who had a sideline as a realtor, they felt "if we start asking him questions he's going to kill us. And my poor summer intern, I don't think ever recovered from it."

As the weeks passed, Romney was trapped in his own special torment. He couldn't really do anything about corruption in the FHA. Firing anyone would compromise the investigation. He had to sit back and let the whole thing play out. He could address procedural issues, though. Congress and the public demanded it. That fall, HUD brought in Donald Carroll to head the Hempstead office and clean up the mess. His job was to make sure people were following the newly clarified procedures for insuring mortgages. Between the grand jury and Carroll's presence, Romney must have thought that at the very least, any ongoing crimes would stop.

While they continued to investigate Eastern Service, the FBI had identified the other largest mortgage banks in New York and in 1972 assigned agents to each firm. Agent Ron Brugger got United Institutional Servicing Corporation, Agent Jeffrey Kay was given Inter-Island Mortgage Corporation, and Springfield Equities went to Agent Dan Kelleher. These were the same four banks mentioned in the press release issued by East New York community activists in the summer of 1971. Agent Walter Ver Steeg, who was investigating officials at the FHA, was also investigating the Veterans Administration (VA) for similar crimes. A lot of the players were the same, and all the agents kept in constant touch, sharing names and other information.

Accetta's grand jury was producing names as well, particularly the names of FHA employees, including appraisers Joseph Jankowitz, Greville Harvey, Charles Joshua, and Edward Goodwin. Accetta, Sniegocki, and other FBI agents got together and went over their list of appraisers, debating who they should try to flip first. Sniegocki and

Accetta both decided independently that they were going to approach Goodwin.

Sniegocki pulled the trigger first. He and Agent Hodges rode out to Goodwin's home to convince him that they had him, and that cooperating was his only way out. Goodwin insisted he'd done nothing wrong. They quietly heard him out. Then, as they sat in his living room, the agents slowly and methodically laid out their case against him. Goodwin didn't talk much after that. "We didn't want him to." This first meeting was not about getting him to confess. They wanted him to feel so utterly trapped and helpless that he'd grab at any shred of hope they offered. They described what witnesses had said under oath about what he had done. We know you've committed a lot of crimes, and we have evidence. The agents were there for about an hour. When they were done they asked him, "Are you going to help us unscramble the case, or are you okay with going to jail with Harry and Rose and all the other realtors and appraisers?"

"Think about it overnight," they told him. "Talk it over with your wife." Before leaving they warned him against getting an attorney who also worked for Eastern Service. The Bernsteins are not your friends. "You should get an attorney who will represent *you*." Consider your own interests, and the position you are in, and not the Bernsteins'."

Soon after, without knowing that Sniegocki and Hodges had already approached Goodwin, Accetta reached out to Goodwin's lawyer. Accetta was the one who could actually make a deal in exchange for Goodwin's cooperation. When he asked if Goodwin was willing to talk to him, his lawyer immediately agreed.

Accetta went out to the attorney's office on Long Island. Goodwin "looked like a Midwestern farmer," Accetta remembered. "He had a sort of round face, glasses, thinning hair." His lawyer didn't say or do very much. Goodwin was terrified. "Which meant he was a man with a conscience. He knew he had done really bad things and had been caught." The meeting took about forty-five minutes. Accetta essentially made the same pitch that Sniegocki had. "I'm here to tell you that you are going to be indicted. We have evidence from multiple people at this point." Kapraki's story alone was enough to get him arrested. "We know that you go to Rose and Harry's office on a regular basis. We even know that you drink Johnnie Walker Black at those meetings."

"Oh my God," Goodwin said. Accetta believes that one sentence turned him, but Goodwin had been hit with a one-two punch. Sniegocki and his partner got him right up to the edge and Accetta pushed him over. "He didn't think about it," Accetta said. "He didn't talk to his lawyer. They didn't go into another room and consult or ask me to step out so they could talk. He said, 'Okay, I'll do it.'"

Our real targets in this thing are Rose and Harry, Accetta told him. "That's who we really want to get. But I do not give immunity. You're going to have to take a felony plea, and you're going to have to cooperate and testify." Thereafter Goodwin's whole life changed. "He was with us almost on a daily basis for the next two years." When Accetta needed evidence from within the FHA office in Hempstead, Goodwin was the one who gathered it. While colleagues all around him continued to commit crimes, Goodwin was right behind them, scooping up the proof that Accetta would later use against them.

Flipping Goodwin was the turning point in the case. Kapraki had given them a lot of good information, but Goodwin was able to tell them what was happening inside the FHA. Goodwin was also the first person to talk to Accetta about Herbert Cronin, the chief underwriter at the FHA. The chief underwriter had a lot of authority. "In terms of appraisals," said John Kennedy, the HUD attorney advisor who worked with Accetta, "it was the most important position," and an important leap up the criminal ladder Accetta was climbing. Cronin, they learned, not only approved the clearly fraudulent appraisals, but could be counted on to increase the final amount when he did.

On January 24, 1972, Sniegocki requested permission to place a body recorder on Goodwin, to tape his conversations with Harry and Rose Bernstein, and with other FHA officials implicated in the investigation. The Bureau was sufficiently excited about their progress to pick up the phone and tell him "yes," instead of sending the usual Airtel. Although they didn't need an okay from Attorney General John Mitchell to put a wire on someone to record conversations, these were federal employees, and they secured his approval. Sniegocki had a month.

Nixon's moratorium on the subsidized housing programs had begun that January. All hope for fair housing was effectively over, for now. George Romney could no longer harbor any illusions. He was not going to accomplish what he'd set out to do. The homeownership programs, he conceded that spring, were "clearly contributing to abandonment and decay." Many of those trapped in East New York were never getting out.

"The really horrible thing about this scandal," Jack Blum would say to journalist Brian Boyer later that year, "are those empty acres of space staring us in the face in Detroit, those square miles of rubble in Brooklyn, Newark, and every other goddam place. Honest to God, it's a real horror show."

10

The Destruction of East New York

1981

The aftermath of the city's budget reductions were everywhere. "Basic city services . . . have been slashed to the point of breakdown," the *Wall Street Journal* reported. "The streets are blanketed with garbage. Robberies, to name one crime, are at an all-time high. The subway system is near collapse, plagued by aging equipment, vandalism, and frequent breakdowns and derailments."

Many believed helping the poor had contributed to the decline in city services and to the rise in crime. George Sternlieb, the director of Rutgers University's Center for Urban Policy Research told the *Wall Street Journal* that what was happening in New York "called into question all the postulates of blind social welfarism . . . which culminated in Mr. Reagan's budgets cuts." The federal budget cuts on top of the city's contributed to the feeling of desperation in East New York and elsewhere, where the decline in city services had been going on for many years.

In February, Congresswoman Shirley Chisholm gave an impassioned speech at the John F. Kennedy Democratic Club, denouncing Reagan's cutbacks as "radical and severe." They "take less from those who can afford to give more, and give less to those who need more . . .

It is the most extraordinary attempt by any president in modern times to redistribute income in this country." Reagan's budget provided more tax incentives and loopholes for the rich, while ending or reducing programs for the poor. East New York, which had never gotten much attention from city officials, and barely existed to most New Yorkers, was pushed closer to the edge by further reductions in services. March was going to be grim, Chisholm warned.

Crime continued to rise. Carmen Enriquez, the director of a volunteer organization called the Civilian Patrol Unit, put out a call for more recruits. Those who came forward spent two months in training and a month patrolling while on probation, before being sent out to help children get home from school, or to accompany the elderly to and from a trip to the local bodega.

In October, responding to a court order to immediately relieve conditions in severely overcrowded homeless shelters, the city dumped four hundred homeless men into an empty school building on Williams Avenue with less than twenty-four hours' notice. The area was mostly industrial and surrounded by vacant lots and the shells of burned-out buildings, but it was directly adjacent to Thabit's Family Area, which East New Yorkers were still trying to turn around. The school had been closed as part of the city's budget cuts, but local leaders had been planning to turn it into a job training and business development center. Not only was the city not helping, they were torpedoing the local efforts to recover.

The city claimed the building was chosen because it would have "minimal impact on the community," but the impact was not minimal. "There's a complete lack of city services in our area: street lights are out, potholes are all over the place, sanitation facilities are shot, and our park is completely devastated, and people are afraid to walk out in the streets after dark." The creation of a homeless shelter, and a particularly large one, made it even more difficult to revitalize.

It also underscored to everyone living in East New York that the city just didn't care. East New York was the city's junk pile, where they'd unload programs they didn't dare try to establish in white neighbor-hoods. In 1950, East New York was 98.3 percent white. In 1980 it was down to 30 percent white. While the administration spent "billions in Manhattan on the Battery Park development, Westway, and the Convention Center," a *New York Amsterdam News* article read, Brooklyn got sewage disposal plants and one of the largest homeless shelters in the city. "If the area were 90 percent white," said Reverend Jacob Underwood of Grace Baptist Church, "this would not have happened."

State Senator Major Owens wrote to Mayor Koch, "You have re-moved from our community millions of dollars in Model Cities funds and thousands of dollars in community action funds, under the pretext of spreading the wealth. But now you dump a heavy concentration of people with serious problems into a neighborhood without resources."

"We had no choice. It was livable and warm," said a city official. As if there was no other space in all of New York City that met such minimal requirements.

After the school had shut down, their children had continued play-ing in the schoolyard. But now that the building was filled with home-less men, the yard was closed. There were no other parks or playgrounds in their corner of East New York so the children played in abandoned lots. When a nine-year-old boy named Paris Turner was murdered the following spring, the homeless men were blamed.

Paris was last seen leaving a playground a little under a mile away from the shelter, with a man who'd been helping him and his friends build a clubhouse. The man had been wearing "dirty clothes," according to the friends. Paris's body was later found in an abandoned lot near the former school. He'd been sexually assaulted, the medical examiner re-ported, before his skull was crushed, killing him. While a homeless man might have been responsible, crime had already been rising in the area, and with no other leads than a man in dirty clothes, the murder of Paris Turner ended up on the Seven-Five's growing list of unsolved homicides.

The EBC continued to move forward, trying to make East New York better by taking on more modest battles that they could win.

Among the complaints raised in house meetings across East New York, Brownsville, and Ocean Hill was the poor quality of food in supermarkets and bodegas in their communities.

Lucille Clark remembered running to the supermarket late one afternoon because she needed some meat to prepare for dinner that night. "I got home, opened it up," and she was hit with the horrible scent of meat that had gone bad. "These are the kinds of things people had to deal with. It was a quality of life issue."

They didn't know there were things like health codes. "The stores didn't have the right temperature for cold food ... and we didn't know it," Sarah Plowden explained. After learning how understaffed the health and consumer affairs departments were, and how long it might take for anyone to respond to their complaints, they decided to do something about the problem themselves.

EBC volunteers surveyed three thousand local residents and collected their comments about the general condition of the food in local stores. They learned everything they needed to know about health codes, how things like milk and meat had to be stored, how garbage should be disposed, and all the rules regarding cleanliness. They compared the prices they paid to prices elsewhere in New York City and learned they were paying 10 percent more for things like flour, chopped meat, sugar, and canned corn, spoiled or otherwise. EBC member Father Edward Mason said they also noticed that prices went up when people got their SSI and Social Security checks, and then went down later in the month.

They formed and trained ten-member inspection teams, volunteers who, after sufficient role-playing, went out to ten markets on a Saturday morning in the summer of 1981. They were armed with clipboards, thermometers, a badge that read "Official EBC Food Store Inspector," and an attitude of authority. Some were terrified, but whether they felt it or not they strode down the aisles with conviction, writing down every health code violation they came across. Father Mason said it was a "thrill for me to watch them walk around that store. They were holding somebody accountable. And they knew it. They believed that something was going to happen." They had taken the power, and "you could see it in their faces, in their body language, and their attitude."

The EBC inspectors found dried blood and rat droppings at the bottom of filthy refrigerators, which made the store smell. They also found moldy produce, ants on drink containers, rusty cans, and food that was stored far above the maximum temperatures. Shoppers who saw what they were doing brought them more evidence of the stores' complete lack of quality control.

Everything was noted on their clipboards. "They didn't just come in and say, 'The food here is bad,'" Father Mason explained. "They gave hard-core specific details. Things like, 'There was a spillage in the milk aisle at 10:00 a.m. At 12:00 p.m., two hours later, it was still there,'" would be added to their report.

Managers yelled at them from their offices on stores' balconies, and some came down to threaten them. But the EBC had alerted the police about their planned action and they directed the manager's attention to the police car waiting outside.

The manager of one of the markets in East New York said one of the freezers they'd inspected was full, "so how could they see if it was dirty?" Another manager, in Brownsville, said the customers made the store dirty themselves and he didn't have the staff to clean up after them quickly enough.

That September a headline in the *New York Amsterdam News* read, CHURCH POWER SHAKES UP SUPERMARKETS. Not all the stores cleaned up their act, but enough did to once again give those involved the satisfaction of having effected change.

The members of the EBC now felt sufficiently emboldened for a larger battle, one that would take on the issue everyone believed had escalated all the troubles that came afterward: abandoned buildings and the lack of decent and affordable housing.

The year 1981 was also a happy and hopeful year for the Arlequin family. Julia Parker now had a baby sister, whom her mother had named Milagros, which is Spanish for miracles.

The FHA Scandal

1972

Soon after getting the okay to wire Ed Goodwin, Sniegocki and Hodges recorded their first conversation between Goodwin and the Bernsteins. Everyone knew about Accetta's investigation by now, and as the most successful perpetrators of the crimes he was unraveling, the Bernsteins were smart enough to know that sooner or later the trail would lead to them. Before talking to Goodwin, one of their chief partners in crime at the FHA, the Bernsteins insisted on driving in and out of the streets surrounding their Hempstead office for forty-five minutes to throw off any investigator who might be trying to tail them.

Once they were sure they weren't being followed, they began to talk. The FBI's goal was to get the Bernsteins to say something incriminating, so Goodwin came right out with it. I met with my attorney, he told them. We've been friends for years. He wanted the truth and I gave it to him. I've been accepting bribes. From you.

The Bernsteins were apoplectic. Go back to your attorney. Tell him you were confused. No wait, just fire him. Tell him to stop his investigation. "Talk to H.C." H.C. was Herbert Cronin, the FHA's chief underwriter in Hempstead. But meet with him outside of the FHA's office, they cautioned him. They pummeled him with demands. Don't let your attorney talk you into anything. If you don't admit to anything, nothing can be proved. When our attorney asks us if we ever paid the FHA we always say no. You should do the same. But the best thing you can do now is just fire him.

Then they made the offer Sniegocki had advised Goodwin to refuse. We'll get you a good attorney, they said, like they were doing him a great favor. Go see your guy tonight and fire him, and then call us as soon as it's done. Use a public telephone. And don't say anything about your attorney. Say this instead: "I've contacted my engineer, and if you do another trench it will remove the hydrostatic condition." The Bernsteins were dealing with a water problem in their King's Point home. It was an easy cover.

The Bernsteins were always very careful, as if the FBI always had a way of listening in. But they never suspected that it was Goodwin they should have feared the most. At that very moment Goodwin was transmitting every word they said straight to the enemy, who, in spite of all their maneuvering, had them surrounded.

What they got on tape that day was good, but the FBI needed more. A week later Goodwin went back to have another recorded conversation with Rose and Harry. This time they were more prepared. Alfred Fayer, their lawyer, was with them in the car. "We have to be very careful," Rose said, "because Accetta, that little guinea bastard, is out to get us." Agents in the chase cars immediately got on the radio and started mimicking her, much to the embarrassment and joy of Tony Accetta, who was listening to every word they were saying.

The Bernsteins continued their efforts to convince Goodwin he should fire his attorney and refuse to talk to the grand jury. As long as you don't say a word, they said, we'll all get out of this okay. If this costs you your job, we'll give you a job in our Florida office, they promised. While the Bernsteins offered enticements, Fayer provided a litany of assurances. If they don't have evidence, they can't do anything, he began. They need copies of checks, bank deposit slips. "For

Christ sake . . . this is something that has to be proven and has to be established . . . So don't be so goddamned nervous."

Accetta added Fayer to the list of subjects in his investigation.

During another one of Goodwin's conversations with the Bernsteins, they mentioned that Donald Carroll, the new state director of the FHA, was an old friend of theirs. They'd known each other for fifteen years, were very close, and got together frequently over the years. This relationship did not stand out to the investigators at the time. A few months later, another revelation about Carroll would.

Through grand jury testimony, subpoenas, and investigative foot-work, a more detailed picture of the crimes was emerging. Accetta learned, for instance, that on their FHA applications someone from Eastern Service would write ORE, for "our real estate," to indicate to crooked FHA assignment clerks which applications were theirs. Those files were then funneled to corrupt appraisers and credit analysts who would rubber-stamp their approval. Goodwin was paid $200 per appraisal.

Fayer was right, though. Accetta's team needed more than they had recorded on Goodwin's wire. They needed physical evidence, a paper trail. What Fayer didn't know was that they had already had a lot of help uncovering that trail. After Goodwin flipped, Accetta and Goodwin went to the HUD office in Washington to get the ORE files and start Goodwin "on a long, arduous process of reviewing those files." They reviewed the actual appraisals, the use of the "chief underwriters' prerogative" (CUP) to bump up the appraised value of the buildings even more, and claims of repairs that were never made. They didn't want Goodwin making things up just to please them, so they had two other HUD appraisers looking over his shoulder the whole time, to make sure that what he said about what they were finding made sense.

While all this was going on, George Romney released the final re-sult of his audit of the subsidized housing programs in February 1972. Unlike the previous year's report, the HUD investigation confirmed the reports of widespread abuse, including the crimes Accetta and the

FBI were investigating. HUD had taken possession of five thousand buildings in Detroit, the auditors discovered, and one out of every thirteen homes whose mortgages they'd insured in Philadelphia. Reforms were immediately put into place. Among them, speculators were required to disclose the price they paid for buildings and the amount spent on rehabilitating them.

Accetta now anticipated having indictments by March. To this end, he brought Ortrud Kapraki, Edward Goodwin, and others before a grand jury and questioned them at length.

"A grand jury is much more relaxed," Accetta said. "There's no defense lawyer there, so there's nobody cross-examining. You don't have a judge." Here is the question the grand jury must decide, Accetta explained. "Is there probable cause to believe that a crime was committed and the target committed it? Those are the grounds for indictment. So you present the evidence. Then you write up the charges, and you present the charges in writing to the grand jury. They vote on each and every count of the indictment."

Many people have probably heard Judge Sol Wachtler's quip, that you can get a grand jury "to indict a ham sandwich." That may be true, but no prosecutor wants to take a case to trial if they don't believe they can win. Accetta believed he had enough to win.

John Kennedy, HUD's attorney advisor, was fully committed to helping him. When he heard Rose Bernstein's "that little guinea bastard" comment "I knew right then and there it was damn the torpedos, full steam ahead," Kennedy said. "We dug up as many cases as we could in the initial complaint." Whenever Accetta said he needed him, Kennedy flew from Washington to New York, staying for two to three days at a time, to debate the pros and cons of each of the statutes they might use to prosecute the Bernsteins and others.

The FBI agents on the case were also frequent visitors to Accetta's office, helping where they could, sometimes working long into the night. Sniegocki and Accetta got along well and came to think of each other as friends.

Everyone who was following the case, and everyone who suspected they were a subject, knew indictments must be imminent, but when questioned by the press, Accetta wouldn't give a date. The Bernsteins and their accomplices, and anyone who'd committed similar crimes, had to wait, wondering if today was the day the FBI would knock on their door and say, "You're under arrest." Special agent Jeff Kay tells the story of driving up to a house in Brooklyn in a black, four-door Ford. He and fellow agent Dennis Lacina got out of the car in their dark suits and ties and walked to the front door. Everything about them screamed feds, and they had the full attention of everyone out on their stoop that day. When they knocked on the door and announced they were with the FBI, the homeowner, who was not a suspect, took off running through the back door.

While Accetta was getting the indictments ready, Senator Philip Hart, who had investigated similar crimes in Boston, announced they would be conducting Senate hearings in New York in May. Brooklyn had lost a substantial percentage of their white population between 1960 and 1970, they discovered, while gaining a large percentage of Black and Puerto Rican residents, many of whom seemed to be "the victims of a plan which was designed originally to improve their lot in life."

Romney was aware of at least some of what Accetta was uncovering, and soon the whole world would know as well. His mood grew increasingly bleak. Several times during this period he would repeat, "The truth is none of us are now sure what are the right things to do." It was like he'd already started to defend himself from the onslaught of condemnation he knew would come. The DOJ and HUD were given advance notice that Accetta would be presenting the indictments to the grand jury on March 28. On that day, in a speech at the Economic Club of Detroit, Romney said, "I acknowledge with deep regret the things that have gone wrong with our housing subsidy program . . . It was a mistake, in part, not to realize the FHA lack of preparation for its role in central cities and their exposure to speculators and fast buck artists."

While Romney was delivering his speech, Accetta was handing out copies of the indictments to the grand jury. They were to read them, ask questions if they had any, and then come back with their decision. In the end, the grand jury believed Ed Goodwin. They believed Ortrud Kapraki, the women from Dun & Bradstreet, the homebuyers, and all the other witnesses brought before them. They came back to the jury room after having voted to hand down all the indictments that had been put before them.

Warrants for the arrest of forty individuals and ten companies were issued immediately. They were charged with varying counts of fraud, bribery, and conspiracy.

Accetta, who was only twenty-nine years old at the time, would soon be overseeing what was at the time the largest and longest trial in the history of the Eastern District of New York. "The low-income Italians I grew up with," he said to the press, "were the same kind of people as the Puerto Ricans and Blacks being victimized here—hardworking individuals trying to get ahead. I don't see how anyone who is Black or Puerto Rican could have faith in the system after being shaken down like this and then losing his house two months later."

"In New York it was the whole goddamn FHA office," said Jack Blum. "They had to back a bus up and lock everybody up." March was just the beginning. There were more indictments to come.

11

The Destruction of East New York

1982

On New Year's Eve, the unidentified body of a boy who'd been shot to death was found on the corner of Pennsylvania and Dumont Avenues. It wasn't the first body police had found on that corner, which was close to Thomas Jefferson High School. The proximity was disturbing, but not surprising. In 1982, Thomas Jefferson was surrounded by mounds of garbage and empty lots. The vacant lots spreading throughout East New York had become fields of peril, and sometimes impromptu graveyards. That spring, a Queens couple beat their five-year-old son to death and buried him in a lot beneath a stretch of elevated train tracks at Pitkin and Van Sinderen Avenues. Perhaps they thought he wouldn't be discovered there when they reported him missing. By the end of the year, Thomas Jefferson was being called the most dangerous school in New York City. The NYPD had lost 30 percent of its uniformed officers by this time; help for that corner was most certainly not on the way.

The EBC was moving forward with their plans to address the abandoned lots and increasing blight. After successfully pressuring the city to either seal or demolish abandoned buildings that were beyond renovation, they were confronted with still more unbroken spans of vacant land. The EBC did not envision themselves as literal home builders, but who else in either the public or private sector was going to build new homes that low-income families could actually afford in all these spaces?

When Michael Gecan, who was now the EBC's lead organizer, first came to Brooklyn, his supervisor handed him a series of articles written by I. D. Robbins, a columnist for the *Daily News* at the time. Several contained a challenge to Mayor Koch: Give me land in the South Bronx and I'll build five homes that are affordable and prove that people will buy them. "Koch hated him," Gecan said, "he hated Koch, and of course they never agreed." Robbins never got the land to make his case. But his ideas were similar to what the EBC were envisioning.

On June 2, 1982, Mayor Koch received a proposal from the EBC for a joint venture with the city to rebuild devastated areas in Brownsville, Ocean Hill, and East New York. It would come to be known as the Nehemiah Plan, and I. D. Robbins would become its first general manager. Inspired by the Book of Nehemiah in the Hebrew Bible, which tells the story of the rebuilding of the walls of Jericho, the proposal began with a quote. "You see our wretched plight. Jerusalem lies in ruins, its gates destroyed by fire. Come let us rebuild the wall of Jerusalem and be rid of the reproach."

Although the city had largely abandoned them, the EBC was proposing they work together, but first they had to lure the city out of retreat.

The centerpiece of the proposal was the construction of one thousand affordable single-family, owner-occupied homes (with an overall goal of five thousand). Lines of modest row houses were their answer to the now cold, indifferent towers of projects the New York City Housing Authority had built in East New York and elsewhere, and which, like Cypress Hills, had become hubs for crime. The EBC would do the bulk of the work. They would be responsible for building the homes, and they'd be done within one year from the start of construction. To accomplish this they would raise $12 million to create a pool to be used as a no-interest construction loan fund. New York City would give them title to city-owned vacant lots that had been abandoned due to fire and nonpayment of taxes, provide $10,000 per home as a no-interest loan to the buyers, and smooth the way by advertising the city's full support, telling all city agencies involved to cooperate and "speed all paperwork, approvals, and procedures," and expedite hearings. The city would also help obtain the lowest interest rates and longest-term mortgage and clean up the nearby subway stations.

They'd moved from modest wins to thinking big. "Any response to the conditions of East Brooklyn must be large in scale," they wrote. "Small-scale or pilot-project approaches, amid the devastation of East Brooklyn, are doomed to defeat." You needed at least one thousand new homes to begin to turn the decline around.

In the plan, a two-bedroom home would cost $40,000. Three- and four-bedroom homes would be higher, but priced up to 40 percent below the market rate. All the homes would be humble in scale, without fancy finishes like marble countertops, but they would also be sturdy and new, with brand-new plumbing, wiring, and heating. It would be the real-life version of the movie *It's a Wonderful Life*, in which George Bailey builds affordable homes for Bedford Falls immigrants in an area that was once a Potter's Field. "Every one of these homes is worth twice what it cost the Building and Loan to build," one of the characters in the movie says, and this would turn out to be more than true of the Nehemiah homes built by the EBC. Reverend Youngblood would later say, "This community was considered a graveyard. Nehemiah saved it."

They expected to break ground the following spring. They got there sooner. Koch was not initially a fan of the EBC, calling them "wackos," but Bishop Francis J. Mugavero, a close friend of Koch's, supported them. A few months before they would send their proposal, Mugavero got the EBC an audience with Koch to pitch their plan. As usual, it came down to money. The story is frequently told about how Koch initially agreed to give the EBC the land, but not the $10 million in interest-free loans for the homebuyers. When Bishop Francis J. Mugavero pressed him for the money, Koch said the city simply didn't have it. "I'll tell you what. You steal the $10 million," Mugavero answered, "and I'll absolve you." Koch found the money.

The EBC raised the $12 million for construction loans from local churches, the Brooklyn Catholic diocese, the Long Island Episcopal diocese, and the Lutheran Missouri Synod, and a contract with the city was signed on August 23. On the same day that the city handed over fourteen square blocks free of charge, the EBC received three hundred applications for the homes that would be erected upon them. That October, Mayor Koch broke ground for the first Nehemiah homes in Brownsville. Five thousand people showed up for the groundbreaking and a choir sang. East New York would have to wait. One neighborhood over from East New York, Brownsville needed affordable housing just as much, if not more.

The following month a memorial was held for Randolph Evans, the boy who had been murdered in 1976 by police officer Robert Torsney. Torsney had been released from the psychiatric facility where he was being held and had been out free for the past three years, along with a lot of other murderers. One hundred eighty-two people were killed in East New York in the last three years, and roughly sixty of the murders were never solved.

Getting away with murder does not take special skills, it turns out. You don't need to be a criminal mastermind. Just do it where there aren't many witnesses, use a gun so you don't have to get close enough to leave biological evidence, and keep your mouth shut. If you want to be really careful, shoot them outdoors, in a street or in a parking lot, and do it late at night. The sort of people who are out then, like kids stumbling home drunk, or prostitutes, or the homeless, are generally considered unreliable witnesses. If you're willing to go the extra mile, follow up after the murder by killing anyone you think might talk to the police.

A lot of murderers have figured out these simple rules. Around 40 percent of all the murders committed in America are never solved, and East New York was on its way to having the highest number of unsolved murders in New York City. That was in part due to a chilling statistic. In New York, you're twice as likely to be murdered if you're a person of color, and your case is four times as likely to go cold.

Julia Parker turned eight years old in 1982, when sex crimes in East New York were on the rise. That summer the police arrested two men who had been paying fourteen children, aged eight to fifteen, to let the men fondle and molest them. This was discovered when one third grader asked her friend why she was so upset. All the children were Puerto Rican. (Julia's father was Black and her mother was Puerto Rican.) After arresting the two men, the police let one of them go, when they discovered he was eighty-nine years old. The other man was released after pleading guilty to disorderly conduct.

The previous summer, a junior high school girl was grabbed on her way home from her graduation ceremony, dragged into an abandoned building, and raped. Her attacker was released on $20,000 bail. Another man was arrested in February for molesting three elementary and junior high school girls. He was given three years' probation and ordered to seek psychiatric treatment.

When responding to the attacks, District 19 School Superintendent Frank C. Arricale, the man who arranged for one of the Gallo brothers to speak to the members of SPONGE in 1966, said protecting the children and keeping them in school and out of trouble was his number one priority. Then, he called the fourteen children who'd been abused for up to three years "hard-core truants." As if it had been the children's fault for not staying in school—which was no longer the safest place to be.

That year, Thomas Jefferson High School started using metal detectors to scan students for weapons.

The FHA Scandal

1972

As soon as the indictments were handed down and the warrants were issued, the plan for the arrests was put into action. Sniegocki had worked on it for two weeks. This was not going to be a routine procedure. Forty realtors, bankers, attorneys, and FHA employees, a manager from Dun & Bradstreet, and nine companies in addition to Eastern Service had been indicted. It was a major operation, requiring precise coordination and timing. (When a company is indicted, no one is arrested; either the firm's lawyer or an executive is served with the warrant and an order to appear before the judge.)

The Accounting Squad only had around twenty agents, so Sniegocki borrowed agents from other squads to put together enough teams to make the arrests. On the day before the indictments, Sniegocki stood before roughly eighty FBI agents. Each was holding a packet he'd prepared for them, containing descriptions and photographs of their targets, their home and business addresses, the addresses of friends and family, and a list of all the other places they might be found. Sniegocki went over the case, the identities of the people they would soon be putting into cuffs, and the schedule for their arrests.

Two days later the seventh floor of the FBI building was packed with excited agents. "Agents are always happy making arrests," Sniegocki said. "This is what they joined for." Sniegocki, however, would not be among them. After a year of gathering evidence, finding witnesses, flipping suspects, and working through mountains of paperwork, he had to stay behind on Sixty-ninth Street to oversee the plan he'd put together and make sure it went off like clockwork. It was killing him. He particularly wanted to be there for the arrests of Harry and Rose Bernstein, whom he'd been investigating the longest. As it turned out, Rose and Harry were in Florida, and were among the three people who were arrested later.

At 7:00 a.m. the agents headed out in about forty cars. Throughout the day Sniegocki was in near constant radio contact with the arresting teams, who'd fanned out to over thirty different locations. Every time an arrest was made, he checked the name off a master list, also noting when the agent called to say he had his target in custody, when they got back to the office, and the time of their arrival at the courthouse. The team assigned to make the arrests at FHA's Hempstead office was the largest of all. Six agents showed up at their door, and minutes later walked out with eight men in handcuffs.

Somehow, in all the planning, the fact that the arrests would be taking place on the first day of Passover had escaped everyone's notice. As soon as Agent Kay was made aware of the plan he looked at Accetta. "My God," he said, stumbling for words, "you're arresting . . . I'm working on a Jewish holiday!" Accetta wasn't about to change the date now. "It created a lot of flak in court that day," Kay remembered. Some of the defendants were Jewish and they complained. "How dare we arrest him on a Jewish holiday?" Accommodations were made. "The Magistrate rushed the arraignments so all were out by the afternoon," Accetta said. It was a courtesy rarely extended to street criminals whose actions cause a lot less destruction. Thirty-seven arrests were accomplished within hours and every one of them was released on $2,500 bail.

It wasn't a dangerous operation. "When you go out to make arrests in an organized crime case," Sniegocki says, "your fear is that you could get shot and killed." When you're arresting bankers and government officials, the fear is that they will hurt themselves. They have families, children. Their careers are likely ruined forever, and they might decide that rather than face all of that and live out their shattered lives they're going to jump out of the car or out a window. The challenge is keeping them alive until they're delivered to the court and are no longer your responsibility.

The arrests were in all the papers. Donald Carroll, who'd known Harry Bernstein for many years, told reporters he was shocked. "Until now he had a good reputation." Although eight people from the Hempstead office were arrested, S. William Green, HUD director of the regional office, told reporters he was still confident in Carroll and his "fidelity to the public interest." They would later learn that their trust was misplaced.

Romney, who could finally act, immediately suspended the eight federal employees who'd been arrested, and barred everyone who'd been indicted from doing business with the U.S. government. "I am angered and determined to eliminate incompetence, conflict of interest, favoritism, graft, bribes, fraud, shoddy workmanship, and forms of 'legal' profiteering that can take advantage of technicalities to defraud the homebuyer and the tax-paying public." Four hundred cases, he said, had been referred to the FBI and DOJ in the past year and a half. Dun & Bradstreet denied any wrongdoing on the part of their employees, and indicted Dun & Bradstreet manager Arthur Prescott requested a leave of absence.

The case involved 2,500 foreclosed homes, U.S. Attorney Morse told reporters, and they expected losses to the federal government would total $200 million. Accetta expressed anger that it had to come to this. "I wish we didn't have to have these indictments. I wish the FHA system hadn't been so thoroughly corrupted."

The investigations in other cities came up in most of the newspaper accounts, as did Senator Philip Hart's Antitrust and Monopoly Subcommittee hearings scheduled for May, covering the operation of the FHA programs and the possible crimes associated with them. Jack Blum, who'd conducted investigations for the committee, would be present.

An employee at the FHA office in Hempstead admitted, "To be frank, we've known a lot of things for a long time." Damage control was already underway. Six new employees assigned by Romney were told to report for work in Hempstead five days after the arrests. Procedures were revised to prevent similar crimes, and to improve the quality of houses whose mortgages they were insuring. S. William Green promised to "weed out corruption, fraud, and bribery." Fifteen speculators who were suspected of wrongdoing were listed on cards in their Hempstead office and were being treated with "utmost caution." Business, meanwhile, continued. Two other mortgage companies in the same building as the FHA quickly picked up the slack left by the now indicted and currently blacklisted Eastern Service Corporation.

Before the Housing and Urban Development Act of 1968 had passed, Senator Charles H. Percy had submitted a competing bill. Now he called for an overhaul of the FHA. Shirley Chisholm, who was running for president, launched a blistering attack. "The FHA, marked by a legacy of racism and profiteering . . . has knowingly tolerated the development of Federal financed slums, the perpetuation and acceleration of segregated housing patterns, and the gouging of the poor by speculators, builders, and bankers who all pocket Federal dollars for violating Federal laws. FHA has turned an official back to the victims of blockbusting and profiteering, it has tolerated corruption in its own ranks, and it has sanctioned a policy of 'separate and unequal' in its administration of the subsidized programs."

In the FBI's annual report for 1972, the Accounting and Fraud division was featured for the first time. Organized crime, gambling, and bank robberies still took center stage, but this year a new section appeared, titled, all in caps, ACCOUNTING AND FRAUD MATTERS. The highlight of the new section was an account of the FHA cases across the country, including the New York arrests, as well as thirty-nine people and five firms arrested in Philadelphia, and seventeen people in Detroit. Overall, 765 FHA fraud cases were being investigated in Boston, Chicago, Detroit, Newark, New York, and Philadelphia, according to their report. J. Edgar Hoover died in May. With his death, white-collar crime investigation began to slowly rise in prestige.

Not long after the indictments, a man accompanied by his lawyer walked into Accetta's office, asking to see him. Accetta didn't know what they wanted to speak to him about, and he sat there with his yellow legal pad, ready to take notes. The lawyer began, "Look, we know you're investigating my client. We want to cooperate, we're fully prepared to take a guilty plea, can you make us any kind of offer?" Accetta had never heard of the guy. He had no idea what his company was, or what crimes he had committed. But he put his pen down and his legal pad aside, and acted like he'd been expecting this visit, and that it was just a matter of time before they'd be sitting across from each other, working out a deal. It was another useful feature of grand juries and indictments. When they're handed down, particularly in large numbers, frightened co-conspirators and people with information come forward.

Fred Fell, the special agent in charge of the criminal division of the FBI's New York office, walked over to Agents Kay and Lacina and said, "I wish you guys would keep this stuff low-key, because I really don't want it to get out of hand." "We looked at him like, are you out of your mind?" Kay said. Agent Kay went to Accetta, "and Tony went ape shit." Low-key was the last thing he wanted. "We're going to take this to the end of the world."

Kay said, "I will tell you that, at times, the four of us [the four lead FBI investigators] had the feeling that even FBI headquarters really didn't want this to go as big as it did, because of the bad publicity it was going to give the Nixon administration."

Later that month, Senator Hart announced that he was calling nine witnesses from New York to testify at the Senate's Antitrust and Monopoly Subcommittee hearing. John Lomenzo, who'd jump-started the investigation that was going to be prosecuted in New York, was among the nine. Unbeknownst to the committee, they also called two people who were currently being investigated by the FBI: Stanley Sirote, of Inter-Island Mortgage, and Edwin Katz of United Institutional Servicing Corporation.

Tony Accetta was drowning in motions from forty lawyers representing the forty indicted—motions for dismissal, severance, pretrial relief, a bill of particulars, investigative reports, discovery and inspection, disclosure of evidence recovered by search and seizure, inspection of grand jury minutes, flowcharts concerning FHA mortgages—there were hundreds of them. Accetta had also made an error on the original indictments and new superseding indictments had to be drawn up. Accetta was overwhelmed and needed help. He asked U.S. Attorney Morse to assign more AUSAs to the case.

Soon after the indictments, Melvin Cardona, the realtor and Eastern Service mortgage solicitor that Sniegocki had tried to flip, lost his company. It wasn't a lot to lose. Cardona was out on bail and would live to see his day in court, while the people back in East New York and in neighborhoods of color across the United States were coping with a "social unmitigated disaster on a scale you'd find hard to believe," as Jack Blum summed up what had occurred. The crimes had "led to the destruction of thousands of perfectly good houses in a neighborhood that had been thriving." Brian Boyer said the FHA scandal was nothing less than an "economic war crime."

12

The Destruction of East New York

1983–1985

In 1983, when only 43 percent of Hispanic Americans were able to purchase a home in America, the Arlequin family had managed to buy two. On a lovely stretch of Wyona Street, in the heart of Thabit's Family Area, Nancy's aunt purchased two buildings, one for herself and one for Nancy and her mother, Nancy's two daughters, and the latest arrival, a son.

About the part of town where their new homes were located, one of Thabit's surveyors had written, "I noticed a marked difference in the streets of most of the area where I worked today, they were much cleaner . . . the buildings were also in better condition. The area struck me as being much more settled . . . The people are obviously more concerned, or have more of an investment. The children in the area were warmer for some reason . . . I think it's an area where most of the people own the buildings."

On Wyona Street, Nancy's three children were able to grow up where summers meant block parties and kids running across the street from house to house, playing tag and opening up fire hydrants while the mothers watched from their stoops. It wasn't quiet, but it was the best kind of noise. Music is a big part of Puerto Rican culture and the spirited and outgoing Julia Parker, with her striking green eyes and dark curly hair, was always an enthusiastic participant in the rhythmic life on the street. Her energy drew those in their close-knit community to her, and amplified the fun. Every Thanksgiving, Nancy and her mother cooked dinner for the whole family, and some of the neighbors. Christmas decorations in the neighborhood went up soon after. Their corner of East New York became one of the merriest spots in New York. Echoing the words of the men describing the Linden Houses in the 1950s and early 1960s, Julia's sister Milagros said their "block was like one big household," where they all felt more like family than friends. It was the idyllic childhood every parent hopes to give their children.

But it was also a block where not too long ago, predators swarmed, destroying the lives of the people who came before them. The children were racing in and out of buildings that were once owned and sold by speculators who'd been indicted by Anthony Accetta for mortgage crimes. Eighteen of the homes on their block were once in the hands of people who didn't care what happened after they were sold, and thirteen of those buildings were eventually possessed by HUD, which meant thirteen families who had lived on Wyona Street lost everything. Eastern Service were the mortgagees for four of the buildings on Julia's block, including one almost directly across the street from where Nancy lived with her family, and the four other banks under investigation were involved with fourteen.

It was like someone had leavened their block with greed and indifference, leaving some buildings to sicken and die, and others to rise above their history of poisoning. Most of Nancy's block recovered, leaving only two vacant lots. The remaining buildings were in better shape, and the next round of buyers had arrived after stricter FHA procedures had been put in place following the arrests and prosecution of Eastern Service and others. The new owners were still families of modest means, but most of them were able to make their mortgage payments and attend to the less drastic repairs. Congressman Major Robert Owens bought and lived in a building on Nancy's block.

The next year, the city took out an ad in the *New York Amsterdam News*, calling for homesteaders to apply to purchase and rehabilitate vacant city-owned buildings. Those who were accepted would get low-interest loans from the city to help them. Three of the buildings listed were on the Arlequins' block and one was a former Eastern Service building.

The following year, a group of East New York residents who were working with the Association of Community Organizations for Reform Now (ACORN) took over twenty-five vacant, city-owned buildings. State Senator Thomas J. Bartosiewicz, who supported the action, said, "There are 2,500 other buildings like this in East New York, and we're going to be back here time and time again. Sometimes this is the only way to dramatize the plight of the residents and to prod the city to take action." Bartosiewicz would be arrested for entering one of the abandoned buildings. Later, the squatters, along with some members of ACORN, formed the Mutual Housing Association of New York (MHANY) and started working with the Pratt Institute Center for Community and Environmental Development. The city, in turn, gave the squatters the buildings they occupied, while creating a revolving loan fund to finance the rehabilitation of these and future buildings.

While things were better, not enough was done to stop similar financial crimes from happening again and buildings continued to be abandoned. East New York was still in decline, and danger was all around them, but the children in Nancy's neighborhood were largely oblivious to it. They all grew up going to the same schools, playing in the parks on Miller Avenue and on Pitkin, and in a field over on Barbey Street. Unless it affected one of their families or friends, they weren't aware of the homes around them that went into foreclosure from time to time. The children weren't following the rise in street crime, which would continue for many years. They didn't pay attention to the ongoing lack of city services and economic opportunity for their parents. They would learn about all that when they were older. In the meantime, the kids in Nancy's part of town were just busy being kids. They looked out on their neighborhood and saw it differently than their parents. At least one person remembered the vacant lots fondly, in particular one lot they called "Looney Lake," because of the standing water that pooled there. In the winter, when the water froze, they'd skate on the ice, jumping over old tires frozen inside the water, like they were part of an obstacle course.

Crime and foreclosure were not the only threats to the health and well-being of the neighborhood children. Opened in 1961, the Fountain Avenue Landfill dump at the southern end of East New York had grown into a toxic waste site, accounting for 40 percent of New York City's garbage. The United Community Centers wrote in their newspaper, *The Link*, about the Sanitation Commission's practice of burying asbestos in the site. While tests showed "more asbestos particles in the air over the landfill than is normal," the commissioner insisted, "It is well below the federal safety standard," omitting the fact that the dump had been classified as a Class 2 site that year, meaning it "posed a significant threat to public health and the environment." Instead he suggested replacing the dump with eight garbage-burning plants, a solution as dangerous as the problem it was supposed to fix.

In 1983, Patrolman Michael Dowd was transferred to the Seven-Five precinct. Assignments to East New York were met with mixed feelings, depending on the officer's response to the threat level that surrounded them. The Seven-Five is one of the largest precincts in the city, and East New York often ranked at the bottom in every quality-of-life statistic. For some, being sent there was a punishment. "I saw it as a challenge," said Derrick Parker, a former detective in the Seven-Five. "I'm going to a high-profile precinct, where you have a lot of murders, you have a lot of crime, so you're going to learn a lot faster than other people that will work in precincts that are slower." Police in the Seven-Five would be getting a little help with all the crime that year, though. A section of East New York was chosen as the site for a $120,000 two-year crime-prevention program, sponsored by the Eisenhower Foundation for the Prevention of Violence. The goal was to bring crime levels down, so that people and businesses would move to East New York and, equally important, stay. The part of town they chose was a relatively large swath bounded by Blake Avenue to the north, Atkins Avenue to the east, Linden Boulevard to the south, and Wyona Street to the west. Julia Parker's family home was two blocks north of that, not within the area identified as troubled.

There was a reason why the foundation chose East New York. Citywide, murder was down in 1983, but it was up in Brooklyn North. Fifty people were murdered in East New York that year. In 1984, when Julia Parker turned ten, sixty people were murdered there. A horrific mass murder was responsible for driving the numbers up. On the evening of April 15, Palm Sunday, a call came into the detective squad of the Seven-Five. Six dead on Liberty Avenue, they were told. Then another call. Make that ten. When they arrived, detectives found eight children and two adults, all of whom had been shot in the head, and one child left unharmed. Two months later, detectives were led to the killer; he was in jail, suspected of trying to rape his own mother.

The year 1985 was seemingly quieter. Only forty-four murders. Had the killer who shot eleven people in their home on February 27 been more successful, the numbers would have gone up that year too, but eight of those people survived. In the course of committing a robbery, seven children who were home at the time of the murders were left alive, but not unharmed. Two of the children had been choked and one was held under water, in an attempt to get one of the men who lived there to reveal to them where the money was. While the killers searched for more to steal, a woman was raped.

A popular local radio station had a well-known motto: "You give us twenty-two minutes, we'll give you the world." If you lived in New York you couldn't help hearing it. Around this time detectives in the

Seven-Five started joking, "You give us twenty-two minutes, we'll give you a homicide." That year the Seven-Five replaced the Four-Six in the Bronx as the precinct with the most felony assaults.

In 1986, an already dangerous situation started to implode.

The FHA Scandal

1972

While those indicted in March were lawyering up, George Romney, after suspending the indicted FHA employees, put a hold on doing business with Dun & Bradstreet and went on an apology tour. It included a lot of backtracking. "We will not solve this crisis if we pretend that it is just a housing crisis." When addressing Congress he said, "Housing didn't take the jobs away ... Housing did not reduce the public services. Housing didn't destroy the quality of education in the schools. Housing didn't bring the drug addiction." Romney said "deep social changes" were to blame. That was as close as he was going to get to voicing the real answer. Racism would always be the root cause.

What was meant to be the next step in addressing that racism, an attempt to give Americans of color a chance to live in a decent home, became instead an opportunity for the unscrupulous to turn a profit at their expense. Their greed had precipitated a housing crisis that in turn exacerbated existing problems, leaving people trapped in neighborhoods with diminished services, inadequate schools and health care, rising crime, and little to no resources to fight the problems that inevitably arose. Racism and greed were responsible, and, as usual, the victims were held to blame.

Romney argued that throwing a lot of money at the problem hadn't solved it. But it also couldn't be solved without it. A lot of it. Romney himself complained that HUD and the FHA were perpetually without the funding needed to do the job they were supposed to do. Enough money was never thrown.

There were many more financial criminals still out there, and Accetta's March indictments were only the beginning. The FBI continued their investigation, which led to more and more FHA employees and officials, and employees at the Veterans Administration (VA) as well.

Special agent Jeffrey Kay had come to the FBI in a similar frame of mind as Tony Accetta's when he took a job at the Eastern District. Kay was in his third year of law school when he interviewed with a number of big law firms. "Their offers sounded as boring as could be, working in some office doing research for a firm partner, being a gofer." Around the same time an FBI special agent in charge came to his law school. They were looking for accountants and lawyers to beef up their white-collar crime initiative. Kay, whose undergraduate degree was in accounting, was intrigued. His roommate dared him to apply. Kay took the dare and that fall he was offered a special agent position and told to report to FBI headquarters for training.

When he was transferred to the Accounting and Fraud Squad in early 1972, Dennis Lacina, who was working the Eastern case, came up to him and asked him, "What do you know about FHA housing fraud?"

"Not a damn thing."

"Great. You're perfect for the job. We need you." Lacina was just glad to have another agent to join him in what would become extensive on-the-job training for all of them, and one with a legal background.

Kay went over to the Eastern District and got a crash course in the case from Accetta. At the FBI, Kay was one of two lawyers in a squad packed with accountants, and he and Accetta quickly became close, discussing legal and investigative strategies. Kay said, "I tease him to this day, that I taught him how to be an investigator, and he taught me how to be a lawyer."

In the early spring, Kay hit the jackpot in his investigation of Inter-Island Mortgage. There was a rumor that Donald Carroll, the head of the FHA's Hempstead office, had taken a trip to Puerto Rico, paid for by one of the mortgage banks. Kay went out to Queens and started walking the blocks surrounding the office, looking for a travel agency. He found one only a block away. "Do you do business with Inter-Island Mortgage?" he asked, while holding out his credentials. They did. There, inside the file, was an airline ticket and hotel reservations for Donald Carroll, paid for by Inter-Island Mortgage. Kay ran to a pay phone to call special agent Walter Ver Steeg, who was investigating Carroll. When Ver Steeg picked up the phone, Kay couldn't stop himself from blurting out, "We got the FHA director by the balls!" They also now had Stanley Sirote, the president of Inter-Island Mortgage.

Accetta started hitting Inter-Island with grand jury subpoenas for all the FHA mortgage file records they'd identified as possibly fraudulent. Kay reviewed the Inter-Island mortgages and found false VOEs (verification of employment) and VODs (verification of deposit).

Not long after that, Sirote and his attorney were sitting across from Accetta and special agent Kay, who showed him the plane tickets, hotel bills, and the mortgage files with phony credit histories. They had him. He was now dangling from a hook and ready to hear whatever hope they offered. Accetta began his pitch as he had with Edward Goodwin and Ortrud Kapraki. Sirote was going to be indicted, but if he was willing to cooperate, Accetta would see what he could do, depending on how useful Sirote's information turned out to be. It turned out to be crucial. Sirote would eventually tell them and the grand jury who he was paying off at the FHA and the VA, how he kept records of the payoffs, and how Donald Carroll had come to do his bidding.

In the fall of 1971, when Carroll was a vice president at Lawrence-Cedarhurst Federal Savings & Loan, he'd made unauthorized commitments for $1 million worth of bad mortgages, which may also have involved fraud. That October, Stanley Sirote, the president of Inter-Island Mortgage, rescued Carroll when he bought the mortgages from the bank at a $30,000 loss. It was a great investment. Later that month, Carroll was made director of the FHA office in Hempstead, and he was in debt to Sirote.

Around this time Jack Blum, the assistant counsel to the Senate subcommittee investigating mortgage crimes, was invited to the FBI's New York office to talk to them about his investigations and theirs. "Talk about the dance that was," Kay said, looking back. They were supposed to be sharing information. But the Senate hearings on the crimes they'd all been investigating were about to begin. One of the witnesses Blum had called was Stanley Sirote. Accetta couldn't let Sirote testify. He didn't want the possibility of a contrary story on record. Sirote had described one set of events, he might tell the Senate a slightly different version, which might later translate to reasonable doubt, or an unreliable witness, in court. It was an impossible situation. "Jack came to New York to help us as best he could," Kay said, "and we couldn't give much back. That made for some frayed relationships, to be quite honest."

Sirote wasn't the only subject of their investigations that Blum would call to testify over that summer, and the Senate hearings would ultimately turn out to be very useful to the FBI and to Accetta.

13

The Destruction of East New York

1986

Murders went up to fifty-six in 1986, and East New York children were increasingly caught in the cross fire. On May 23, five-year-old Aurelio Martinez was shot by a stray bullet. He'd been playing with his sister in front of his home when he suddenly fell, bleeding from the back of his head. At Brookdale Hospital his parents were told nothing could save their son. His organs were donated for transplants, and reward posters went up around the neighborhood soon after. The posters didn't help. Aurelio's case went cold, and white roses were planted on his block in his memory. Aurelio wasn't the only child whose murder that year remains unsolved. Elizabeth Ramirez, who died from blunt force trauma, was only one, and no one was ever arrested for her murder.

Some parents responded to the growing threat by arming their older children. The year before, one Thomas Jefferson High School student said, "My dad gave me his gun, registered in his name, and he told me I should carry it every day. He said it was very important for my own protection."

Four of the people murdered that year were killed in vacant lots and abandoned buildings. Vacancy seemed to create a murder-vortex, which spread as each building was evacuated, and later, many burned to the ground. Two of those murders were closed by "exceptional clearance." Homicides can be closed by exceptional clearance when an arrest is impossible due to circumstances beyond the control of the police, such as the death of the perpetrator, or when the perpetrator is living in a country that doesn't have an extradition agreement with the United States. A case can also be exceptionally cleared if the perpetrator is already in prison for another crime and the DA does not want to bring the case to trial. The district attorney has to agree that the evidence is strong, however, and sign off on the clearance, and he is not the only one.

To get an exceptional clearance the detective would write up the case, document the merits, and note the reason for asking for an exceptional clearance. The clearance must then be signed off on by the detective's commanding officer, commanding officers up the line, and the DA. There is nothing alarming about closing a case by exceptional clearance, but two cases were closed by exceptional clearance in 1985, ten in 1986, and the number would continue to rise. The increase appeared to coincide with the arrival of a new commanding officer, Detective Sergeant Michael Race.

Around this time a new form of cocaine called crack was gaining popularity. Because it was less expensive to produce, crack was cheap, around $2 to $20 a pop. "It's all too darn easy," a lieutenant from Brooklyn North Narcotics told a *Daily News* reporter. The high was immediate, intense, and very addictive. Every morning, people on their way to work would find the street curbs littered with empty vials, left there the night before.

On October 6, detectives in the Seven-Five got a tip that a robbery and assault suspect they were looking for was holed up on Bradford Street, a block away from the Arlequin home. They didn't find the suspect, but they did find two teenagers and 269 vials of crack. It was a crack house. They'd just recently found another in an abandoned building on Miller Avenue. They would soon find many more. Use of crack was spreading and there were plenty of abandoned buildings in East

New York where those with little money to spare could buy a few short minutes of a high many of them would never stop craving. The euphoria and sense of well-being was so great, and the subsequent crash so unbearable, that many got caught in a downward spiral that sucked the life and humanity right out of them. Their constant, doomed attempts to claw their way back up to that first high turned them into agents of destruction in a neighborhood already under siege. Wherever there was poverty and despair, there was crack, and East New York would go on to become one of the biggest crack hubs of the city. One young mother regularly left her baby outside an abandoned building on Miller Avenue for hours, while she lost herself inside. Her child was eventually taken away. Legislation in response to the appearance of crack was almost immediate. The Anti-Drug Abuse Act, establishing a mandatory minimum sentence of five years without parole for people found in possession of five grams of crack, passed in 1986. Congress did not feel the need, however, to mount a similar and swift defense against financial crimes, which had almost completely destroyed neighborhoods across the country before crack had even appeared, supplying plenty of places for its dissemination and usage once it did.

The East Brooklyn Congregations' (EBC) efforts to do something about the abandoned buildings in East New York had stalled. Mayor Ed Koch had announced plans to build 1,550 Nehemiah homes in a twenty-block area of East New York, but the city later removed twenty-seven buildings scheduled for demolition from the plan. Build around them, the EBC were told. The EBC immediately objected. It would increase the cost of construction and the final cost of the homes. They also didn't want to build a home here and a home there. "Nehemiah is not a housing plan, it's a neighborhood plan," Father Edward Mason of St. John Cantius would later explain, as the conflict went on. "Nehemiah is a community building program." They accused Brooklyn Borough President Howard Golden of sabotaging the plan, but Golden wasn't the only one opposed to the demolition. There was resistance from homeowners in the community. Carlos Bristol's home on Cleveland Street, the one that his parents had bought twenty-three years before, was among those scheduled for demolition. There was nothing wrong with his building and he wanted to keep it. It was nicer than the Nehemiah homes, and bigger. The Nehemiah homes were dollhouses in comparison, one person said.

Carlos Bristol began working with Diane Golden, who'd formed a homeowners' association to block the demolition of his home and others. They'd seen the results of slum clearance and forced relocations from earlier urban renewal programs. Communities disappeared and were never reestablished. They were just gone.

There was another problem. The Board of Estimate modified the plan to include blocks west of Pennsylvania Avenue, in the area identified by Thabit as the "Industrial Quadrant." It was one of the worst sections in East New York. The EBC had already planned to put up homes there, but only after the original plan to build east of Pennsylvania had been completed.

The EBC had received a lot of positive responses to their plan, but they were also used to resistance. There will always be people who resist change, no matter how constructive that change might be. "Every phase of Nehemiah was a battle," Michael Gecan remembered. "A battle with the city, a battle with other people, a battle with some activists." But some of their complaints, like those of Carlos Bristol, were legitimate. After a promising beginning in Brownsville, things were starting to unravel in East New York. Within a year, the Messiah Baptist Church would start organizing protests and buying space in the *New York Amsterdam News* to proclaim that the reverend Johnny Ray Youngblood was throwing eighty-two-year-old grandmothers out on the street.

Also threatening East New York was a rise in crime within the Seven-Five precinct itself. In 1986 the NYPD's Patrol Borough Brooklyn North Field Internal Affairs Unit (PBBN/FIAU) opened their third corruption case involving Police Officer Michael Dowd. The first, for harassing his girlfriend, and the second, for having sex with a prostitute in Bailey's Bar, were closed as unsubstantiated. But the third allegation came from the commanding officer of the Seven-Five, who said Dowd was stealing money from drug dealers, prisoners, and dead people. Four days later they opened a fourth case; there had been claims of brutality by Dowd and other officers from the Seven-Five.

Julia Parker, now twelve, went from the private school at St. John Cantius to I. S. 292, the public school. Ashmat Ali, who would later become friends with Julia, had attended I. S. 292 a few years before. "It was rough," Ali said. He wasn't scared exactly, but every day "I was just hoping I don't get in a fight today." I. S. 292 was in the middle of East New York, and a little to the west. "You had the guys from Pitkin projects, and then you had the guys from Unity. And then you had all the neighborhood people, too, going to the school," Ali explained. "So you always got a little beef . . . one guy try to act tougher than the other guy. 'I'm from Pitkin projects,' or, 'Fuck Unity projects.'"

As a result, there were fights every day. "Somebody step on your sneakers back then, it's a fight. Somebody bump you when you walking through the hallway, oh, it's a fight. Stupid shit. Now that you're older and you think about it, it's stupid. It's stupid. But back then in that neighborhood, you couldn't back down. Once you back down, you're the one that's going to get picked on all the time. So you couldn't back down."

Julia would learn to never back down. "She was a little thing," her sister Milagros said, only five feet, one inch. She had to defend herself any way she could. "When you're living in East New York you're on high alert because you don't know if you're going to be robbed, you don't know if you're going to be shot, you don't know if you're going to be stabbed." Four girls tried to jump Julia one day, but she was prepared with razor blades. The fight ended quickly. Julia cut one of the girls, punched another, and, like that, it was over. She got through her junior high school years the same way she got through everything else. She was the kind of girl who helped people with their schoolwork, and their problems, while also carrying razor blades to deal with anyone who tried to mess with her. She had all the skills needed to survive junior high in a neighborhood where the number of murders, already inconceivable, would almost double by the time she got to high school, and would continue to rise from there.

The FHA Scandal

1972

On May 1, the Senate hearings on the housing programs for the poor began, chaired by Philip Hart, the senator from Michigan. Initially meant to take place in New York, other Senate business required changing the location to Washington.

Senator Strom Thurmond was a member of the subcommittee; his contribution to the Civil Rights Act of 1968, which for so many others had been about ending housing discrimination, was the anti-riot amendment, which, among other things, made it a crime to cross state lines or use interstate facilities such as the mail or a telephone to participate in or incite what was referred to as a riot. When Thurmond said his amendment would "protect society from the extremist element which advocates the destruction of our nation," he was talking about groups like the Black Panthers, whose Free Breakfast for School Children Program was destroyed by the FBI and the Chicago Police, and not the Ku Klux Klan and other white supremacists, who were firebombing churches, and murdering children and civil rights workers. Martin Luther King Jr. was specifically named by proponents of the amendment as one of the outside agitators America needed protection from.

Thurmond never said a word during the two months of the hearings. Later, when the Carter administration sought greater power to enforce the law against housing discrimination, Thurmond was opposed. "I am a bitter opponent of the federal government's injecting itself in every facet of people's lives."

Over seventy witnesses were scheduled to testify that summer. The hearings opened at 10:30 a.m. with a brief opening statement by Hart, who set the tone when he said their investigation caused him to become painfully familiar with human misery, and that for some families it was normal that their babies were bitten by rats while they lay in their cribs. He was followed by members of the National People's Action on Housing, the Latin American Coordinating Council, Inc., and other representatives from community groups from around the country, who read from opening statements outlining problems with the FHA housing programs.

Their statements were greeted by cheers from the audience, but it was Gale Cincotta, chairperson for the National People's Action on Housing and a seasoned activist, who set the room on fire. "I am here today to testify before the Subcommittee on a specific case of conspiracy, the outright murder of our neighborhoods . . . aided and abetted by the Federal Housing Administration, the mortgage industry, the insurance industry, and the unscrupulous real estate industry," she said, throwing down the gauntlet. "These four institutions are working together to systematically destroy what is left of America's cities. What for so long have been considered natural phenomena—changing neighborhoods, deteriorating cities—are not natural. It's an outright plan, and the government, the realtors, and the big-money people are making a lot of money out of changing neighborhoods, out of the communities we call home."

After the statements were read, and questioning began, Senator Hiram Fong from Hawaii immediately went for Cincotta.

There were already laws against all the alleged crimes, Fong argued, and these problems should be handled locally, in court. But the problem was too large and too widespread, Cincotta argued. "The people cannot keep up with it. It has to be handled by your committee. To give it to the people who are suffering, to say you fight it through the court system, that is impossible. We are going to lose . . . We are talking about mortgage brokerage houses and realtors using FHA in a conspiracy," a problem that was not going to be solved by dragging one realtor at a time into courts all over America.

"We would be very happy if you can give us the evidence to show this," Fong replied.

"The evidence is the city," Cincotta shot back, "the deterioration of one community after another. There are whole files of it . . . Call the head of HUD here. Call in the realtors. Call in mortgage bankers, the Metropolitan Insurance Co. They write all the mortgage papers on FHA-insured money and never take a risk . . . The proof is, we are losing our cities. We are losing our communities. The Blacks are saying it, the whites, the Latinos. I don't know how much more proof the people can bring to you, plus their own misery, to get you to understand this is happening."

"Just by making statements is not going to prove your case," Fong said. "You have to give us concrete evidence that there is collusion . . . And then, this committee will act."

Jack Blum and others, who knew what Cincotta was saying was true, who had already seen the proof, must have inwardly groaned. Blum said later it was a healthy exchange. "I was hoping we'd be able to break through and get him to understand what was going on, on the ground, as opposed to a theoretical notion of how it was supposed to work."

Senator Hart stepped in and said, "I think before these hearings are concluded, there will be various specific evidence in this record."

"We shall see," Ms. Cincotta responded. She never backed down. "She was one tough cookie, and a terrific witness," Blum said. "She really represented her people. She was a community organizer in the best sense of the word."

Fong's answer was to read from a *Wall Street Journal* editorial hold-ing President Johnson and the HUD Act responsible for the current situation.

George Gould, a lawyer from Community Legal Services Inc., in Philadelphia angrily responded that the 1968 act reiterated that the homes insured by the FHA "must comply with local housing codes . . . the 1968 Housing Act did not, in any way, say that shoddy homes should be sold."

"Have the lenders and the FHA people, which would be Romney's people, have they colluded so that inspections have been negligent, so that sometimes there is no inspection, faulty things have been let go so that the people who bought them bought really substandard homes that did not come up to specifications?" Fong asked.

"That is correct," Gould replied. Although the crimes being de-scribed were no longer news—they were being reported nationwide—Fong was completely taken aback by what he was hearing. "Fong had a lot to learn," Blum said.

Later, when Fong tried to defend Romney, saying that Romney fully recognized the problem and had asked the FBI to look into 750 cases, a priest from Chicago said thirty thousand houses had foreclosed there. How many of those were being investigated?

"Are you saying that the thirty thousand homes, which were fore-closed, are all Romney's fault?"

"It's not ours," Cincotta answered. She was cheered.

Fong persisted. "What percent of these thirty thousand homes were foreclosed due to Mr. Romney's fault?" He was booed while other members of the audience called out, "Whitewash!"

James Sporleder, a consultant to the Greater St. Louis Committee for Freedom of Residence, explained how this kind of response was a large part of the problem. "The biggest difficulty we have is convincing the housing officials and politicians and the president that, in fact, there is a conspiracy, that these are not isolated, unrelated, unconnected incidents. That this is an organized, exploitive process that destroys the city." Then he made an appeal. "When Lockheed was in trouble, this government figured out a way to help it. When the oil industry was in trouble, we helped it then. When ITT got into trouble, somebody figured out a way to help it. And now the people are in trouble. The people are hurting and asking for help."

If there were any other committee members who still needed convincing, the subcommittee had lined up witnesses, including mortgage and commercial bankers, representatives from Fannie Mae and Ginnie Mae, politicians, realtors, accountants, lawyers, and, unbeknownst to the committee, several people whose companies were currently under investigation by the FBI. When Blum visited the FBI's New York office the agents couldn't tell him that one of the people he called to testify, Stanley Sirote, from Inter-Island Mortgage Corporation, had flipped.

Sirote was the subcommittee's last witness on May 4. He'd been served a subpoena and he came accompanied by his lawyer.

"You have the right to refuse to answer any questions you feel may tend to incriminate you," Senator Hart told him, as he fully explained Sirote's rights. "Do you understand this?" he finished.

"Yes, sir."

"Are you willing to waive your rights and answer questions at this time?"

"No."

Hart decided to give it a try anyway. "When you negotiated the purchase of mortgages from United to complete Inter-Island's GNMA pool 642, were you aware that United was planning to sell you below-average-quality mortgages?"

"On the advice of counsel, I respectfully decline to respond to the question on the grounds that the answer may tend to incriminate me."

"Is it your intention today to invoke your Fifth Amendment privilege to any and all questions relating to conduct of your mortgage business?"

"Yes, sir."

Sirote certainly didn't want to incriminate himself, but he was refusing to testify because he was one of Accetta's chief cooperating witnesses against the FHA officials Accetta planned to indict, and both Accetta and Kay told him not to testify. The next day the Securities and Exchange Commission (SEC) suspended trading of Inter-Island stock.

The FBI weren't the only ones holding back. Blum had an informant for his investigation, who was "one of these characters who floats on the edge of the underworld," and who wanted to be paid. The Senate doesn't pay informants, so Blum arranged to have him be paid as a consultant. To be a consultant, the informant had to get a full field security investigation by the FBI. When Blum had been in New York, meeting with the FBI about their task force, someone had asked, "Did you ever run across a guy named . . ." and named Blum's consultant. "We really want to catch up with him."

"If you want to know all about it," he answered, "somebody downstairs is doing a full field investigation." "The rookies," he later explained, were the ones "doing the security clearance work."

Blum's informant was the one who told them about Mr. Oliver Diaz (not his real name), the drug dealer who had a side hustle in the real estate business and who had frightened Blum's summer intern. Secretary of State John Lomenzo's office had dealings with Diaz as well. When Patrick Cea, the counsel to the secretary of state, learned that Diaz had moved out of state and was no longer their problem, he received the news as if he'd been give an unexpected gift.

At one point they heard from a man who had been subpoenaed because his signature was on the mortgage papers for one of the buildings they were looking into. From his appearance, he might have been a homeless person, and he had no idea why he had been called. When they advised him of his right not to testify he immediately answered, "I think I'll be doing that," and left. They made no effort to stop him. The investigators had come across many instances of buildings that were unlivable, or that didn't even exist, and were nonetheless bought and sold to buyers who might be equally imaginary, or like this gentleman, had no idea what they had signed.

The committee talked to commercial bankers, who loaned the money to mortgage banks like Eastern Service, and learned that in spite of the arrests, it was business as usual. When Blum asked Edwin Katz, the former chairman of United Institutional Servicing Corp, if the banks were upset about Eastern Service after the indictments and if they might withdraw lines of credit, Katz said, "They were very upset about it." But, "Nobody threatened to withdraw any lines of credit."

"The banks," Blum explained, "underneath it all, were the silent source of the real grief because they were the ones who wanted to get out from under the conventional mortgages that had declined in value and they wanted to convert them to FHA. So they were perfectly happy to go along with the loans and all of the things that kept this whole circus afloat."

Or, as John Vogel, the president of the National Bank of North America, put it at the Senate hearings, "We do not believe that our responsibility as a supplier of interim funds includes making an independent appraisal of the hundreds—or perhaps thousands—of properties which are the underlying collateral for the mortgages pledged to us. Nor do we believe that we should make an independent credit check on the home purchasers. These are functions which should be fulfilled by the originators themselves, by the insuring agency, and by the permanent lender." And in spite of thousands of foreclosures, indictments, and numerous reports substantiating the claims of abuse, they would continue to loan money to the mortgage banks involved.

Everyone was doing it. Frank Caruso, the vice president of Empire National Bank, which had recently acquired United Institutional Servicing Corporation, and which was currently being investigated by the FBI, was questioned by Blum.

"Since the time Eastern Service has been suspended by HUD," Blum asked, "had you been approached by officials at Eastern that handled closings which they were no longer permitted to do? Did they ask to be paid for the deals they referred to your company?"

Caruso answered that they were purchasing loans at a discount. After a few more questions Blum asked if Eastern was "finding it possible to circumvent the effect of suspension?"

"Yes."

"The suspension really does not mean very much to them?"

"Maybe not to them." Nor to Empire National Bank, apparently.

Accetta wanted to go after the banks. "Specifically, I wanted to go after Chase Manhattan, who was Rose and Harry Bernstein's main bank." Chase had extended a $20 million line of credit to Eastern. But, "I could not make the connection. How would I prove that Chase Manhattan knew the source of their loans was bad?"

Of all the reasons that had been introduced to explain what was happening, the most pernicious was the idea of the unsophisticated buyer: Black buyers had little or no experience in homeownership and the problems were due to their ignorance and naivete.

George Gould, the lawyer from Philadelphia, said that when he first went to Washington in 1970 to talk about the problems, George Romney said there was no problem. "Now, he says there is a problem and he said the problem is caused by poor people failing to understand the responsibilities of homeownership . . . The issues are that he has failed and his staff has failed to properly inspect these homes, and homes are being foreclosed because people cannot afford to pay for homes that are literally falling apart."

Although there had always been cases of FHA fraud, for the most part, low- and middle-income white buyers, many first-time homebuyers, had safely managed FHA-insured mortgages for decades. How had these unsophisticated buyers come through the process unscathed? Because white-collar criminals hadn't collaborated with government officials to defraud them. The white buyers weren't more sophisticated; they just weren't targeted. Many argued that had the minority homeowners been properly counseled, this never would have happened. Counseling would certainly have helped, but unless the counseling had included "FHA employees are taking bribes from the realtors and the mortgage banks, and the building they have appraised as sound and up to code is a death trap," it would not have prevented the catastrophe.

Instead, as Ronald Yelenik, an attorney from New York Legal Services, Inc., explained, "The federal government is left with thousands of shells for which it has paid out millions of dollars . . . The frustrated, disappointed poor, the real victims who have been bilked, cheated, and exploited, are faced with another failure of the system, and the failure of a program which, if administered properly, could make tremendous strides in accomplishing the goals of the National Housing Act."

An exception was Wisconsin FHA director Lawrence S. Katz, who made counseling work by also weeding out corruption. He had houses thoroughly checked to make sure they were up to code, and actually made sure that buyers had jobs and sufficient income to make the modest mortgage payments. Lawyers representing the buyers were present at the closing and a fund to help with the expenses related to maintenance and repair was established. Keeanga-Yamahtta Taylor points out that he succeeded, "but he did so in overbearing ways that infringed on the freedom of the Black women who were in the program," which included regular home inspections that white homeowners were not subjected to. In the end, Katz was fired in 1971 for not insuring enough mortgages.

The hearings would continue through June, yielding key evidence that in a few months would help with still more indictments.

14

The Destruction of East New York

1987–1988

One-fifth of East New York was now vacant land, and what remained continued to decline. The 207-bed Baptist Medical Center closed in 1987. The homeless shelter on Williams Avenue in the old school building, however, was still in operation. The shelter now shared the former school with the Local Development Corporation of East New York (LDCENY), an organization that formed in 1979 to promote business in East New York. It was a desolate place to work. There were no other buildings around them then, just vacant lots. Carey Shea, the program director of LDCENY, remembered coming to work one day, and finding "a dead dog, a big one, on the sidewalk in front of our office." She called Animal Control.

"There is a really big dead dog on the sidewalk here."

"Where?"

"Williams Avenue, East New York."

"Okay, this is what you do. You get two trash bags and you double bag it, and then you put on gloves . . ."

Shea interrupted them. "What? I'm wearing a dress and high heels. What are you talking about? You put on gloves!"

Williams Avenue, with all that vacant land, had a reputation. Buildings that had been rehabilitated and converted to co-ops as part of the Vest Pocket program, Mayor Lindsay's early effort to restore the neighborhood and implemented by Walter Thabit, had once again fallen into disrepair and were taken over by the city, which meant they were abandoned and subsequently taken over by drug dealers. "Williams Avenue was one of the most famous blocks," for just how bad it was, said Father Edward Mason. The Animal Control people were not anxious to travel there.

There were two entrances into the school, "Boys" and "Girls." The homeless entered through the boys' entrance and the LDCENY staffers went through the girls'. Shea spoke of the men fondly, but not sentimentally. At night the men slept on cots, and "they were put out during the day, so they'd sort of hang around. The sex workers would come in the evening and there'd be a little thing going there with some of the guys," Shea said. "It was mayhem." Richard Recny, the director, told her, "Hire somebody to clean the office," meaning the homeless men. She did, and everything was stolen. "There wouldn't be a stapler left. It was really something."

For the most part, the shelter wasn't a problem for the LDCENY. Once, two of the men were fighting out front. "One of them had a golf club, and he went for the backswing and he smashed the windshield of my little 1972 Volkswagen." He apologized, she said. "He wasn't trying to break my windshield. It was an accident while he was trying to hit the other guy. My only question was, 'Where did you get a golf club?'"

The homeless problem was growing, while still relatively low compared to what it would become. A 1988 article in *The Link* noted that there were only between sixty thousand and eighty thousand homeless in all of New York City. It wasn't yet in people's faces. "There were hundreds of abandoned buildings where people could find shelter," Michael Gecan pointed out. "So street homelessness was not apparent." By the end of the decade *The Link* reported that the central section of East New York would soon have the largest concentration of homeless shelters in New York City. Andrew Cuomo, who had founded Housing Enterprise for the Less Privileged (HELP) in 1986, contributed by building a shelter in Walter Thabit's Tenement Section. "It was a big deal," Carey Shea said. At the time, the shelter was considered innovative. It provided temporary housing units for families versus the old-style giant room full of cots. "Took up an entire city block," Shea continued. "Put Andrew on the housing map, which eventually led to him becoming the secretary of HUD." But *The Link* complained that the shelter went up in an area that was "isolated and deserted" with "virtually no stores or readily available services. Its schools are old, troubled, and deteriorating."

While shelters filled a need in the short term, the long-term solution was truly affordable housing. The LDCENY wanted to get more involved in residential housing, but they were legally limited to developing industrial and commercial projects. In 1988 they spun off a separate group called the East New York Urban Youth Corps (ENYUYC) to focus on residential housing and youth programs. Carey Shea left the LDCENY to become the ENYUYC's first executive director. While the LDCENY continued to attract business to the industrial park area, the ENYUYC selected one of their first housing projects, the renovation of a vacant nineteen-unit fire-ravaged building owned by the city, at 611 Pennsylvania Avenue.

The EBC meanwhile were moving ahead, ultimately agreeing to the East New York homeowners' demands and consenting to what is called "infill housing." Where viable buildings stood, they would build around them. Infill housing made Nehemiah "more successful in the long run," Richard Recny maintains, "because it didn't destroy the neighborhood that remained at the time they started their project." The homes that were not demolished "helped stabilize what they did." The EBC did their best to work with their detractors and came to an agreement with everyone who opposed them, including the Messiah Baptist Church. "I don't think everyone was happy," Gecan said, "but I recall a kind of ceasefire at some point." Carlos Bristol, who'd fought

Youngblood on the original plan, came to respect him and would soon call him his pastor. The EBC even changed the design of the homes based on feedback from the residents. The kitchens, for instance, which were originally going to go in the back of the home, were moved to the front, so mothers could watch over their kids who congregated on the stoops, their preferred hangout spot.

Nehemiah homes were sold by lottery, before construction began. Due to the concessions made, work would begin on 1,100 houses in East New York, and not the 1,500 originally planned. But the buildings would go up. "This is a poor man's dream, owning one of these houses," said one Brooklyn resident, and 1,100 families would soon become proud, new homeowners.

There were now at least three community-based housing efforts: EBC, ENYUYC, and the newly formed Mutual Housing Association of New York (MHANY), who were working with the Pratt Institute Center for Community and Environmental Development. If it weren't for the crack epidemic, which accelerated the rise in crime, it would have seemed like things were looking up for East New York.

One night in October eight crack houses in Brooklyn were busted and shut down. When one hundred cops converged on a building on the corner of New Lots and Alabama, the dealers set the building on fire, trapping themselves inside. Firefighters had to chop open an escape route on the roof for them, where they were greeted by cops with automatic weapons. As the police took the men away, a woman looking on yelled, "Thank God. At last. Get them away from here, so we can at least walk on the street again." New Lots and Alabama were known as areas with the heaviest drug traffic. Despite all the building, fewer and fewer places in East New York felt safe. When asked which parts of East New York were the worst in those days, Ashmat Ali answered, "Everywhere."

That year, when Julia Parker turned thirteen, East New York led the city in rape, robbery, assault, burglary, and car theft; eighty-two murders were reported. Sixteen of them were cleared by exceptional clearance, a total that normally would have been hard to ignore, but the twenty-two detectives at the Seven-Five had sixty-six other murders to solve, along with all the other crimes. No one had time to question sixteen closed cases. A former officer said, "East New York Brooklyn, the Seven-Five precinct, back in the late '80s, was the deadliest precinct in the country."

"I felt often that my life was in danger," LDCENY director Richard Recny recalled. "My life was threatened many times . . . There were people in the neighborhood who didn't want me to be in the neighborhood making the place better because it displaced their ability to make money." He started walking around with a loaded .38 caliber Smith and Wesson revolver on his hip. "I was licensed with the City of New York. It was a legal gun. I had to show that gun many times to people who were messing with me. That's how bad East New York was then in the '80s . . . I would come upon the aftermath of a murder, where there was a body laying in the street or the sidewalk covered with a sheet. I saw that many times."

Wherever Nehemiah homes went up, crime on those blocks went down. Reverend Youngblood's head must have exploded in the summer of 1988, when he read Housing Commissioner Abraham Biderman's quote about the Nehemiah plan in the *Washington Post*. "Nehemiah is a successful program, but it's of limited application. There isn't that much vacant land, and we're not giving them Central Park. It's a wonderful concept, but it probably has a better future in other areas." Not much vacant land? It wasn't possible for a housing commissioner to have been more out of touch. "It was absurd," Michael Gecan said. "There was vacant land everywhere. We built twenty homes to an acre." Youngblood immediately wrote to Koch. The city wasn't turning over vacant lots fast enough. The year before they had to stop taking names on their waiting list for homes because they were already up to 5,300. Referring to their first meeting, when Koch promised his support for Nehemiah, he wrote, "Do what you did more than four years ago: risk, lead." Biderman left the public sector in 1989.

That summer, Julia was walking down Wyona Street when she was almost run over by a car. She immediately started cursing the driver. He stopped to say he was sorry, but she kept right on cursing. The driver, seventeen-year-old Ricardo Nelson, thought, "Damn. I like this chick. She's kinda feisty." And very pretty. He drove away, but he couldn't stop thinking about her. He returned to Wyona Street day after day, hoping to catch a glimpse of her and find out where she lived. He would sometimes see her sitting out on a stoop with her grandmother, but it wasn't until he saw Julia out walking on Sutter Avenue that he tried to talk to her. She was friendlier this time. They talked for hours. After that, Ricardo returned again and again. Within a few months they were a couple.

In the fall, Julia started her first year at Franklin K. Lane High School. I. S. 292, the junior high school she'd just left, was getting even worse. A thirteen-year-old was shot there in 1988, but survived. It was a rough place to go to school, a seventh grader who was interviewed said. "Some of the kids here are very bad. Some of them carry guns and knives."

When Nancy sent her daughter to school at Franklin Lane, she likely hoped to avoid the perils that existed at Thomas Jefferson High School. Ashmat Ali described Franklin Lane as "calm," compared to Thomas Jefferson, which the year before was once again rated by the Board of Education as "the most dangerous high school in New York City." The *New York Amsterdam News* reported thirty-four assaults at Thomas Jefferson for the 1986–1987 school year, along with twenty-five incidents of weapons possession, four robberies, and two sexual assaults, and those were the ones reported. Most of the kids knew better than to complain to the police. As always, Julia got along with almost everyone at Franklin Lane. She was fearless, open, and friendly. "She was my homegirl," Ashmat said proudly and affectionately. But Julia made everyone feel that she was their homegirl, and people gravitated to her.

Wyona Street continued to be relatively safe. Milagros remembers watching Julia and her friends Wanda and Jeanette putting on shows there for their neighbors. "I saw pictures where they were dressed in white leotard shirts with red skirts and skippies [shoes], which I thought was so cool." On Halloween, all the kids on their block went from house to house, collecting candy without a care in the world because they knew they'd be all right. Nancy Arlequin had always done a good job protecting her children, especially on Wyona, where she was like the mom of the neighborhood. "Whenever one of the kids fell," her youngest daughter remembered, "she'd fix their wounds. They always came to her and she'd come running out with gauze and first aid." But drugs were coming closer to Wyona Street, and at least one significant drug operation was only a block away.

When the LDCENY was given a grant to address rising crime, one of the things they did was establish more block associations, which had some success at keeping the dealers at bay. The block associations were almost always run by older Black women. These were "the people who hadn't fled," said Carey Shea, "and they were determined to try and hold on and not let the neighborhood completely fall apart." A few years later, on one particularly bad block along Williams Avenue, the ENYUYC and the NYPD community officer Ricky Perez got the Department of Parks and Recreation to designate the block a "play street." Every day, "at nine o'clock in the morning," Carey Shea explained, "our staff would go out, put up the cones and the barricades, put the sprinkler thing on the fire hydrant," and let the kids take over. "We had big boxes of chalk and stuff for the kids to play, and lots of sports equipment, balls and everything." They took back that block, but for only eight hours, five days a week. "So it disrupted a little bit, but I'm sure they found another place."

The biggest obstacle to fighting the drug trade was the money to be made. To give the young people of East New York better options, the EBC started a program they called the Nehemiah II Project, where 250 jobs were set aside for East New York and Bushwick high school students at participating banks. But turnout for the interviews was low, and while Franklin Lane was one of the largest schools to join the project, they had the fewest students apply. One of the problems was that banking was never going to be the "industry of overwhelming choice" among teenagers, a vice president of the New York State Banking Association conceded. "Banking is not something that comes to mind when they think about what they will do when they grow up." The other problem was money. Although students were told they could be earning $20,000 in five years' time, they knew that entry-level transit workers made almost as much their first year, and drug runners could make $400 to $500 a day and more. Never mind that promotional opportunities were better at the banks than they were for transit workers, or, more to the point, the life expectancy for bankers was higher than it was for drug runners. But they were kids, and "the youngsters, because they are youngsters, don't see the whole picture," read an editorial in *The Link*.

They didn't see the dark side of working in the drug trade. They saw their parents living life on the edge of poverty, working day in and day out for low pay, while those hustling drugs were draped in expensive clothes and jewelry, walking around in the best sneakers, and driving "BMWs and Bronco 4 x 4s." Dealers made the "big bucks" while everyone else made "chump change." They saw the money and glamour, and not the homeless addicts and prostitutes. If they did notice the horror, like every other kid before them when faced with a possible bad outcome, they were sure it wouldn't happen to them. They would be smarter.

Only eight banking jobs went to students at Franklin Lane, the largest school in the program. In the end, one hundred students were hired, which meant 150 positions went unfilled.

It wasn't just naive schoolkids who found the drug trade irresistible. By the end of 1988, the NYPD's Internal Affairs Division reported nine allegations of corruption against Officer Michael Dowd and his associates. Four informants had come forward that year with details about Dowd's involvement with a local drug operation. Dowd and his partner, investigators were told, were being paid $8,000 a week in exchange for protection and information about upcoming raids. They were also committing armed robberies against the operation's competition, then selling the drugs they'd stolen on Long Island. The very people who were supposed to be fighting drug-related crimes had become drug dealers. All the allegations were referred to the PBBN/ FIAU and Sergeant Joseph Trimboli, who was conducting the investigation almost entirely alone. He reached out on several occasions to Internal Affairs for help. They declined. When Trimboli's commanding officer followed up and repeated the request for assistance, they shut him down as well.

In 1988 the total murders in East New York hit 105. Twenty-two of the murders were closed by exceptional clearance and twenty-five of those cases have never been solved. Most of the victims were killed out in the street, and seven were murdered in abandoned lots or buildings. Juanita Buggs-Cost, who was eighteen and whose murder is one of the twenty-five cold cases, was stabbed to death in a vacant lot on Cleveland Street. Sixty of those killed that year were Black men, twenty-eight were Hispanic; five Black women and four Hispanic women made up most of the rest. The victims ranged in age from one year old to sixty-seven, and twenty-one of them were just teenagers, who probably thought that this would never happen to them.

The FHA Scandal

1972

When the Senate hearings resumed in June, Accetta's investigation picked up an unexpected assist. The day after pleading
the Fifth, Stanley Sirote, the president of Inter-Island Mortgage, met
with Donald Carroll, the director of the FHA's Hempstead office. It
is not known what the two men discussed, but a few days later Sirote
wrote a letter to Carroll. On the day Sirote had refused to answer
questions at the hearing, auditors from the General Accounting Office
testified to having uncovered nine bad mortgage loans funded by Inter-
Island that could have involved fraud. This was the matter addressed in
Sirote's letter, and he was writing Carroll for help. "As a former banker
you are cognizant of how an audit is conducted," he wrote, then he
asked Carroll to reach out to Senator Hart and Assistant United States
Attorney Anthony Accetta. "I do not intend in any way to discredit the
capability of Messers Lyons and Roemer, however, not being familiar
with the mechanics of mortgage banking and not having discussed
their findings with us I do believe they drew erroneous conclusions involving the above mentioned nine mortgage loans." Carroll could easily
clear the matter up, and Sirote wrote that he would "deeply appreciate
your cooperation in this matter."

That letter would be included in the record of the hearings as "Exhibit 5: Letter From Stanley Sirote to Donald Carroll Dated May 8, 1972."

What made Sirote think Carroll would be inclined to grant this favor? The hearings provided the answer. In their testimony, various bankers explained how they swapped their bad conventional loans with FHA guaranteed mortgages, thereby transferring the risk and the loss to the FHA. Bernard Roth, the former president of United Institutional Servicing, the second largest mortgage bank in the east, who was also under investigation by the FBI, took the Fifth. Gerard Orsi however, the president of Carroll's former place of employment, Lawrence-Cedarhurst Federal Savings and Loan Association (which had since changed its name to the Century Federal Savings and Loan Association), testified to his bank having made such swaps with Stanley Sirote.

"Who, at the bank, was responsible for working out the details of the arrangement?" Jack Blum asked.

"A vice president by the name of Donald Carroll."

"Is he with the bank presently?"

"No. He is director of the FHA right now in Hempstead."

"He resigned. When was it?"

"October of 1971."

"He became director of the FHA office in Hempstead in October 1971?"

"Yes." [It was actually November 1, 1971.]

Accetta had already learned all about Carroll and the swaps from Sirote. But Accetta now had the letter and additional testimony on record. During his debriefing, Sirote explained how he knew that Carroll was about to take over the FHA office where his biggest competitor, Eastern Service, held all the FHA cards. Sirote needed his own guy on the inside. Carroll needed to get rid of the bad commitments he'd made on the nine loans. The two men made a deal. In exchange for Sirote having bought Carroll's bad loans, and at a loss to Inter-Island,

Carroll promised to promote John Daly to assistant chief underwriter and Patrick Lama to the assistant chief of mortgage credit, where they would personally oversee the Inter-Island business. Daly and Lama really made out. On top of their promotions, they would receive regular payoffs from Sirote.

Accetta, who was swamped with motions and appeals, had reached out to his boss, Robert Morse, for help. Ronald DePetris was the first to join the prosecution team. George Bashion, who would come on-board next, said, "DePetris was like a brain." Before joining the U.S. Attorney's office as an AUSA in the Criminal Division, DePetris had been a law clerk for a federal judge in the Eastern District of New York. "You don't get that position because you look nice in a suit," Bashion would say. Robert Morse believed DePetris had the expertise they would need to take on the increasingly complex case. He was "in-valuable," according to Accetta. "Whenever there was a legal objection, or a motion to do something, Ron would take the lead."

Finding George was serendipity. Accetta was out at the Westbury courthouse when he saw Bashion giving his summation in a loan sharking case. His calm, easygoing manner made Accetta stop and listen. Bashion owned that room. Accetta knew they'd be going up against eleven well-paid defense attorneys. "I want this guy," he told Morse. Bashion was an experienced prosecutor who already had a rep-utation as a brilliant trial lawyer. "Fine. You got him," Morse answered.

Over the summer, Jim Sniegocki, who had a wife and three chil-dren and was looking for a smaller office in a place with a lower cost of living, was transferred to St. Louis, where he was assigned to a Criminal Squad that also handled accounting and white-collar crime cases. Agent Dennis Lacina was put in charge of the Eastern Service case. It was now up to Lacina to help bring the case to the finish line, the trial. Lacina turned out to be "as essential as any other agent who worked these cases," Accetta said. "Dennis was hardworking, insight-ful, dedicated, and effective." With him on the team, "We didn't miss a beat."

Agent Jeff Kay's investigation into Inter-Island was moving forward at the same time. Stanley Sirote agreed to wear wires so the FBI could gather evidence of people at the FHA who were guilty of fraud. One of their targets was the new assistant chief of mortgage credit, Patrick Lama.

"Nasty, nasty guy," was former agent Jeff Kay's response when Lama's name came up. "He was arrogant." After flipping, Sirote told Kay he was paying cash to Lama under the table. The accountant in Kay immediately asked, "How did you generate cash out of the business?" Sirote explained that he would write an Inter-Island check made out to cash, and in the corner of the check he would write the initials of the FHA employee he was paying off. That way he had a record.

Lama refused to talk to the FBI so Kay and special agent Dan Kelleher met with Sirote on a Saturday morning at the FBI's office on Long Island, to record a conversation between Sirote and Lama. These were the days when you recorded phone conversations by placing a rubber cup on the phone and attaching it by wire to a tape recorder. "Stanley, I can't talk to you," Lama said when he picked up the phone. "The FBI's got my phone tapped." [Not true.] "Call me in ten minutes, at this number."

Ten minutes later Sirote told Lama, "We got a problem. The FBI came to my office and got my records and all my checks. The checks are made out to cash, and they have your initials on the corner of the checks."

"How dumb can you be," Lama screamed. "They're going to track all this money to me."

"Thank you, Mr. Lama," Kay said out loud, back at the Garden City office, where he was listening in. They already had him for a trip to Puerto Rico. In the same file where they'd found tickets to Puerto Rico for Donald Carroll, paid for by Inter-Island, were also tickets for Patrick Lama. Now they had him on tape admitting to having accepted bribes.

They also went out to talk to Lama's wife about his trip to Puerto Rico. They knew he had taken his girlfriend and not his wife. When

Mrs. Lama learned that another woman had gone to Puerto Rico as "Mrs. Lama," she said, "I'm going to kill him when he gets home." "He hated us for doing that, but you got to do what you got to do," Kay said.

As the investigation continued, the FBI and the Eastern District of New York (EDNY) had to maintain a delicate balance as they worked with the FHA to investigate their own people. They got "good support from FHA in Washington, and the FHA Inspector General's office in New York," Jeff Kay said, but there was always a certain amount of friction between them. "Here's the FBI, getting the bulk of the publicity, and we're stealing their thunder and making them look inefficient." Kay was also in the same difficult position that he was with Blum and the Senate subcommittee. He couldn't tell the FHA all he knew.

Publicity was exploding as cases all over the country were proceeding. That June, the Philadelphia grand jury indicted forty-six people, including the former head of the FHA's Philadelphia office. In July the Chicago grand jury indicted four FHA officials, seven contractors, and two real estate brokers. Detroit had indicted sixteen people and was working toward more, as were Cleveland, Los Angeles, Portland, Seattle, and Tampa. Hundreds of investigations were moving forward.

Accetta's first case went on trial at the beginning of the summer. The defendant was Milton Berlin. "It was a run-of-the-mill FHA fraud case," Accetta said, "but everybody was looking at that case. Everybody." Not only was the Eastern District of New York watching, but federal courts in other states pursuing similar cases were also keeping tabs. The prosecutors wanted to know if a case like this could be won. Defendants wanted to see what their chances were of going to prison. The stakes were high. "When I got into the Berlin trial, I knew I had to win that case."

The outcome was swift. The trial lasted only a day, and the jury deliberated for six hours. Milton Berlin was guilty on two counts of supplying false information to the FHA.

Afterward, "I wasn't jumping up and down and shouting, 'Hallelujah!'" Accetta said. But, "it was a tremendous relief. I knew the impact that it would have, and what the impact of an acquittal would have had. I knew he was guilty. That doesn't mean the jury's going to buy it." They did. In August, Berlin was sentenced to one year in prison and a $2,500 fine. He appealed in December, and while one count was reversed, the other was upheld, and he went to prison.

15

The Destruction of East New York

1989

The year Julia Parker turned fifteen, there were ninety-eight murders in East New York, and a 45 percent increase in violent crime over the previous four years. Every morning, as she set out from her home on Wyona Street, it must have felt like she was facing a 5.6-square-mile death trap. Her mother would have been sure to remind her to stay away from Miller Avenue, a stretch with so many murders the children in the neighborhood called it Killer Miller. Like all of East New York, Miller Avenue was only getting worse. Six people had been murdered on that street since 1985, and in 1990 six people would be killed on Miller in that one year alone.

The neighborhood had become a literal shooting gallery and the number of places to avoid kept increasing. The police noticed an uptick in murders along Williams and Blake Avenues, in front of the Unity Plaza housing projects. Since 1985, nineteen people were murdered in the projects and in the surrounding streets; the housing police had taken to calling Unity the "slaughterhouse." The intersection where the Linden Houses stood, once described as the most wonderful place to grow up, was now called the "four corners of death."

East New Yorkers were taking their lives into their hands by merely venturing outside. Ashmat Ali always planned his walks carefully. "At night, I would go where I know where my friends are. I wouldn't go any other route or direction. Say I'm at Sutter or say I'm at New Lots, I'll take my own route. I know, well, I got a friend here. I got a friend there. It's not like I'm avoiding anywhere, but I know where to go because my friends are there. So if anything happens, I have a friend here."

Elizabeth Margoshes, then a clinical psychologist in the Department of Child Psychiatry at Brookdale Hospital Medical Center, remembered how "Brookdale Hospital paid for car service for us to go to the schools because it was deemed too dangerous to take public transportation or even drive our own cars and park on the street. More than once, the windshields of the car service cars had bullet holes in them."

Sister Margaret Smyth, who taught at St. John Cantius Church, where Julia went to school for a time, said, "It was not very easy, the area was violent, and girls were a target. Parents took their daughters and kept them more secluded. I was driving down the street one evening. As I drove . . . a girl that I knew was walking on the opposite side of the street on the sidewalk. I saw her being shot. She was by herself, and someone came up behind her and put a bullet in her head." This hadn't happened on a dark quiet corner. "There were people on the street, there were always people out on the street. There was so much drugs in the neighborhood, and everyone participated." The girl, who was only in her teens, did not survive.

Sister Margaret remembered how, "on Sundays, when we'd start mass at 10:00 a.m., we'd have maybe twenty or thirty people. By the end of the mass we'd have one hundred. People would say, 'I'm so sorry we're late, but our building was shut down due to a murder.'"

Yvonne Harris was stabbed fifteen times a block from where she lived. The man who was arrested for her murder was later found not guilty. A juror said, "The police did a very sloppy job investigating this case. They better go out there now and find the real killer." But they

almost never did. Once a suspect is arrested the case is closed. The
NYPD rarely goes back to change the status of a case if the suspect
is later freed or found not guilty. In a list of homicides for that year
Yvonne's case is still marked as closed and no one is looking for her
killer.

The corner of Pennsylvania Avenue and Dumont continued to be
particularly lethal. Twenty-year-old Julio Banos was killed there on
October 28. Like several other murders on this corner, his case was
never solved. In spite of the dangers, the spot had become something
of a hangout among the people in the neighborhood. Thomas Jefferson
High School was right up the block and Ali's Deli, run by Ashmat
Ali's father, Ahamad, was the corner store of choice. That was all due
to the generosity of Ahamad Ali. If people didn't have money for food,
Ashmat's father would give them credit. "Instead of stealing, if they
would walk up to him and say, 'Yo, I'm hungry,' he would make them a
sandwich. At the end of the month when they get the food stamps or
the SSI check," they would pay him back.

As the murders rose, so did the pressure to clear the mounting cases.

On January 14, Antonio Valesquez was found on the corner of
Arlington Avenue and Bradford Street, stabbed in the back with a
folding knife protruding. A witness to the murder said the killer, who
was his friend, was drunk and had taunted Antonio and chased him
toward Bradford Street. He then saw his friend's hand up in the air,
with the knife in it, coming down on Antonio's back. Shaken, the alleged killer walked back and said, "I fucked up. I don't know if he's
alive." He wasn't. Depressed, the killer left East New York, and shot
himself a year later. It was a clear-cut story, but was it true? Although
there was another witness, the case was exceptionally cleared without
corroborating the account.

Toya Turner was shot repeatedly in a hallway in the Cypress Hill
projects in May. She was taken to Brookdale Hospital, where she died.
An informant told them that a Black man named Bishme, and who
was recently murdered in Red Hook, had confessed to killing Toya. The

detectives contacted the Seven-Six precinct to verify Bishme's death. A Black man was killed there a couple of weeks earlier, they told him, but his name wasn't Bishme. The informant was shown a photograph of the victim, whom he identified as Bishme. The case was closed by exceptional clearance that same day, based on that one testimony alone, and without showing a photograph of the alleged killer to the other four known witnesses.

You need more than one witness to make a case. The informants could have been pointing to people who had conveniently died in order to get the police to close the case without looking for the real killers.

Twenty of the ninety-eight homicide cases in East New York that year were closed by exceptional clearance. Without those clearances, 40 percent of the murders that year would have remained open. But with them, the Seven-Five had among the best clearance rates in the city.

That year, Michael Gecan wanted to show Governor Mario Cuomo just what life was like in East New York. They drove around in a van with tinted windows making their first stop on the corner of New Lots Avenue and Georgia Street, where they watched a drug deal take place. They drove to the next block and watched another drug deal. The next block was a repeat of the first two, and on and on it went. Afterward, they went to St. Paul's to meet with Reverend Johnny Ray Youngblood and thirty members of the EBC. "They wanted Cuomo to send money to back up drug sweeps with prosecutions," Gecan would later write in an editorial. "Moreover, the 75th precinct was so unable or unwilling to respond—so divorced from any accountability—that one priest suggested it be put into receivership by the state, a tactic similar to New Jersey's approach to school districts that collapse."

The EBC asked to meet with Cuomo again in ten weeks. Cuomo said it was too important to wait ten weeks. They would meet again in five weeks. Four years later, when the story about the Seven-Five's involvement in supporting the drug trade in East New York came out, and the Mollen Commission was finishing up their investigation of corruption in the NYPD, they still hadn't heard from Cuomo.

The NYPD expanded their $110 million Tactical Narcotics Team (TNT) program to deal with the crack epidemic into East New York. Soon after, a notorious crack house at 447 Vermont Street, which sat on the same block as the Danny Kaye school and a block away from St. John Cantius, was demolished. But East New Yorkers complained that it was not enough. "There was so much crack you could smell it through the walls," said Maryanne Schretzman, the former deputy commissioner for Policy and Planning at the Department of Homeless Services, who grew up in East New York. In the March/April 1989 issue of *The Link*, a headline ran, "Crack and Crime Plague ENY, 'TNT' Can't Turn Tide." Despite an impressive 1,500 arrests in the first two months of operation, they called the program a "dud." Crack dealers were still openly doing business. The dealers who lost their operations when the Vermont Street building was demolished had already found a new home nearby on New Jersey Avenue, across the street from P. S. 149. "There is too much money to be made in drug dealing and too few alternatives for youngsters and crack addicts for these policies to work." A long-term solution was needed. A real war on drugs would mean more drug treatment facilities and school programs, but most of all, a war on poverty. "Poverty and hopelessness, the causes of drug use, must be conquered. It will require a major effort to rebuild our neighborhoods, cities, and our country." But twenty years after the Kerner Commission's report the country still wasn't prepared for the "massive and sustained" effort required.

While doing what they could, community leaders continued to sound the alarm. Vivian Bright, who replaced Richard Recny as the chief executive officer of the LDCENY, told a *New York Times* reporter, "We have four main problems here: abandoned housing, sanitation, crack, and unemployment." The LDCENY had established its own nighttime security patrol for the sixty companies in the industrial district, training and paying local East New York residents to conduct the evening patrols, and to check on all the building alarms. "I mean, all this stuff was brand new back then," Carey Shea said of the early

LDCENY days. "They brought in businesses, they kept businesses going. They created a security force!"

The ENYUYC would eventually finish their work at 611 Pennsylvania Avenue and other buildings, providing rental homes to low-income families. It was decided that eight of the units at 611 Pennsylvania Avenue would go to people made homeless by fire. The Fire Department of New York's Engine 290 in East New York was still one of the busiest engines in New York City, and every year fires created more people with nowhere to go. Carey Shea described how people would "come in and sign their lease and get their key and we'd go and we'd open up the door of their beautiful apartment and they'd cry. One woman actually dropped to her knees in the middle of the living room, knelt on the floor, and cried." By the end of 1989, the ENYUYC would be working with Pratt to complete a housing plan for a twenty-five-block area west of Pennsylvania, well-known as one of the poorest and most "drug-infested" sections of East New York.

Renovating buildings in East New York was always a challenge. "Before you could renovate a building, you had to have an asbestos inspection," Carey Shea explained. When the city took over a building they put roll-down gates over all the front doors "so they could have access, but everyone else was locked out." The drug dealers would cut off the city's locks and put on their own. "So they controlled the building." On one occasion, when she sent out an inspection team, "The asbestos inspectors tried to use the key, and the drug dealers were like, 'Back the fuck off.'" The inspectors called Shea. "We are not going back out there."

Shea called the Seven-Five. It was the Animal Control people all over again. "They said to me, 'Well, what you do is, you get your contractor to fill up his truck with dirt and then go dump the dirt in front of the gate so the drug dealers can't get in,' and I was like, 'You dump the dirt!'"

She reached out to a friend who was a transit cop. "Call up the police station," he told her, "get the same guy and just say, you need the correct spelling of his name, because you'd like to send a letter describing how we have this problem and the two of us can't seem to agree . . ." She called up, "and fifteen minutes later, the cops were out there clearing the whole thing."

The EBC, which was becoming nationally known due to the early successes of their Nehemiah Plan, continued work on the 1,100 homes in East New York while planning more for west of Pennsylvania Avenue. The problem was that they couldn't build fast enough. Where they built the area was transformed. But everywhere else continued to decline. Between the drug traffic and the ever-increasing stock of abandoned buildings, it was almost impossible to gain enough ground. The EBC had proposed building in the area known as Spring Creek, but they were told by the city that the Department of Environmental Protection and City Planning had determined that toxicity problems precluded any building there.

Crime inexorably rose. The homeless shelter on Forbell Street and Sutter Avenue was now a minimum-security prison for women, many of whom were being incarcerated due to crack.

At a town meeting on October 7, Congressman Major Owens called on Governor Cuomo and Mayor Koch to declare a state of emergency in East New York and Brownsville to combat crime. "As a measure of last resort," Owens was asking for military police and the national guard to help the NYPD to disarm and arrest the "heavily armed crack gangs." Budget cuts at every level, for "schools, day care centers, housing, youth services, and health care have created an atmosphere of disease where substance abuse and crime flourish." He called for the "restoration of funding for all schools and other programs" to the pre-1975 levels.

Like most East New York teens, Julia Parker had grown up fast. The year 1989 was the year she got pregnant and dropped out of high school at Franklin Lane to give birth to a baby boy. She was fifteen. Once she gave birth, her baby was always with her. "She never went anywhere without that baby," the father said. Julia Parker was now a single mother with a child to support and protect in a world that was only becoming more dangerous.

The FHA Scandal

1972

The March indictments left Donald Carroll, the head of the FHA's Hempstead office, scrambling. The pressure was on to respond to the charges. He began by blacklisting mortgage insurance applications from certain sections of Brooklyn. "We are not abandoning the inner city," Carroll was very quick to point out. "We are trying to upgrade the areas in the hope that we can begin insuring them again. But until they are rehabilitated, we can no longer insure them." It was redlining all over again.

In the wake of the fallout, like many others, Carroll resorted to blaming the victim, with repeated references to "unsophisticated buyers." But he also acknowledged the unscrupulous speculators, who were buying houses for $3,000 to $5,000 and selling them for $20,000. The FHA would now make sure repairs were made, and that homes that were once appraised at $20,000 would be valued in the area of $13,000. In what was perhaps a nod to the office's in-house problems, applications would receive what he called "quality processing." They were scrutinized more carefully, and what used to take five days now took three weeks. Carroll took all the precautions he could, but he couldn't undo the crimes that he himself had committed. Nor did he know just how much the FBI knew about them.

In other ways, it was business as usual. In only two weeks the FHA resumed business with Dun & Bradstreet, with the exception of the office named in the Brooklyn indictments. The Veterans Administration (VA) never stopped doing business with Eastern Service, and the FBI continued investigating the VA. "The VA fraud was not as extensive as the FHA crimes," Agent Jeff Kay explained, because the victim had to be a veteran. But the speculators were just as ruthless. Local real estate agents hired runners to scour the streets and bars for veterans who hadn't used their benefits. "They'd pull guys off the street and ask them if they were veterans, and they would use their veteran's benefits to sell a house to them," which would later turn out to be worthless.

In August, Stanley Sirote began negotiations with Granite Management Services, Inc., to buy his company, Inter-Island Mortgage Corp. He knew it was just a matter of time before he was indicted and the value of Inter-Island plummeted. If he timed it right, as the owner of two-thirds of the company, he still stood to make millions from the sale.

That summer a conference took place in Warrenton, Virginia, attended by Romney and all the FHA field representatives. Romney had invited Accetta to speak about investigating mortgage fraud. HUD's Attorney Advisor John Kennedy, who was working with Accetta, knew that Donald Carroll was going to be there. He also knew Donald Carroll was going to be indicted. On the limo ride with Romney to the convention center, "I explained to him what was happening and what we knew so far." Romney was incredulous. "He was an extremely honest man and he just couldn't believe people would behave this way." Kennedy had to break the news that they had clear and convincing evidence. Carroll was going to be sitting in the meeting that evening, and "I didn't want him to be blindsided," Kennedy said. He didn't want Romney saying anything that might prove awkward later when his director of operations in Hempstead was indicted.

When Accetta gave his talk, Romney was sitting on the dais, along with HUD General Counsel David Maxwell. Donald Carroll was sitting in the front row. At one point Accetta began a familiar setup. "Look to your left. Look to your right. There's a high probability that the person you just looked at is going to be indicted soon." Carroll came up to him afterward and asked, "Am I one of them?" "And I looked at him, and said, 'if the shoe fits.'" Carroll blanched, and Accetta walked away. "It had the exact effect I wanted it to have." Later that summer, Carroll would join the list of indicted.

Tensions between Romney and Nixon were at an all-time high. Newspapers frequently covered the rift between the two men, often highlighting Romney's lack of influence in Nixon's administration, further humiliating the embattled Romney. As Nixon had intended, he'd successfully sidestepped much of the responsibility for the housing problems, and blame for the crimes increasingly fell at Romney's feet. Nixon and civil rights opponents would also begin what would turn out to be a successful campaign to reframe the narrative about what had happened. According to Vesla M. Weaver, author of *Frontlash: Race and the Development of Punitive Crime Policy*, "Fusing crime to anxiety about ghetto revolts, racial disorder—initially defined as a problem of minority disenfranchisement—was redefined as a crime problem, which helped shift debate from social reform to punishment."

Romney, who once thought he could make a difference, had to bear the recriminations from the rightly angered victims of fraud, while reading lines like author Joseph P. Fried's, in his book *Housing Crisis U.S.A*, "The vision of an America acting to provide a decent home and a suitable living environment for all its citizens seems as realistic as the hope of a palace-studded Camelot suddenly arising out of the squalor and decay of Brownsville in Brooklyn."

On August 7, Nixon made another demonstration of just how little he thought of Romney. Without giving him a heads-up, Nixon released a statement saying he'd ordered Romney to Wilkes-Barre, Pennsylvania. The area was suffering from the aftermath of Hurricane Agnes. One hundred eighteen people had been killed, thousands were homeless, and the citizens and local government were angry about the lack of response from Washington. Romney learned of his trip when he read about it in the newspaper along with everyone else. The press conference he traveled to on August 9 turned into a shouting match among Romney, the governor, and a crowd of flood victims. At one point a sixty-three-year-old grandmother yelled at him, "You don't give a damn whether we live or die."

When he got back to Washington, a message regarding Accetta's New York investigation was waiting for him. The DOJ and HUD were given advance warning prior to indictments, and Romney now knew a second round of indictments, involving still more FHA officials, was imminent.

On August 10, Romney submitted a letter of resignation, prompting Nixon to do something he hadn't done for a while. He invited Romney, who'd tried repeatedly to meet with him to work out their differences, to the White House. When they met, he convinced Romney to stay in his position at least until after the election.

Throughout the summer, the FBI and the EDNY continued to work on the investigation. Now that Accetta had solid evidence of Patrick Lama accepting bribes from Stanley Sirote, he brought Lama in to testify to the grand jury. Before going in, Lama approached Accetta in the hall, "with tears in his eyes and a heart full of sincerity, telling me he never, ever took a dime from anybody," Accetta said. "He swore on his mother's grave. When an Italian does that, that's a big deal. He was so believable that I actually would have believed him, except for one thing: in my pocket was a cassette tape of him and Stanley Sirote conspiring to cover up the payments."

In the grand jury room, Tony questioned him. "I'm setting up a perjury wrap, because I now ask him and basically get him to repeat everything he's told me outside the grand jury room. Then I play the tape." The grand jury listened to Sirote and Lama cooking up a story about the trips and the payments, and about Sirote paying Lama to do credit reports. "He just dropped his head as if to say, 'Oh, shit.' He had to plead guilty." But he wasn't immediately ready to accept that.

On September 11, Granite Management announced that they had agreed to buy Inter-Island Mortgage. The SEC subsequently lifted the suspension they had imposed on over-the-counter trading of stock. Similarly, the FHA lifted their suspension of Inter-Island as an approved FHA lender. Stanley Sirote, who'd made a deal with Accetta and knew he would eventually plead guilty and go to prison, must have been confident that at least he wouldn't come out a poor man.

16

The Destruction of East New York

1990

The first murder of 1990 happened just an hour after people had cheered in the New Year. The victim was nineteen years old. Two other murders quickly followed. East New York was now openly referred to as the Killing Fields. Over five hundred children were victims of gunfire in 1990. Most survived, like thirteen-year-old Karina Dinolis, who was hit with a shotgun blast outside the Pink Houses, one of the more notorious projects in East New York. Others were not so lucky. Twelve-year-old Laykama Taylor, nicknamed Sugar, was shot and killed while she sat in the courtyard at the Cypress Hills projects. A neighbor pushing a baby stroller pointed out the crime scene to a *Daily News* reporter and spoke freely about what had happened. Her husband tried to stop her. "My children knew that little girl," she snapped back. He pleaded with the crowd around them. "Somebody shut my wife up. You get killed easy out here." Never solved, Laykama Taylor's murder was added to the rapidly growing cold case list.

Twenty-three of the 109 people killed that year were under twenty-one. "So many kids I knew died," said Sister Margaret Smyth. "I spent a lot of time going to wakes. A lot of wakes, and no one had ever died of natural causes." It was not unusual for murder to work its way through a family. "A boy's grandfather was shot over drugs the year before," Sister Margaret continued, "and they asked me to take the grandfather's picture. This was something that was done. The next year, the grandson, who was just a teenager, he gets shot and killed. I went to his wake and people there said, take his picture too. Last year you took his grandfather's picture, you gotta get his picture too.'"

Nine-year-old Veronica Corales was hit with a stray bullet while she slept in a car in her mother's arms on July 22. Two days later, and three hours after the shooter was arraigned, she died and was later buried in a white party dress her stepfather had only recently finished paying off. On the day Veronica died, one-year-old Yaritimi Fruto and her father were shot while they sat in a car at a stop sign. Edward Fruto died immediately. Yaritimi died two days later, a week after celebrating the first and only birthday she would ever have.

That year, a familiar and horrific crime returned to East New York. On February 10, twenty-eight-year-old Merdis Carter was raped, stabbed three times, and thrown naked from a seventh-story building in the Cypress Hills projects. She landed on the first-floor roof of a children's community center, where she was found at 1:00 a.m. after neighbors heard a loud thump and her agonized cries. Merdis was taken to Brookdale Hospital, where she later died, but not before identifying her killer, a man who was out on parole after being convicted of a similar crime nearly ten years before. In 1980, Michael Steedly had followed a twenty-three-year-old pregnant woman and forced her to a roof at knife point, where he raped her, took her jewelry, and stabbed her three times. The prosecutor believed that Steedly threw Merdis from the roof because stabbing his 1980 victim hadn't been enough to end her life.

Five months later, while he was playing with friends, three-year-old Dashiell Phillips Johnson was lifted up by a stranger and carried to the roof of a nearby building, also in the Cypress Hills projects. Neighbors heard him crying "no, no, no," as he was thrown to his death. If you stood in the right spot down below, you could turn around and point to where Laykama Taylor, Merdis Carter, and Dashiell Phillips Johnson were murdered, all within months and yards of each other.

Under pressure to do something about all the killing, the NYPD had launched Operation Take Back a few weeks after Dashiell was thrown from the roof. They increased the number of cops on patrol in the top six crime-ridden precincts, which included the Seven-Five. Eight months later they checked their progress. In all the precincts homicides had either gone down or stayed the same. Except the Seven-Five. Nothing they'd done had slowed down the carnage one bit. In those eight months homicides increased 28 percent. Murder was not the only ever-present danger in East New York. CompStat records showed 133 women were raped there in 1990. A significant percentage of the rapes in East New York occurred in abandoned buildings according to a retired detective sergeant in the Seven-Five. "Women going to or returning from shopping or work would be dragged into these buildings by predators" who knew the location provided the perfect "physical cover and concealment."

The NYPD also brought back the Tactical Narcotics Team (TNT), which had been suspended in East New York. They added officers to the foot and car patrols in the neighborhood. "But they cannot be everywhere," an editorial in *The Link* read. East New York was now number one in New York in rape and robbery. It would have had the highest number of murders in 1990, but the eighty-seven victims of the Happy Land Social Club arson fire pushed the Four-Eight precinct in the Bronx to the top that year. For the young men who were most likely to be killed, carrying a gun and using it felt like their best chance at staying alive.

The city was as unresponsive as ever to the calls for more schools and health centers, and consistent sanitation pickups. Instead, Mayor Dinkins responded with budget cuts. Over at St. Paul Community Baptist Church, the reverend Dr. Johnny Ray Youngblood was doing his best to address crime, and he pressured the NYPD to recruit more officers of color.

The NYPD remained largely indifferent to mounting allegations against Officer Dowd, which continued coming in, as did informants who confirmed what all the previous informants had said. One of the claims was passed on to them by the federal Drug Enforcement Task Force (DETF). It became the twelfth case referred to the PBBN/FIAU. Like every other allegation against Dowd, it would be closed as unsubstantiated.

East New York community groups and activists did what they could. In addition to the patrols started by the LDCENY, other groups like the Stanley-Van Siclen Merchants Association paid for their own security teams. Contractors for ACORN building projects hired security guards to protect their construction sites.

On February 24, Congressman Major Owens continued his call for help from the National Guard by touring East New York and Brownsville with representatives from the New York State National Guard. "Governor Cuomo agreed that the Guard could be involved in cleaning up vacant lots in our communities and turning these lots into community parks," the *New York Amsterdam News* reported. After the tour, Owens said that "despite its size, the 75th precinct has only between twenty [and] thirty police officers on duty at night. This is totally inadequate and it is the reason we are demanding a law enforcement support role for the National Guard."

While Congressman Owens toured East New York with the National Guard, life in Manhattan went on, for the most part oblivious of the carnage. In 1981, the EBC wrote, "Like Moses and the Israelites, Black church leaders and Black Americans are in exile. Down the road from slavery but not yet near the Promised Land." Most Manhattanites had little idea just what was going on only a few subway stops away. East New Yorkers were as alone and cut off from the rest of New York as they had been back when Lindsay's aides admitted that City Hall "hardly knew of its existence." They knew now, but as long as East New York remained virtually unknown to the rest of New York they could do little with almost no blowback.

A few days before the congressman's tour, students from Franklin K. Lane High School testified at the New York City Board of Education budget hearings on February 21. "In a city as large as New York, where costs are high and a teenager can easily just get lost," a student told the board, "public health clinics in the high schools are a necessity. They would help solve the problems of teenage depression and suicide, sexually transmitted diseases, drug abuse, and unwanted pregnancies." Julia Parker had dropped out the year before, at fifteen, to have a baby. Public health clinics, the students suggested, "would make it more possible for teenagers to do well in school and prepare for the future."

At a rally on March 9, after violence had broken out at a library, Arthur Camins, a spokesperson for the United Community Centers (UCC), said, "The city can't keep cutting back on our schools, our libraries, and our kids, and expect that nothing will happen." Jose Camacho, also speaking for the UCC, said, "They are the victims of years of budget cuts and reduced city services." In an interview for the East New York Oral History Project, Richard Rabinowitz, who grew up in East New York, would talk about the public services in his time, the 1950s and early 1960s. "We were all given this gigantic boost, but it didn't come through family . . . the system of public support, for housing, for transit, for education, for health care, that came through the public sector, was so significant in creating the conditions for prosperity in the next generation." It was the difference between success and failure. But the city had withdrawn that support.

In May, representatives from Mayor Dinkin's office met with East New York residents to talk about the cuts. Mel Grizer, the director of the United Community Centers, said that "after twenty years of neglect, East New York needs a massive infusion of funds, not new budget cuts. Life is extremely difficult on the streets of East New York."

A member of a block association complained that, "Each mayor makes promises. Seven years ago Mayor Koch promised at a town meeting at Gershwin Junior High School that the city would rebuild New Lots Avenue. But this promise was never kept." Another block association representative said the rebuilding of New Lots Avenue should be the "first step in the revitalization of East New York."

In the midst of all the mayhem, some East New Yorkers were working to carve out islands of calm, areas that were peaceful and livable. Marlene Wilks, who taught math and science at the Philippa Schuyler middle school, had been on a waiting list for a Nehemiah home for three years when she was finally able to buy one on Schenck Avenue in 1990. In an abandoned lot across the street, the builders had left behind piles of discarded materials. It was an eyesore in the middle of what had been transformed into a nice, clean block, and abandoned lots were known to invite crime. Wilks hired a truck to move all the garbage out. Around the same time her twelve-year-old daughter planted watermelon seeds in their yard, which successfully grew into enormous, delicious fruit. "It was exciting," Marlene said. And sitting right in front of her was an unused lot with more space to grow watermelons and anything else they'd like to try. It wasn't long before Marlene and her neighbor across the street were planting gardens in the formerly abandoned lot. More neighbors joined them later.

The New York City Department of Parks and Recreation had established the GreenThumb Garden program in 1978 to foster volunteer community gardens. They granted leases on the lots to the people who had essentially taken them over. A Community Development Block Grant from HUD helped provide supplies and training to the gardeners. Eliza Butler, who lived on Schenck Avenue and had joined the group of gardeners, became a driving force behind the garden. She went through the process of registering their garden and getting a lease a couple of years later. Every garden got a name, and they named theirs the New Visions Garden. In the summer they'd close off the street and hold block parties to celebrate what they'd done. Reggae musicians were hired to provide music. Other gardens like theirs had already been established in East New York and many more would be added in the years to come.

While East New Yorkers worked hard to convert the vacant lots, another danger had emerged. On March 8, 1990, forty-nine-year-old

Mario Orozco was walking along Atlantic Avenue when he saw a man in a ski mask holding a gun. He turned to run and was shot in the back. Mario fell, and when the man stood over him, pointing the gun at his head, Mario didn't move. The gunman, thinking he was dead, didn't shoot again and Mario survived.

Twenty-one days later, Jermaine Montenesdro, thirty-three, was shot on Jamaica Avenue. The bullet went through his liver, but he too survived. Twenty-one days after that, seventy-eight-year-old Joseph Proce was shot in Queens, one hundred feet from the boundary of the Seven-Five precinct. A note was found nearby that read "Zodiac—Time to die!" Proce wasn't killed by the gunshot, but the wound became infected and he died three weeks later.

In June, a writer from the *New York Post* received a letter from the man who would come to be known as the New York Zodiac Copycat (after the California serial killer). In the letter, he claimed that he'd killed three people, and would kill twelve in all, one for each sign of the zodiac. As if East New York didn't have enough problems, they now had a serial killer on their hands. Seven months earlier, the Seven-Five had received a similar letter from the New York Zodiac. "The first sign is dead . . . the Zodiac will spread fear." He also wrote about seeing a lot of cops from the Seven-Five, "But you are not good and you will not get the Zodiac." The Seven-Five was drowning in murders, and the letter, which was vague and seemed more than a little crazy, was ignored. After the second letter, police were able to track down the Zodiac's first two victims. The Zodiac was not aware that the first two people he'd shot had survived, they realized. The NYPD formed a task force.

The New York Zodiac always struck on a Thursday, every twenty-one days. The night before he was expected to hit again, police flooded East New York and the Queens border. Presumably due to the show of force, the New York Zodiac shot his next victim, Larry Parham, in Central Park. He also survived. Fifty detectives were working the case, fielding one thousand tips a week. They amassed hundreds of pages of logged phone calls in a tip book, and one hundred cassette tapes of messages. Rewards were offered, a psychic was consulted, but no solid leads were produced. Then the New York Zodiac disappeared. He would not strike again for two years.

Life in East New York, such as it was, went on. A crack house opened on the block where Julia Parker lived with her family and her young son, bringing danger still closer to their door.

In 1990, Nancy Arlequin pulled Milagros out of St. John's and enrolled her at P. S. 149 for the fourth grade. "I hated it. I cried every single day," Milagros said. "I got picked on, and pushed," and all her music lessons at St. John's—piano, violin, and flute—came to an end. But Nancy had to take her brother out of St. John's and she thought it was unfair if Milagros got to stay.

Julia Parker's son turned one that year, the same year that thirty-one of the 109 murders in East New York went cold.

The FHA Scandal

1972

Over the summer, the guilty pleas began. Rubin Oringer, the president of one of the indicted realty firms, and the secretary of another, was the first. Among other crimes, Oringer confessed to bribing FHA appraiser Edward Goodwin. FHA appraiser Frank Dreis admitted to taking bribes from Ortrud Kapraki in exchange for understating the need for repairs. Former Eastern Service vice president Frank Fey pleaded guilty to fraud and conspiracy. Other defendants filed motions to be severed from the case. Indicted Brooklyn attorney Douglas Hollenbach, who'd filed a slew of motions, including one for a separate trial, managed to get removed from the case in the least desirable way. At the end of July, his attorney wrote to say that Hollenbach had died. By the time the case came to trial in October 1973, of the original fifty people and companies indicted, nine defendants would stand trial.

Harry Bernstein fired his original lawyer, a generally cooperative Wall Street attorney whom Accetta described as the "best gift he ever gave us." Bernstein wised up and replaced him with Abraham Brodsky, a former assistant United States attorney who went on to make a reputation for himself defending organized crime figures. Brodsky also had a reputation for winning, and would make a formidable opponent, as would Dun & Bradstreet's attorney Otto Obermaier, a future United States attorney for the Southern District of New York.

By now they'd flipped realtor Ortrud Kapraki, FHA appraiser Edward Goodwin, Inter-Island president Stanley Sirote, and, most recently, FHA director Donald Carroll. Once Agent Jeff Kay had Sirote's confession to buying Carroll's bad loans in exchange for FHA favors, and the records of Carroll's stay in Puerto Rico to throw down in front of him and his attorney, Accetta called them both into his office. "We gave him the facts of life speech on each potential bribery count," Kay said. He could go to trial or cooperate. "Carroll decided to cooperate."

Along the way they also picked up Rose Cohen, a clerk at the Hempstead FHA office who funneled mortgage applications to appraisers like Goodwin, who were accepting bribes, and former Eastern Service vice president Frank Fey, who initially noticed something was off with the applications submitted by Kapraki, but later became a part of the scheme. Most of Sirote and Carroll's information had to do with the Inter-Island investigation, the second of the five main investigations currently underway, the others being Springfield Equities, United Institutional Servicing Corporation, and the Veterans Administration.

Accetta was now ready to bring a second round of indictments to the grand jury. On September 26, the day of the indictments, Jeff Kay was waiting for Accetta to call and let him know that the indictments and arrest warrants had been filed. These were the indictments Romney learned about when he got back from his trip to flood-ravaged Pennsylvania. He knew things were about to get a whole lot worse for the FHA.

At 2:00 p.m. the call came in. Indictments were returned against Stanley Sirote and a slew of FHA executives: director Donald Carroll, assistant chief underwriter John Daly, chief mortgage credit officer Bernhard Fein, deputy chief Patrick Iannuccilli, deputy director Michael Jancovic, and assistant chief of mortgage credit Patrick Lama.

Sirote and Carroll were cooperating, so they turned themselves into the FBI office in Garden City. The rest were located and arrested at their offices and homes, then brought to Garden City and then on to the courthouse in Westbury, ten minutes away. Accetta drove out from Brooklyn and met them at the courthouse with the paperwork. That was when one of the defendants pointed out to him that, yet again, he'd chosen a Jewish holiday to make the arrests. It was Sukkot. "He actually threatened to kill me," Accetta said, "and called me an anti-Semite."

It was early in the evening when the men were finally led into the courtroom. Everyone pleaded not guilty except Donald Carroll, who was cooperating, and who looked "tired and sad" according to a newspaper account, with "his hands locked behind his back." (Accetta didn't want Sirote to plead guilty yet, because they didn't want the others to know Sirote was cooperating.) The rest would all eventually plead guilty once their lawyers got a look at the case against them, with the exception of Bernhard Fein. His indictment was dismissed on a technicality. Patrick Lama, who'd now been indicted twice, held out for five months before finally accepting there was no way out. He pleaded guilty and admitted to accepting bribes from Stanley Sirote. The Inter-Island case never went to trial.

Romney immediately suspended the newly indicted executives and replaced them with HUD executives who were flown in from Georgia, California, Kansas, and Oklahoma. Business with Inter-Island ceased.

Newspapers speculated about how much money the now indicted Stanley Sirote would make if he successfully sold his company. (Three years later the company was running under a different name and Sirote was still the principal stockholder.)

On September 28 and 29, a meeting of top HUD officials scheduled prior to the indictments took place in Washington. At the same time, a memo prepared for the meeting was leaked to the *Washington Post*. The author of the memo, William Whitbeck, the director of the FHA office in Detroit, offered a frank appraisal of their efforts to provide housing for the poor. "Far from learning from our mistakes, we appear to be resigned to repeating them." The regulations instituted after the scandal had broken had only succeeded in shutting down their efforts in the inner city. HUD was no longer insuring mortgages in low-income neighborhoods in New York, Chicago, Detroit, and Los Angeles. Brian Boyer would write how families of color who were paying their mortgages and keeping up their homes were screwed. If they wanted to get out of their rapidly declining neighborhoods, they couldn't sell their homes because potential buyers would no longer be able to get a mortgage. Between the recent indictments and the leaked memo, the tone of the meeting must have been bleak.

Across the country, twenty-eight FHA officials were indicted in 1972, including the top six officials at the FHA's Hempstead office, and the FBI was investigating 1,930 possible cases of fraud.

Richard Nixon was reelected on November 7, 1972. Two days later Romney delivered his letter of resignation. Once again, Nixon would not miss an opportunity to show Romney how insignificant he was to him, and he waited until November 27 to accept it.

On December 4, Philip Brownstein, the former assistant secretary of Housing and Urban Development who'd once stood before a large group of FHA employees and said, "I am asking you and every employee of FHA to enter into a new crusade. We're going to improve housing conditions for the poor and resurrect the inner city," now appeared before the Joint Economic Committee to continue to plead his case.

"Experience has shown that where such families acquire a satisfactory house, the failure rates are no higher than are those of unsubsidized mortgagors . . . the critical question for the seventies is our willingness to commit the resources necessary to house low- and moderate-income families. Until we are willing to make such a commitment, until we are willing to reorder national priorities and make adequate funds available, a successful housing program will elude our grasp." Senator Proxmire reiterated the need to find "some method to make certain that the house will not require some repair item right after purchase." But they had a method. It simply wasn't followed.

One of the many things that were missed when focusing on "unsophisticated buyers" was the fact that the FHA, by approving the inflated appraisals and signing off on repairs that hadn't been made, had left low-income buyers more economically vulnerable than they would have been had they paid a fair price for a home in sound condition. They had less money for standard home maintenance and the repairs that were never made. Sellers could still have made a profit at a fair price, it just wouldn't be as fantastic as it had been when they were committing fraud.

Lawrence Katz, the only FHA director in the country to run the housing for the poor programs successfully, also spoke at the hearing. The programs were only as good as the people running them, he said. In Wisconsin buildings were carefully inspected, and properly appraised and underwritten. They made sure that all required repairs were made. The areas being supported also had to be backed up by the local government with proper schools, and police. It would require a great deal of money to administer the programs effectively, he conceded, but with that, and counseling for homeowners about home repair, the programs could succeed. Wisconsin had done well, in part, because they spent more.

On December 1, Romney wrote to Brian Boyer, for inclusion in Boyer's book about the FHA scandal, *Cities Destroyed for Cash*. In his letter he continued to rationalize what happened, and he repeated the nineteenth-century practice of dividing those with low income into the worthy and unworthy poor. In the 1800s, when it became apparent that society was unwilling to make the investment necessary to address the problems of the poor, they pared down the number they would help by classifying some as "unworthy." Unless you were disabled (or a widow, or a child), your poverty could only be the result of a moral failing and you were therefore undeserving of assistance. Social issues such as fewer opportunities due to race, gender, and other biases were not considered.

Romney's twentieth-century version was the "good poor people" versus the "prostitutes and the pimps and the drug pushers and the drug addicts," as if they were responsible for the crisis, and not the result of it. "The good and stable poor people are at their mercy," Romney wrote, not acknowledging that white-collar criminals, and the government who aided and abetted them, had created the situation and then trapped the "good poor people" with the "prostitutes and the pimps and the drug pushers and the drug addicts" when they refused to encourage integration elsewhere. Like his nineteenth-century counterparts, Romney was implying that the people asking for help were the ones responsible for the decline, continuing the long history of criminalizing the poor and absolving the rich.

But Romney hadn't stopped wanting to help low-income families buy homes. At the end of the year, he would leak the news that a moratorium on all new construction of subsidized housing would begin in January, and that funds for urban renewal and the Model Cities program would be frozen. Romney did not support the wide-ranging embargo, writing Nixon that it "will only be taken by the American people—and especially those in the central city—as further evidence of a hardheaded, coldhearted indifference to the poor and racial minorities." Perhaps he thought the leak would generate a tsunami of criticism that would put a halt to Nixon's plans.

17

The Destruction of East New York

1991

The first person to be murdered in East New York in 1991 was killed forty minutes into the new year and it took place in the housing complex police called the Slaughterhouse. From there, someone would be murdered once or twice a week until July, when that number went up to an average of four. It's not that no one saw this coming.

Dr. Kenneth B. Clark laid it all out to President Johnson's Kerner Commission decades before. "This society knows . . . that if human beings are confined in ghetto compounds of our cities, and are subjected to criminally inferior education, pervasive economic and job discrimination, committed to houses unfit for human habitation, subjected to unspeakable conditions of municipal services, such as sanitation, that such human beings are not likely to be responsive to appeals to be lawful, to be respectful, to be concerned with property of others." But the warnings were not new, and as they had repeatedly been in the past, they were largely ignored.

Julia Parker turned seventeen in March. Her son would turn two in September. By now it was difficult to find a block in her neighborhood that hadn't been festooned with yellow crime scene tape at one time or another. Before the year was out, the number of murders would rise to 116.

It is not known how and when Julia first became involved with the drug trade in East New York. The police never found out, and her family and friends are not talking. "But a lot of girls were carrying drugs," Sister Margaret said. This was something that was done in the neighborhood, and among the teenagers it didn't carry the stigma others attached to it. When speaking of the girls who became involved with drugs, Sister Margaret insisted, "These were good girls, they were lovely." Some girls were doing this to help out their boyfriends, she explained. "When you're in love and young, you make a lot of very poor decisions." By 1991 Julia was making money as a drug courier, likely to help support her family and her young son.

In May, a twenty-three-year-old man came up from North Carolina to visit his uncle who was undergoing dialysis. We'll call him Mr. Fayetteville. During this trip he met a young drug dealer who ran his operation on Vermont Street, between Sutter and Belmont, around the corner from Julia's home on Wyona. We'll call him VSB. VSB told Mr. Fayetteville that there was money to be made in North Carolina, and he would help set him up.

VSB may have seen Julia in the neighborhood and might already have recruited her. Because soon after, on May 8, a young man came up to Julia and told her that VSB wanted to talk to her. They went around the corner. VSB asked her if she wanted to carry his "stuff" down south. "Yes," Julia immediately answered, "but what am I going to get out of it? What's in it for me?" VSB told Julia that she knew he'd take care of her, indicating that this is not the first time Julia and VSB had done business together.

"Be ready when I come to get you." After that, things happened quickly. VSB and another man came by Julia's house at 6:15 p.m. and found her sitting on her stoop. "Are you ready to go?" Julia went inside to pack a bag. Ten minutes later she was in VSB's jeep and on her way to Penn Station. As a precaution, they'd be traveling down south separately. VSB gave her a brown paper bag filled with cocaine and $200 for transportation and food. Mr. Fayetteville gave her his parents' number and told her to "Be careful." "What are you, the police?" Julia answered. "No, I ain't no police, I'm just telling you to watch out for the police." Julia left New York City at 8:30 p.m.

She should have heeded Mr. Fayetteville's warning. At the last stop before her final destination, the police were waiting for her. A joint task force of the DEA and the local police were on to VSB and Mr. Fayetteville, and they were staking out the train station to look for young people arriving from New York. Julia was arrested carrying six ounces of cocaine. The investigators weren't after Julia. She was only the courier. They wanted the guys who'd hired her. Julia quickly agreed to cooperate. The police outfitted her with a wire and put her on the next bus to Fayetteville, with a female detective sitting nearby.

When they arrived, Mr. Fayetteville and another man drove up to take Julia to meet VSB at Horne's Motel. Law enforcement followed. Once there, the men were arrested. Mr. Fayetteville flipped imme-diately. "The ones you want are in room 260 and 261." Julia couldn't help them with all the men who were arrested, but VSB was the one who gave her the drugs, she told them. Mr. Fayetteville admitted to knowing Julia, but claimed he was just being paid to pick her up. He didn't know about the cocaine, he insisted, but would later change his story.

Julia promised she would come back to North Carolina to testify and was released. Mr. Fayetteville was brought to New England, where he was wanted for the sale of narcotics. VSB made bail and was back in Brooklyn a day after Julia.

VSB's drug operation wasn't the only one law enforcement had learned of. The United States Attorney's office was aware of the alle-gations against police officer Michael Dowd and his partner, and they passed along contact information for two new informants to Internal Affairs. They were now up to eight. The latest informants gave the same story as all the ones before them. In addition to providing protection and information to the dealers that were paying him, Dowd gave them police radios, guns, and shields, and ran drugs for them in his police car. Dowd was not just a drug dealer. He had also become a drug courier, just like Julia Parker and other teenage girls in East New York.

There was now 27.8 million square feet of vacant land in East New York. Parents of children in a day care center had to walk their toddlers past a pack of stray dogs who'd made their home in a vacant lot next door, along with colonies of rats thriving in the growing piles of trash. As always, the empty lots provided plenty of space for mischief and garbage.

By the end of May there were thirty-nine homicides in East New York. A relative of Julia's shot David Winston to death on Killer Miller on June 8, bringing the body count up to forty-one. Thirty-one teenagers had been murdered from 1990 to 1991 alone, and the principal of Thomas Jefferson High School would establish a "grieving room with a counselor to counsel the kids because so many of them had lost their peers" due to gangs and gun violence.

Father Edward Mason came to St. John Cantius in East New York in 1991. He'd been in Brownsville, and Bushwick just before that. "I thought Bushwick was bad at that time. And it was. Then I got to East New York. They called it the Killing Fields." The murder rate was rising sharply in Father Mason's first years in East New York. "The median age of funerals at the church for one calendar year was twenty-three." Like Ashmat Ali, when Father Mason had to get somewhere, he'd carefully plan which streets to take. "If I were walking, even driving in my car, I would take a route based on avoiding large numbers of abandoned buildings. I just didn't feel good or safe walking down a block. So I would change how I was traveling somewhere because of the abandoned buildings that were there. But sometimes you had no choice. You're visiting someone who lives on the block, so you have no choice."

Father Mason talked about Father Brendan Buckley, a pastor at St. Michael's parish. "He had sixteen funerals of young people that he knew. Not random people . . . sixteen kids that he knew personally from his church in one year."

A month after Julia's relative shot David Winston, and twelve homicides later, Julia's friend Darryl Jenkins was shot at the corner of Wyona and Sutter, only half a block away from the house where Julia and her family were living. Darryl was number fifty-four. Julia's little sister Milagros saw it happen. She was nine years old.

It was a warm evening, the beginning of a heat wave, it would turn out, and a light rain was falling. Milagros had fallen asleep on the couch on the first floor when she was awoken after midnight by a man yelling, "Get him! Get him! There he go!" She peeked out the living room window and saw Jenkins running toward Sutter Avenue. Two guys were following, shooting at him. They'd shoot him eleven times. When Darryl's mother arrived on the scene to find her son bloody, and wet from the rain, the police asked her for her son's Social Security number. "I'll never forget that," she said. Milagros remembers Julia talking to detectives after Darryl's murder, but her answer to every question was, "I don't know anything."

Over the next week the temperature went up to 102.

The FHA Scandal

1973

When the new secretary of HUD, James T. Lynn, took the helm from George Romney in February 1973, he summed up his understanding of the cause of the housing problems. "People who had been given homes didn't understand the concept of homeownership." Given homes? "When the furnace needed repairs," he continued, they didn't understand that as the owners they had to fix it. Instead, if they didn't have the money to make repairs "they simply abandoned the property and defaulted on their loans." Is that what had happened?

It was the unsophisticated buyer argument that wouldn't die, with a characterization of flagrant irresponsibility thrown in for good measure.

The homeowners didn't cause the crisis. The scandal happened because government officials across the country had teamed up with white-collar criminals to become the largest and most extensive organized crime operation to date, relying on the racism that built this country to act as an accessory to their crimes. But accepting responsibility and facing hard truths was not something the current administration aspired to. They were focused on finding someone else to hold accountable.

To that aim, Nixon would blame the homebuyers as well, but he also said things like, "It now is clear that all too frequently the needy haven't been the primary beneficiaries of these programs." However, his response to this admission was to go back to blaming the needy and the programs meant to improve their lives. In a March 4 radio address about community development, Nixon dug in. "Some of our programs to help people buy or improve housing are also backfiring. Too many of the owners fail to meet their payments, and the taxpayer gets stuck with the bill." After giving a few examples of unsuccessful housing projects as proof, he announced that they were going to tighten the budget and stop the "programs which have failed." Once again it was the programs which had failed, not those who had implemented them.

The FHA scandals turned out to be politically useful to Nixon. In his book *Knocking on the Door: The Federal Government's Attempt to Desegregate the Suburbs*, author Christopher Bonastia explains how the scandals enabled Nixon to use them as an "escape hatch." They allowed him to retreat from any real effort to end housing discrimination and to further fair housing, "without enduring attacks for reversing civil rights gains."

Four days after Nixon's address, former FHA deputy chief Patrick Lama pleaded guilty to conspiring with former FHA director Donald Carroll, and to taking bribes from Stanley Sirote.

Lawsuits against the FHA started piling up. There were civil suits for damages for FHA-insured homes that had been falsely appraised as up to code with all repairs made. In the essay "Federal Compensation for Victims of the 'Homeownership for the Poor Program,'" the author cites one civil case naming Romney in which the buyer's mother died from pneumonia due to the building's lack of heat. Community groups in East New York sued the FHA to prevent their sale of one hundred abandoned buildings at the bulk price of $97,000, a move that would foster urban decay, they argued. The injunction they sought was part of an action to stop the FHA's policy of evicting all tenants in the event of foreclosure.

HUD took additional steps to prevent more crimes. They created the Office of Inspector General (OIG), which combined their audit, investigation, and security units into one. In their fiscal year 1972, the OIG conducted 2,500 investigations, some with the FBI, leading to 146 indictments naming people and firms. In the next fiscal year they sent 2,093 cases to the Department of Justice, resulting in 251 indictments as of November 1973. Under the act that created the Inspector General offices in a number of agencies, the OIG operated independently, and had the authority to investigate and audit any program or participant in the HUD programs. Even the secretary couldn't stop the OIG from conducting an investigation.

Critics complained that they were just scratching the surface. "We knew there were a lot of cases out there," said former attorney advisor John Kennedy (who left HUD an associate general counsel). "We also knew that the U.S. Attorney's office couldn't possibly spend that many person hours" on all of them. HUD would continue to refer criminal and civil cases to the Department of Justice when needed, but, "We wanted to have administrative remedies that we could take." They already had debarment and suspension, which prevented companies from doing business with the FHA nationwide, pending correction or a hearing. But that was something that was done at headquarters in Washington. "We wanted the local offices to have a similar kind of authority to take immediate action," Kennedy said. This ultimately led to the creation of the Limited Denial of Participation (LDP) procedure. Local FHA directors would still refer cases to headquarters for debarment, suspension, or possible criminal or civil prosecution, but once LDP procedures were in place, they could stop or suspend lenders from doing business with the FHA in their jurisdiction, also pending correction, a hearing, or an appeal.

One of the companies suspended was the Brewster Reserve Corporation, an affiliate of Eastern Service run by Louis Bernstein, the son of Harry and Rose Bernstein, who had been indicted along with his parents in March 1972. There was a hearing later that year and the decision to suspend Brewster Reserve was upheld. In July, Louis filed a motion in the Eastern District to have the suspension overturned, naming George Romney and the assistant secretary in his motion.

Judge Anthony J. Travia, who would preside over the Eastern Service trial, upheld the suspension.

Donald Carroll pleaded guilty and was sentenced to ten years in prison on January 22, 1973. Former FHA appraiser Francis Dreis and realtor Rubin Oringer were sentenced to four years. Oringer's two companies, Jabin Realty and Rite Properties, were fined $30,000.

As everyone was preparing for the trial, Accetta continued to go back to the grand jury and indictments were handed down every month between April and August.

Indictments were increasing across the country as well. Philadelphia was up to 116 indictments and twenty-four convictions as of May 1973. The grand jury in Detroit handed down forty-six indictments naming ninety-three defendants, with the prosecutor promising more to come. (By 1976 the number of indicted would surpass two hundred.) Chicago had indicted forty people as of April 1973.

The Eastern Service trial was set for October 1. The preparation required was massive. The process of discovery, turning over documents in a case that size, when much of the evidence was on paper, was enormously time-consuming. They didn't have computers. They didn't have the internet. Transcribing the tapes from the wire records took hours and hours, day after day. "Every time we listened we found something different," special agent Jeff Kay remembered.

The trial would take place in the Eastern District's building at 225 Cadman Plaza East. The relatively small, six-story building sometimes felt like a small town. Federal judges, attorneys, court personnel, U.S. Marshals and defendants all rode the same elevators and passed each other in the halls as they moved in and out of the offices and courtrooms, often eating together in the cafeteria in the basement, where they might cross paths with members of the Federal Organized Crime Strike Force, who were housed in the basement. The Eastern Service trial would take place in Federal Courtroom number 9, Judge Travia's courtroom.

Jack Blum called building cases like the one against Eastern Service "ball-busting work." They were about to see what all that work would amount to.

18

The Destruction of East New York

1991

It was a Wednesday evening, the golden hour before sunset, and the temperature was in the midnineties. Someone was watching Julia Parker's baby, now a toddler, and she was free to hang out with Ashmat Ali and other friends. They met at the corner of Pennsylvania and Dumont, where Ashmat's father had his store. "Summertime," Ashmat said, "everybody's on the block at the corner. That's how New York is. Everybody's outside. Everybody's doing something." They were sitting on Ashmat's uncle's car, when Ashmat realized he had to get back to work. He was working with his father at the grocery that day, each of them taking turns watching the store. His father would work one hour, then Ashmat would work an hour.

"So I'm talking to Julia, I'm walking backward, telling her, 'I got to go inside, I got to go inside to work.' She was smiling and we were happy. And then the guy just came up behind her. Pop, pop, pop. I guess her face just froze." And then she fell.

The gunman kept shooting. At first Ashmat didn't move. "I just stood there, looking at her," he said. He was hit in the arm, and another bullet went into Julia. Then Ashmat ran inside the store. "My uncle was there too. He was like, 'You're bleeding.' I look at my arm. I didn't feel nothing. And then five minutes later, my arm started burning." His uncle grabbed him and pulled him outside.

The EMTs put Ashmat in the ambulance with Julia. "They had her laying down. They had me sitting by the door. They tried to resuscitate her, but she was gone. She was gone." Julia and Ashmat were taken to Brookdale Hospital, where Julia was pronounced dead. Ashmat was treated and released.

Julia used to come by the store all the time to hang out. "Everybody used to hang out at the corner," Ashmat said. There was a fire hydrant there and in the summertime they'd open it. Or they'd play basketball. "We didn't have basketball hoops on the street. We used to cut up a milk crate. That was our hoop." But most of the time, "We just chilled, just chill at the corner and hung out."

Three days before she was shot, Julia ran into VSB. According to her mother, he'd said, "You better do the right thing," referring to their arrest in North Carolina. VSB knew Julia would be called back to testify at the trial, and he wanted to make sure she wasn't going to say anything that would send him to prison. "I know what to do," she assured him. "I'm no rat."

If VSB didn't believe her, he would know that the corner of Dumont and Pennsylvania was one of the places he could find her.

That evening, July 17, the streets were bustling with people and activity. Mateo Alvarez (not his real name) was standing in front of his home on Dumont Avenue, when he heard the first shot. His wife and son were sitting on their stoop. The shooter fired four more times, according to Alvarez, and then he started running, waving his gun at everyone he passed by. Alvarez ran to cover his wife and child. Others ducked behind cars.

The police canvassed thirty-seven buildings looking for witnesses, but only eleven people opened the door, and three of the buildings with a view of the murder were abandoned and empty. Everyone believed Julia was killed because she had spoken to the police after her friend Darryl's murder. So it was understandable when people insisted, "I didn't see anything." Ashmat couldn't help, explaining that the murderer's "height was the same as Julia and he was behind her so I couldn't see his face." Later he remembered the guy had on a black hoodie.

"It's every man for himself out here," Julia's mother said to a *Daily News* reporter. "There's a chain of people who know each other who have been getting killed for a while now." At the suggestion that her daughter was killed because she had spoken to the police, Julia's mother insisted, "My daughter didn't say a thing to police." But she had.

The detectives wouldn't say which leads they were following. Maybe she was killed because she'd talked to them after her friend was murdered. Maybe it was related to her relative's killing of David Winston, or drug activity in the area.

Decades later, Ashmat said, "I always think about her. We just clicked, and we had a good time. I was always happy to see her, always. You know how you see somebody and they put you in a good mood? That's how she was. Everybody that we moved with liked her. She was cool."

About her involvement with drugs, Ashmat says softly, "To me, she was a good girl. She did what she did. She probably had to do what she had to do because a lot of people were poor in that neighborhood.

"The thing is, too, everybody in the hood know the drug game. Once you're dealing with drugs, everybody knows that either you're going to get locked up or you're going to die, one of the two." Why did they do it? "The money. A lot of money."

"I know I'm giving you a grim story, but it was a lot more fun, a lot more happiness than the bad stuff. Bad stuff happened, but it's not like we was trying to escape from anything or that. She would come to the corner, and we went to go see somebody or, 'Let's go to a house party.' It was always about a good time."

When Julia died, her sister Milagros was sitting inside the front door, behind a screened gate to get some air. That's where she was allowed to sit when no one was available to watch her. It was where her mother could keep an eye on her. A friend of the family came running inside. "Where's your mother?" Upstairs, Milagros told her. Seconds later her mother was crying and running out the door. Milagros didn't know what happened until her mother came back sobbing, "They killed my daughter, they killed my daughter."

"Before that, my mom was always full of colors," Milagros said. "She was always happy, always taking us out. When my sister got killed everything was darkness." Life forever changed for Julia's young son, who until that night was rarely out of her sight. He would now have to grow up without her.

Julia was the fifty-fifth person to be murdered in East New York that year. Sixty-one more people would be killed, bringing the total for the year to 116. Like every other year, most of the murder victims in 1991 were shot, a few were stabbed, and one person died in a fire that had been deliberately set. On September 12, firefighters were called to 495 Atkins Avenue, an abandoned building where three people had been murdered over the past four years (and several more nearby). As firefighter Kevin Kane was making sure the people who were squatting in the building got out alive, the ceiling fell on him. Eighty-two percent of his body sustained second- and third-degree burns. He died the next day.

On the morning of November 25 at Thomas Jefferson High School, a fourteen-year-old shot and killed a sixteen-year-old and wounded a teacher, all while trying to protect his older brother whom he believed was about to be shot. "I did what I had to do," he would later say. It's not difficult to comprehend. By 1992, homicide was the number one cause of death for young people aged fifteen to nineteen in New York City. Twenty-six percent of high school students were carrying weapons to school, according to one survey. In newspaper reports the fourteen-year-old was referred to as the "gunman" as if he wasn't just a child, fighting for his life and his brother's.

More than three decades later, forty-three of the murders committed in 1991, including Julia's, remained unsolved.

People who grew up in East New York in the 1950s, '60s, and '70s look back on their childhoods with longing. "The greatest times of my life were spent on New Lots and Wyona," someone posted on an East New York website. "The best of everything was right there." Today, on a map of East New York, New Lots Avenue and Wyona Street are jammed with push pins, each representing a murder, many of which have never been solved.

When Romney ticked off his list of the bad poor people responsible for what East New York had become, seventeen-year-old single mother Julia Parker would have neatly fit on his register. Father Edward Mason, who'd only just arrived in East New York, presided over Julia's funeral. "I wasn't even officially there yet. I took over in September." The death of this child shook him. She made a bad decision at a bad time and was "in the wrong place," Father Mason said. There was "a culture of violence" around her. "I can't imagine what it's like to grow up in that environment. I grew up in a neighborhood where we didn't lock the doors."

The EBC and so many others were racing to return East New York to the thriving working- and middle-class neighborhood it had once been. By the end of 1991 the EBC had added 1,100 affordable homes to the battered neighborhood, with still more planned. "It was a time of despair and hope living side by side," Mason said. "Put a few criminals in a large building, you have a crime wave," I. D. Robbins told Congress. A neighborhood of single-family homes, however, would "handle the problem very easily." Joseph Dunne, the commanding officer of the Seven-Five, said the best anti-crime strategy in New York City is Nehemiah. But they weren't building fast enough to save Julia.

Like Ashmat Ali, Father Mason still thinks about Julia Parker. "The senselessness of it, the randomness senselessness of it, stuck with me." Her mother would never recover. "I never had trouble with her and she never had any trouble with anybody," she cried when it happened, adding, "I'll be the first one to get revenge if I find out who did this."

The FHA Scandal

1973

In addition to pursuing mortgage fraud cases across the country, the Department of Justice was also investigating other violations related to the Civil Rights Act of 1968. In the past few years their civil division settled two large cases involving housing discrimination with consent decrees, one in Los Angeles, and one, more recently, in New York. (Like a settlement, a consent decree is not an admission of guilt, but it is an agreement approved by a judge and enforced by the court. The Vera Institute describes consent decrees "as a legally binding performance improvement plan.") The New York case was settled in 1971 with Samuel J. LeFrak, one of the largest builders in the city, and it involved 21,000 apartments in 150 buildings.

After the Department of Justice settled with LeFrak, the New York City Commission on Human Rights referred another discrimination case to the DOJ, based on allegations from the New York Urban League (who had also filed the initial complaints against LeFrak). The DOJ investigated and on October 14, 1973, they brought a suit in the Eastern District against a smaller, although still substantial builder, Trump Management, Inc. The Trump case involved 14,000 apartments in thirty-nine buildings in Brooklyn and Queens.

The New York Urban League had sent potential renters to Trump properties and found that Black renters were either told there were no available apartments, or were sent to other, predominately Black buildings. White applicants were immediately offered apartments. The DOJ's investigation confirmed that some Trump buildings contained few minority tenants, some as few as 1 percent, and that employees marked applications from Black renters with "C" for "colored," or "No. 9," and were told to rent to "Jews and executives." Donald Trump, who was named in the suit along with his father, Fred C. Trump, denied the charges. Making the same kind of claim he continues to make today, Trump later said, "When these stories hit the national wire services, I received many calls and letters of surprise from tenants and community leaders expressing their shock and disbelief that our organization should be charged with such outrageous lies."

Discrimination cases like these were important because they contributed to funneling people of color into neighborhoods that were underserviced and prevented them from living in neighborhoods that were thriving. While Accetta and those working alongside him were prosecuting people who were scamming fair housing programs that had been established for families of color, other related housing crimes were being committed that put fair housing even further out of reach. It was just the kind of case HUD would have referred to the DOJ if the New York Urban League had come to them first, and it was exactly the kind of case they originally thought would be their sole focus.

The Trumps had twenty days to respond to U.S. Attorney Robert Morse, who was also overseeing Accetta's mortgage fraud case, which would begin selecting their jury the following day. Twice, the Trumps asked for and were granted more time to respond.

The Trumps finally answered the charges with a press conference at the New York Hilton Hotel, and a countersuit. Trump could have settled, as Samuel LeFrak had done, but, as he wrote in his 1987 autobiography, "I'd rather fight than fold, because as soon as you fold once, you get the reputation of being a folder." Instead, they filed a countersuit asking for $100 million in damages. They characterized the government's suit as an attempt to force them to rent to welfare families who could not afford their moderate or "luxury" apartments. Roy Cohn, who had been Senator Joseph McCarthy's attorney during McCarthy's communist hearings and the prosecutor in the trial of Julius and Ethel Rosenberg, was the Trumps' lawyer. He asked that the case be dismissed due to lack of evidence. Judge Edward Neaher, who had hired AUSA Tony Accetta, scheduled a hearing for January, to consider the request.

On January 25, the Trumps and their lawyer made their way to the courthouse at 225 Cadman Plaza East. If they were traveling from the Trumps' office in Gravesend, at the southernmost end of Brooklyn opposite Coney Island, they had a bit of a trek. The Eastern Service trial was in progress at the time. When the Trumps came to the courthouse, they were sometimes directed to courtroom nine, Judge Travia's courtroom, and the one where Eastern Service was being tried. Judge Neaher was apparently using the courtroom on days when the Eastern Service trial was not in session.

Judge Neaher would ultimately bat away each of Trump's maneuvers. He dismissed Trump's suit for damages saying, "You would be wasting time and paper from what I consider to be the real issues." Cohn responded by asking for a freeze on press releases regarding the case. Neaher denied that motion as well, citing the public's right to know, but he did instruct AUSA Henry Brachtl to concentrate on the case and let the press do their job gathering the facts.

The next hit the Trump team would suffer was their attempt to discredit the AUSA Donna Goldstein. Cohn claimed that when Goldstein came onboard, the investigation "turned into a gestapo-like interrogation," and that his employees were being badgered and threatened. In July, the Trumps filed a motion to have Goldstein held in contempt and for a protective order against the United States.

Neaher denied those motions as well. "I find no evidence in the record that anything in the nature of gestapo tactics was permitted by the

FBI in doing the tasks assigned to them." Trying everything, Trump lied and said he only learned of the lawsuit when he read about it in the newspapers. But the DOJ had contacted the Trump organization prior to filing suit.

Ultimately, Trump had to choose between going to court or settling. He settled. Or, as he would say, he folded. The consent decree (a.k.a. improvement plan) Trump signed on June 10, 1975, required the Trump organization to "thoroughly acquaint themselves personally on a detailed basis" with the Civil Rights Act of 1968, and to implement a plan for compliance with the act. They also had to provide a weekly list of vacant apartments to the New York Urban League, offer apartments to financially able tenants on a first come, first serve basis, and place ads for two years informing the community that they would be abiding by the Act.

Trump could have gone to court. He had a bulldog of a lawyer perfectly capable of fighting for him. Instead, he gave in, insisting to this day it was a win. In reality he'd conceded even more than LeFrak had. LeFrak didn't have to send civil rights groups a weekly list of their vacancies or give them the first shot at providing qualified applicants in predominantly white buildings (for every fifth vacancy). The Trumps also had to file a report three times a year on their fourteen buildings, that among other things provided the racial makeup of each building, and listed the number of people, by race, who had inquired about an apartment, were accepted for occupancy, or were rejected. If someone was rejected, they had to supply "a detailed statement of the reason(s) for rejection and supporting information." In an attempt to frame the settlement as a win, Donald Trump told reporters that his agreement didn't "compel the Trump organization to accept persons on welfare as tenants unless as qualified as any other tenant."

The government was happy to settle. They got what they wanted without the trouble of a trial. They could now turn their attention to the trial they'd been working toward for the past two years.

19

The Destruction of East New York

1992

The year 1992 started out with a murder, just as it had in 1991 and 1990. According to a retired detective, officers of the Seven-Three in Brownsville and the Seven-Five in East New York had a yearly pool to see which precinct had the first murder of the year. Whoever arrived at the crime scene first collected the money. In 1992 the body of a sixteen-year-old Hispanic girl, Jennifer Negron, was found on the corner of Stanley Avenue and Elderts Lane in East New York on January 1 at 5:00 a.m. Five days after turning sixteen, Jennifer was beaten, strangled, and stabbed four times in her head and neck. Two men were found guilty of kidnapping her (the murder charge was thrown out due to lack of evidence), but the convictions were overturned in 2014. The detectives had based their case on the testimony of one witness, who was shown to be unreliable, and evidence that could have exonerated the men had been withheld. As with other murders in which the NYPD learned they had the wrong guy (or guys), the status of Jennifer's case was not changed. It is still listed as closed and no one is looking for her killer.

Sergeant Michael Race, who would retire the next year, would later tell a *New York Times* reporter that only one of the 750 murder investigations he'd overseen while at the Seven-Five, which would include the Negron case, was "done the correct way, from A to Z."

Ninety-two more people were killed that year in East New York, including three on Killer Miller, three at the Slaughterhouse, and two at Thomas Jefferson High School. "School is like Vietnam," the father of a student there told a reporter. Brooklyn Assembly-person Roger Green agreed, telling the *New York Amsterdam News* that some children were "showing signs of post-distress syndrome—similar to what combat soldiers internalized during the Vietnam War." Nineteen of the people killed in 1992 were teenagers like Julia Parker or younger, including a seventeen-year-old who was gunned down a block from where Julia was shot, and an unidentified one-year-old who'd been strangled to death and left out in the street in an area of East New York known as The Hole.

Like an urban valley, the twelve-block span of The Hole sinks ten to fifteen feet below the streets around it. The water table here comes close to the surface, making drainage a challenge. The streets flood when it rains, but also sometimes when it doesn't. Compounding the problem is the lack of a functional sewage infrastructure. Homes in The Hole are not connected to New York City's sewage system and instead use septic tanks and cesspools, which can also overflow in the rain. Poorly maintained tanks spring leaks, which flow into lakes of sewage that residents must regularly wade through. The Hole is more forsaken than it is menacing, but it's not surprising that a murderer would leave a body there. In the 1980s, the Mob used an area in The Hole as a burial ground.

East New York continued to collect colorful, morbid nicknames. One block west of Pennsylvania Avenue, in the middle of the Unity Plaza projects, a.k.a. the Slaughterhouse, was a stretch across the street from an elementary school that the locals referred to as Death Alley. "We buried a nineteen-year-old parishioner this year," Father Mason said of a young girl who was killed in Death Alley in 1992, when she got caught in cross fire.

While most of the people murdered in East New York were in their twenties or younger, that didn't mean people who made it past that age were in the clear.

For more than three decades Frank Falleti left his West Hempstead home on Long Island to sell coffee and sandwiches in East New York. He'd grown up nearby and was familiar with the area. Brooklyn was where he met his wife. When Frank came up with the idea of a food truck, nobody in his family was surprised when he planted his new business in a place that was like a second home to him. His customers—factory workers and people from the neighborhood—were his people, and his family knew he'd be happy there.

"This guy was a prince," the owner of a security firm in the area told a reporter. "Anybody that was broke, he'd feed them. A hooker was broke, he'd feed her. He'd give credit to the entire world. That's the way he was."

On a Friday morning in 1992, Frank set up his truck in front of 737 Atkins Avenue. He'd been there since the 1950s. Five years earlier, he'd been shot in the leg during a robbery there. Even though he was seventy-two years old at the time, and his family wanted him to retire, as soon as he recovered he went right back to working in the same spot. Now seventy-seven he still wasn't ready to retire. "If I retire, what am I going to do? I meet all the people and I enjoy myself," he told his family.

According to witnesses, around 11:35 a.m. that Friday, two men came up to Falleti and told him to hand over all his money. When he resisted, they shot him three times in the chest and once in the stomach. As he lay bleeding and unable to defend himself, they went through his pockets, exploring his body for plunder, like ants working over a carcass. He was pronounced dead at the scene.

He would have fed them for free, if they'd told him they were hungry.

As if things weren't bad enough, in 1992 the New York Zodiac returned. So far he hadn't been entirely effective as a serial killer. Three of the first four people he'd shot survived. But this year he hit upon a more successful strategy, which Sergeant Joe Herbert would figure out later, when victims started showing up in Highland Park. In one of his letters, the Zodiac had written about watching the cops from the Seven-Five standing at Jamaica Avenue and Elderts Lane. "I went to that location," Herbert said, "and it's underneath the Jamaica Avenue el train. Right there is Franklin K. Lane High School, which is a very large complex. In front of the high school is a running track." The Zodiac would sit in the stadium seats at the track, Herbert determined, where he had an elevated view to target victims coming off the train. On August 10, the Zodiac spied Patricia Fonte, a troubled young woman from the Bronx who for reasons that were never determined decided to travel to East New York that night.

The Zodiac quickly rushed to her side and lured her into nearby Highland Park with the promise of cigarettes. She was a disturbed young woman and that was all it took. The Zodiac walked her to a reservoir bridge that was overgrown with bushes, weeds, and vines. There, he shot Patricia twice, but he was foiled by his poorly functioning zip gun. When that didn't kill her, he started stabbing her. The bridge was so dense with vegetation, "Nobody could travel, or walk through there," Herbert said. If she screamed, no one heard. "He had all the time in the world to stab her one hundred times. It was a really gruesome event." A second task force was formed.

The Seven-Five had enough on their hands with all the other killers in East New York. In 1992, the detective squad had eight detectives on each shift who comprised what is called the "catching team." As each homicide case came in, it would have been assigned to one of the eight detectives in turn. By the end of 1992, every detective on the team would have caught nineteen more homicides, and that was on top of any unsolved cases from previous years. On average, a third of all the murders in East New York went cold every year. As the piles of case files on their desks grew higher, the commanding officer would at some point have told them, Look, If you're not going to solve that one quickly, move on.

The detectives who'd caught Julia's case didn't move on immediately, but there was never a lot of activity.

Making the detectives' job still more challenging at the time was the fact that some of their own were working against them. The NYPD had received four more allegations of corruption against Michael Dowd, sixteen in all. Retired Detective Denise Thomas, who worked undercover narcotics in Brooklyn, said, "He was jeopardizing our lives too. If something would've happened and we got caught up in some damn shoot-out ... Everybody that had a hand in knowing that it was going on and kept it at bay was really jeopardizing all the narcotics bureaus that were working to rid these areas of drugs and drug dealers."

The NYPD determined that the allegations against Dowd were unsubstantiated and the cases were closed. The Suffolk police and United States Attorney Otto Obermaier (the former defense attorney for Dun & Bradstreet in the Eastern Service case) concluded otherwise. The police on Long Island were investigating a drug operation in their jurisdiction when they intercepted Dowd's telephone calls about his drug sales in their area. They arrested Michael Dowd and his partner on May 6, 1992. Sergeant Trimboli, who for years had tried to get the NYPD to launch a full-on investigation of Dowd, read about it in the papers. Two months later Dowd was arrested on the federal charges.

While out on bail, Dowd planned an escape that involved being paid by drug dealers to kidnap a woman they intended to execute. "This is the plan," Dowd told his partner Ken Eurell. "She'll be tied up in back. And if they want her, you got her in a hotel room somewhere, and that's it." Eurell was wearing a wire at the time, and investigators were able to intervene to save the woman. Dowd denies that murder was part of the plot.

Dowd, who pleaded guilty in 1993, was not the only member of the force undermining the efforts of the detectives at the Seven-Five. In addition to his partner, the Suffolk County Police arrested four other officers. A detective working out of Brooklyn North Homicide Squad, Louis N. Scarcella, has had more than a dozen murder convictions based on his investigations overturned, with more being added all the time. A case from 1996 was overturned in January 2024. The improper investigations have led to millions in settlements. Scarcella denies any wrongdoing.

And then there were all those exceptional clearances. One hundred and seven homicide cases were exceptionally cleared on Sergeant Michael Race's watch. If the clearances were not sound, that meant up to 107 murderers were still out there.

Men hired by various organizations to take up the slack left by the police were often sitting ducks. Forty-five-year-old James Dyson was shot to death on July 14 while working as a security guard protecting abandoned buildings on Sheffield Avenue that were being renovated by ACORN. Sheffield Avenue was one of the worst streets in East New York. Six people would be killed along Sheffield that year. For Dyson, protecting the much-needed housing rehabilitation project was a mission. A fine artist as well as a martial artist, Dyson was described as affable and kind. "Why would anybody have to kill somebody who was so gentle?" a friend asked. When ACORN couldn't find anyone willing to take his place, ConEd refused to send men to complete the electrical work. After the buildings were finally completed, it took them a while to find anyone brave enough to move in. Forty-two murders from 1992 have never been solved, including James Dyson's.

The city still wanted the EBC to build Nehemiah homes in the same area, west of Pennsylvania Avenue, a section where some of the streets "are in such poor condition . . . as to be almost impassable," according to the city's Department of Planning. But the EBC held out until the city gave them enough land to build the number of homes they'd need to actually make a difference in the area. "If we can't build enough Nehemiah homes to change the culture of a community, that's not Nehemiah," Father Mason said. In 1996, construction would begin on 696 homes that would be completed by 2003.

"When Nehemiah came in," said Carey Shea, of East New York Urban Youth Corps, "they built these row houses and it was transformative." But it was effective because they didn't build one or two at a time, but hundreds. The East New York Urban Youth Corps were a smaller operation, but they were making their mark as well, and in 1992, they completed rehabilitating thirteen buildings.

"The home is the center of life," wrote Matthew Desmond, the author of *Evicted: Poverty and Profit in the American City*. "It is a refuge from the grind of work, the pressure of school, and the menace of the streets . . . without stable shelter, everything else falls apart." Put simply, "Without a home, nothing else is possible."

At the end of 1992, in an otherwise terrible year in Brooklyn, early EBC member Sarah Plowden, who got up before dawn every morning to walk the streets and write down where signs were missing, happily bought a Nehemiah home of her own. "I did not have a lot of furniture to move into my new house, just a bed in a couch," along with a few dishes, and some sheets and towels. But after a thorough scrub down "I was glad to have a place to put them," and a home that was all her own.

The FHA Scandal

1973–1974

They'd been preparing for this day for over a year. A steady stream of FBI agents, HUD attorneys, and other personnel made their way to Accetta's office to pitch in. Gale Drexler, a legal assistant, talked about Sally, their secretary, who would become one of many who felt invested in the Eastern Service case. "Nobody at the Eastern District wanted her as a secretary because she was older and she walked slow and she talked slow and she was a cat lady. We ended up with her and we loved her. We adored her and she adored Tony." There wasn't anything Sally wouldn't do for them, and she was going to see it through to the end.

Of the original forty people and ten companies indicted, seven people and two companies were going to trial. Some were to be tried later, six people had pleaded guilty, one pleaded nolo contendere, and one defendant died. Accetta would later fume that "every functional level of the FHA regional office was on the take. From low-level clerks to the regional administrator, almost everyone was on Eastern Service Corporation's payroll, and that spread to many other mortgage companies. It was pay to play on a mass scale." He couldn't prosecute them all at once. He began with nine.

On October 1, 1973, the Eastern Service trial finally began. It would become the longest in the history of the Eastern District at the time, ending nine months later on July 9, 1974. Judge Anthony Travia put everything he had into what would be his last time in charge of a court; he retired at the end of the trial. Having grown up in East New York, ending his career on a case that addressed crimes in his hometown may have felt particularly fitting.

After various preliminary procedures and jury selection, Accetta made his opening statement on October 25. "He has a very compelling presence," George Bashion said. He remembers Accetta sweating. "It was dripping off his hands, but it was a good sweat." Accetta was about to begin the trial of a lifetime.

Rose Bernstein would go through the entire trial wearing a neck brace, even though she was observed in the ladies' room with the brace off and her head leaning forward toward the mirror to put on makeup. On more than one occasion, "Rose would come screeching into the bathroom complaining about everything," Drexler recalled. "And I'd have to say, 'Mrs. Bernstein, I'm in here.' She would huff and puff like how dare I come into the bathroom." Rose, who was about five feet, four inches, had bleached blond hair, wore heavy makeup and glasses, and was often imperious, obnoxious, and loud. At one point during the trial they played the recording of Rose calling Accetta "that little guinea bastard." The jury thought it was hysterical. Rose Bernstein never tried to make herself agreeable to anyone. It was not a winning strategy.

The first two witnesses were from the FHA, and they described the process involved in insuring a mortgage. That took a week. For the most part, the proof was in the paperwork and there was a mind-numbing parade of it throughout the course of the trial. Every count was explained, every single evidential document was displayed, identified, and pored over. Hundreds of false figures and claims were carefully and slowly spelled out and exposed. It was not an exciting trial.

Gale Drexler was responsible for making sure the many boxes of evidence and case files they were using each day were in the courtroom.

"I had this cart that had the files on them, and I used to have to push this heavy cart around." The only person who ever offered to help her was Arthur Prescott, the Dun & Bradstreet manager who was accused of okaying Eastern's false credit statements. Prescott "was appalled that I had to push this heavy cart," Drexler said, "and he wanted to push this cart for me. It was so sweet. I couldn't let him, but every day he would say to me, 'Are you sure I can't push this cart?'"

As the months wore on, "we all began to get to know everything that was going on in one another's lives," Drexler said. They had to show up each day and if they weren't there Travia would explain why. When anyone fell ill, everyone knew. When Drexler's step-grandfather died, the court was told. "It didn't matter whether you were the prosecution or the defense. We knew that we were going to be there for quite a while, and everyone really tried hard to be civil to one another."

Ortrud Kapraki took the stand on November 5, to testify for the prosecution. "Tony had problems with Ortrud," Kay remembered. "She came across as Attila the Hun."

Her presence should have provided some relief from the tedium, but Ortrud was on the stand for nineteen days and Accetta had managed to coach her from Attila the Hun to monotonous. A *New York Times* reporter described how she gave "detail after detail, speaking in a quiet monotone, her mouth turned down." When the second week of her testimony began, a juror fell asleep. The next day a court clerk fell asleep.

In her testimony, Kapraki explained how she would figure out how much income the buyer needed to get a commitment from the FHA, and make up the buyer's job and salary accordingly, sometimes while working together with Cardona, the Eastern sales person who'd recruited her. "We're going to put down that he's a painter," they'd conspire, "and he makes $10,000 a year." A lot of painters were buying houses in East New York those years. When testifying at the Senate, Secretary Lomenzo joked that if all the people in the mortgage applications were actually painters "they would have painted half of Brooklyn." So many people laughed it was recorded in the court transcript.

Ortrud Kapraki was still testifying on the morning of December 4, when U.S. Attorney Robert Morse, who'd assigned the Eastern Case to Accetta, walked into the chambers of the chief judge of the Eastern District, and told him that he wanted to resign. After that he went home and at 2:10 p.m., jumped to his death from the fifth floor of his Brooklyn Heights apartment on Montague Street. Five hundred people attended his funeral. It hit Accetta hard. He thought, "Why didn't you talk to me, maybe I could have helped you." Edward Boyd stepped in briefly for Morse, until David Trager, a former AUSA and a professor at Brooklyn Law School, was appointed the new U.S. attorney.

Lengthy trials are "absolutely exhausting for everybody," Accetta said. Your day isn't over when court is adjourned at the end of the afternoon. "You're reading transcripts at night and preparing for the next day's testimony. It was all-consuming. You didn't do much else for nine months."

As the trial proceeded, more indictments were returned, and guilty pleas continued to slowly filter in. Investigations into similar crimes across the country also continued. A Justice official told a *New York Times* reporter, "Everybody seemed to be in the same game. What we find in one city, we're finding in other cities in almost the same pattern of activity."

The Dun & Bradstreet government witnesses testified in January, taking up almost the entire month. Edward Goodwin, the FHA appraiser, testified soon after. Accetta took him through hundreds of cases. Using simple and clear language, Goodwin explained how the whole operation between Eastern and the FHA worked. But when cross-examined, "He decided he was a lawyer and got cute. He wouldn't answer the questions and started evading." Accetta immediately stood up and asked for a recess. When they got back to his office he yelled, "What do you think you're doing? Are you out of your mind? You answer their questions the same way you answered mine." Goodwin was a bland, "milquetoasty like guy," Accetta said, and it wasn't difficult to bring him back in line. Properly chastened, "he went back and did his job." That took sixteen days.

One by one their witnesses came forth, and the boxes of documents Drexler dutifully wheeled in and out were emptied and displayed. Frank Fey, the former Eastern Service VP, testified about who was involved at Eastern and who had knowingly submitted false information to the FHA and had bribed their employees. Rose Cohen, the FHA clerk, testified that she accepted bribes to funnel Eastern's applications to the appraisers, who would also happily take their bribes. The last two witnesses for the prosecution were two FHA appraisers who'd gone through all the paperwork to find and verify the phony files. On March 21, 1974, four years after Secretary of State John P. Lomenzo found evidence of massive fraud, which he brought to the Eastern District, Accetta stood and announced, "The prosecution rests."

20

The Destruction of East New York

1993–1994

According to a *Daily News* article, two years after Julia Parker was murdered, a sergeant in the Seven-Five was alleged to have stood up at his retirement party in 1993 to say, "I'd like to thank all the young men in East New York who gave their lives so I could buy my house." He denies having ever made such a statement.

That year, 1993, would produce the highest number of individual murders to date in any one precinct in the entire history of the NYPD: 128. (The Four-Eight precinct's higher total included the Happy Land fire mass murder.) The 128 victims in East New York included seventeen-year-old Toya Gillard, who, in the midst of gunfire on a playground, ran to save her two-year-old son. Just as she reached him she was shot in the head. The detectives found her slumped over the playground fence, her arms still held out for her little boy. They would later learn that Toya, a junior in high school, was killed by another child, Anthony Knowles, who was only thirteen. They both lived in the Pink Houses. "I hate the projects," Anthony's mother told reporters.

Thirteen-year-old Maria Negron Luz died from blunt force trauma. Her body was left in Highland Park in June. When a child is murdered, the police go all out, but despite their efforts, Maria's case went cold.

Sergeant Joe Herbert, who'd replaced Detective Sergeant Michael Race when he retired in 1993, later wondered if Maria might have been a victim of the New York Zodiac. The Zodiac had tallied up three more victims that year, all in Highland Park, and Maria's body was found 150 feet from his eighth, Diane Ballard, who survived. The Zodiac's murder success rate had improved since he'd started killing in Highland Park, but in the end more of his victims lived than died. The Guardian Angels posted a police sketch of the Zodiac around Highland Park that year with the message, "Guardian Angels to the Zodiac 2 [to distinguish him from the Zodiac killer in California] your horoscope says your time is up." Soon after, the Zodiac went underground once again, this time for three years.

In 1993, the lives of Julia Parker's remaining family grew still sadder, and more difficult. The year before, the family was forced to move out of the Wyona Street home due to financial difficulties. Not long after that, their beloved grandmother, whom Julia was named for, passed away. The two Julias were buried together, their pictures and two doves adorn their gravestone. That year Julia's sister Milagros had a vision of Julia. It wasn't clear; at first she could only tell it was a person. Then, as the wispy image before her came together to form a face, she saw that it was Julia. "Please take care of Donavon," Julia said. Her son. Milagros was only twelve. She was just a kid herself. "Please just take care of Donavon," Julia repeated. "Always look out for him." "Okay," Milagros told her. "I'll always help him."

The nightmares were worse. "I would see her at her gravesite, and there were two men, they were digging up her grave and when they pulled her out they started shooting her." Every single night for two months she'd wake up crying, going to school in the morning distraught.

Milagros believes she had the nightmares because she never knew exactly what had happened to Julia.

The killing in East New York went on and on, and every year the number of unsolved murders climbed. The murders from 1993 would add fifty-five more cold cases to the grim total. People who already mistrusted the police saw this as proof that they just didn't care.

At the end of 1993, six months after Police Officer Michael Dowd pleaded guilty to dealing drugs and protecting drug gangs, Governor Cuomo proposed extending the Combat program (Coordinated Omnibus Municipally Based Anti-Drug Teams) into East New York. The program involved residents supplying information to the police about drug activity and the police increasing surveillance and arrests accordingly. (As long as the drug dealers were not the police, apparently.)

The last person killed in 1993 was Michael Rivera, who was shot to death the day after Christmas. His murder has never been solved.

Earlier that year, Father Brendan Buckley, who lost nineteen children from his congregation in one year, wrote to the Mollen Commission. Mayor Dinkins had created the commission to investigate police corruption following Michael Dowd's arrest. Father Buckley asked for the opportunity to testify to the commission. He wrote of the "deadly ten-year riot of drug-related crime" and the "detached and defensive police investigators" who failed to adequately respond. "Hustlers and thieves both in and out of uniform know how to fill this vacuum." Dowd and his partner, two of the hustlers in uniform, were making $208,000 a year each protecting the drug dealers who were killing people like Julia Parker, and that was on top of their NYPD salary and whatever they were making selling drugs. Buckley was never invited to testify. They had other "more expert" witnesses scheduled, he was told.

The year 1994 was turning out to be as miserable as the year before. In Walter Thabit's book *How East New York Became a Ghetto* he wrote about a recent survey of junior high schoolers in East New York. Thirty-three percent said that in the past four months they'd "badly beat" someone, 26 percent had carried a weapon, 15 percent had robbed someone, and 13 percent, around 110 children—sixth graders—had been arrested. Only a third of East New York students were reading at or above their grade level.

Many East New Yorkers didn't have a family doctor, and instead would literally spend days in emergency rooms waiting to see a doctor. In collaboration with the NYC Health and Hospitals Corporation, the Maternity Center Association had been trying to open the Childbearing Center of East New York in the health center on Pennsylvania and Pitkin since 1992. There was an alarming shortage of obstetric and gynecological care in the neighborhood and infant mortality was high. But the 1992 opening was postponed, as was the opening planned for 1993. When the work group met to discuss what to do next, one member expressed the concern that a 1994 start "would be ruinous," financially. "How do I think this will end?" she later wrote to the board of directors. "Badly." The Childbearing Center of East New York never opened.

Over at the NYPD, a cultural shift had begun which would lead to changes that continue to be debated today. When William Bratton, then chief of the New York Transit Police, was appointed police commissioner of the NYPD in 1994, he brought Lieutenant Jack Maple along as his deputy commissioner of Operations. Maple had instituted a crime-tracking program for the transit police that they called their "Charts of the Future." It was simple. They stuck pins in maps that allowed them to track crime in the subways. It seems astounding, but until the Charts of the Future, no one was methodically monitoring crime in this way. The Charts of the Future evolved into an important piece of a new system the police were developing around crime statistics, called CompStat.

They went after petty crimes first, like graffiti in the subways. Known as the "Broken Windows" theory, the thinking was that these small crimes created an atmosphere of lawlessness that led to bigger crimes. Studies have found problems with the theory and its implementation. Years later, Professor Bernard E. Harcourt, director of the Columbia Center for Contemporary Critical Thought and author of *Illusion of Order: The False Promise of Broken Windows Policing*, said at a Columbia Law School talk, "There is no evidence that policing disorder lowers crime or that broken windows works. But it has had a tremendously disproportionate impact on African American and Hispanic communities."

The NYPD also put together a database of all the crimes committed in New York (an updated Charts of the Future) and started holding meetings twice a month in which all precinct and operational commanders in a patrol borough got together to grill the precinct commanders with the highest crime rates. John Timoney, who was made the NYPD's Chief of Department, had started reorganizing the command structure of the seventy-six precincts. One of the things he did was take the ten worst precincts and designate them "A houses." The next thirty became "B houses," and the remaining thirty-six were "C houses." The Seven-Five was classified as an A house. Once a precinct was named an A house, the commander had to come up with a plan to improve it and present the plan at the next CompStat meeting.

It's hard to understand why the NYPD didn't have a database before, if only on paper, and why the numbers they did have were often months behind, or why they weren't routinely responding to spikes in crime with meetings and plans. But it's not surprising that murders (and other crimes) started dropping once they were following the newly established procedures. But CompStat was not the only reason for the falling crime rates. Crime was decreasing across the United States. The crack epidemic that had amplified the crime rate was subsiding and that wasn't all due to the police. The National Institute of Justice would study crack's downturn in 1997 and write, "Ethnographic evidence suggests that the crack epidemic in New York City entered a decline around 1990 when youths began to disdain crack use." Nonprofits and community groups were a factor as well. A 2017 study found that cities with ten or more organizations "focusing on crime and community life" saw reductions in murder, violent crime, and property crime. The East New York Urban Youth Corps (ENYUYC), for instance, transformed a block on Williams Avenue by buying three abandoned buildings and rehabbing them. "You get rid of the crack house by buying it and making it a decent home for people," Executive Director Martin Dunn would later say at a Senate subcommittee hearing on Crime and Community Opportunity. The ENYUYC also provided an apartment to the police for surveillance, which led to hundreds of drug arrests, organized a block association, and created a community garden out of a vacant lot. In time, people returned to sitting on their stoops or in lawn chairs, watching their children playing on the sidewalks while they chatted with their neighbors.

In August 1994, the Zodiac was heard from one more time before disappearing again. He sent a letter to the *New York Post*, listing five victims, although the police were only able to identify four. The letter contained chilling lines, like "Sleep my little dead how we loathe them." And then, like before, he was gone.

Eighty-eight people were murdered in East New York in 1994, 32 percent fewer than the year before. Murder rates were finally starting to fall.

The FHA Scandal

1974

After Accetta, DePetris, and Bashion finished presenting the government's case, the defense attorneys made a flurry of motions to dismiss or acquit, which Travia denied. The show would go on.

Bernstein had been trying to get himself severed from the case, and on March 27, 1974, Abraham Brodsky, Harry Bernstein's lawyer, informed Judge Travia that Harry was currently in the hospital, having suffered chest pains at 5:00 a.m. that morning. Perhaps a possible heart attack would get it done.

To this day, all the living members of the prosecution speak highly of Abraham Brodsky. "A perfect gentleman with a knife-edge wit," as Accetta described him. "I really liked him," Gale Drexler said. "Wonderful gentleman. One of those people that could have the jury eating out of his hand because he was nice. He was polite. He was an old-school attorney. He treated everybody respectfully."

Brodsky asked Travia to call Harry's cardiologist, Dr. Charles Poindexter, who told the judge that there hadn't been any incremental damage to the heart, but to continue, "where he would probably be exposed to examination and cross-examination," would not be "safe, or wise." Another doctor wrote to AUSA George Bashion. "I believe that this individual would always be at risk if he were subjected to continued emotional strain that would be required during a court trial. This would be particularly true if he would have to take the witness stand."

On April 4, Brodsky attempted to sever Harry from the case due to health concerns. Harry was a tall man, but not imposing. He was also a quiet man, and Accetta could not remember having ever heard him speak. Rose generally did all the talking. But "he made a great actor as he lay on a gurney trying to convince the court his heart couldn't stand a trial," Accetta said. Travia wasn't buying it. Do you have any plans to have Bernstein testify? he asked Brodsky. No. Then he can attend and sit there, Travia concluded. Accetta remembers Travia said Harry could bring his doctors to court, and if needed, "we'll let you lie in bed." Harry sat stoically through the rest of the trial.

Like Brodsky, Judge Anthony J. Travia was greatly admired, at least by the prosecution. He was a "wonderful, common-sense guy," Accetta said. "He wouldn't take any nonsense. The defense would prod him, he wouldn't take the bait. They would say things intended to get him upset so they could get a mistrial, but he was too savvy for that." Drexler agreed. "He took no prisoners. He had his rulings. He wanted it run a certain way, and that would be it. But within those parameters, he had a tremendous sense of humor. He was a spry old man."

A week later Dr. Poindexter wrote to Travia, making a slightly different argument for severing Harry from the case. "I still feel that the anxiety and nervous tension created by being in the courtroom and hazarding the outcome of the jury's verdict, even though Mr. Bernstein is not subjected to direct and cross-examination, is very likely to be dangerous and to precipitate another attack of coronary thrombosis, which in turn, may be fatal." Travia did not change his decision and listed his reasons. Among them: the tests taken after the attack were "basically negative," the court would provide medical assistance, and as long as his wife remained on trial he was going to be anxious regardless.

While the trial went on, investigations by HUD, the FBI, and U.S. Attorney's offices were still underway in twenty cities, and efforts were also being made to stop the crimes before they started elsewhere. HUD's first inspector general, Charles Haynes, sent people around the country to educate their employees about mortgage crimes and how to prevent them. Perhaps with East New York in mind, HUD imposed stricter property standards and requirements for "life safety from fire," that had "to be complied with before the FHA will insure mortgages covering the structures."

The defendants would rest their case within a month. "There wasn't much that the defense could do from a legal perspective," Accetta said. The prosecution had the paper trail and the witnesses. They were cornered. At one point one of the witnesses testified that Rose Bernstein had been meeting with the FHA clerk on the staircase at the FHA office in Hempstead to make the payoffs. Joseph Soviero, Rose Bernstein's lawyer, tried to refute the claim. Look at her, he said to the jury. Can you imagine this lady, this sophisticated woman, going down a staircase and paying a bribe? She should be out on the golf course. "Everybody cracked up. It was so ridiculous that I think it helped convict her," Accetta said.

Once, during what was supposed to be a sidebar, Soviero and Travia got into an impassioned dispute when Soviero accused Travia of belittling him before the jurors using facial expressions. (The following exchange has been edited down.)

"Mr. Soviero, I want you to stop right there."

"No. I am not going to stop."

"That is the most insulting thing that you have done so far in this case . . . I have purposely made it my business not to even breathe. And when I have coughed, I have put my hand up . . . You are not going to tell me how to sit on the bench, whether I should put my hand toward my cheek, or whether I should put my hand under my chin, or whether I should sit with my legs crossed."

"This is not a sidebar any longer," Brodsky politely pointed out, when it was clear everyone in the courtroom could hear every word.

"May the record indicate," Soviero said, "that Your Honor is making the statement in front of the jury."

"Yes."

They continued quietly, in an actual sidebar, where Soviero accused Travia of snorting at one point and then trying to cover it with a cough.

Dun & Bradstreet's defense amounted to, "This is just a few grains of sand on a beach," Accetta said, summarizing their case, "and how can you hold an entire organization accountable for what some obscure manager in one of our offices did?"

They did not rebut what the Dun & Bradstreet credit analysts who testified had said. "They did not deny that there were false statements in their reports," Accetta said. "They had to concede that. They were left with, 'Well, this doesn't mean that the entire organization is at fault.'"

All the defense attorneys rested by May 15, 1974. Following another flurry of motions for acquittal, which were denied, the summations for both sides went on for weeks.

The FHA, meanwhile, had been phasing out the Hempstead office and consolidating it with their office in Manhattan. Sixty-four of the 145 people who worked there resigned rather than make the move.

On June 17, the jury retired for deliberations. "We all waited. Very nervously," Accetta said. The jury came back with their first verdict the very next day. They found FHA appraiser Joseph Jankowitz not guilty. George Bashion remembers Jankowitz's lawyer leaving the instant his client's verdict came in. "I never saw a lawyer leave a courtroom faster than that guy. He got up and left. He didn't say 'thank you, Your Honor,' he just walked out." Although all the defense lawyers were getting paid every day, they still had to sit through a nine-month trial when perhaps only twenty minutes applied to them.

Accetta was disappointed with the verdict, but not overly concerned. Jankowitz was "small potatoes" next to the other defendants.

"I think the jury felt sorry for him," Accetta concluded. "I was pretty sure he'd never take another bribe, and the time he spent from indictment through trial was punishment enough." He went back to waiting very nervously for the verdicts for the people he cared about the most. Harry and Rose Bernstein.

21

The Destruction of East New York

1995–1996

The homicide rate in East New York continued to fall. In 1995, forty-five people were murdered in East New York. Two years earlier, the number was 128. It wasn't just East New York either. Homicides in New York City overall had declined almost 48 percent in the last five years, tangible evidence that something was getting better. No one knew if the same could be said about financial crime. Twenty-one years after the defendants in one of the largest and longest trials of white-collar crime to date were convicted and sentenced, no one had a clue if white-collar crime was going up or down.

Every year, police departments across the country voluntarily report to the Federal Bureau of Investigation every murder and nonnegligent manslaughter, every rape, robbery, aggravated assault, burglary, larceny-theft, and car theft in their jurisdiction. The FBI publishes the results in a report called "Crime in the United States." There was no such report for white-collar crime. No one was gathering and compiling corresponding statistics. No one in the DOJ, FBI, the SEC, or in Attorney General offices across the country could have said if white-collar crime was getting better or worse. The SEC published how many cases it was working on, but without knowing the total

number of crimes committed, it was not a terribly enlightening figure. "Suspicious activity reports" (SARs) were filed with the Financial
Crimes Enforcement Network (FinCen), but not all financial institutions were required to file reports, which primarily address things
like possible money laundering or tax evasion. Also, banks that are
complicit are not going to generate a report on themselves. A year after
the Eastern Service trial concluded, the American Bar Association's
Committee on Economic Offenses had warned that the federal government was unable to "measure accurately its own efforts against
white-collar crime and to assess the impact of such offenses on the
country as a whole." Worse, what little data they had collected was of
"questionable validity." Not much had changed.

Granted, there are challenges to tracking white-collar crime. As
noted before, the evidence of financial crimes isn't splattered all over
the place as a clear indication a crime has been committed. In "The
Changing FBI: The Road to Abscam," James Q. Wilson sums up the
problem. "Many laws the FBI enforces—particularly those pertain-
ing to consensual crimes such as bribery—place heavy reliance on the
skill and energy of agents and field supervisors who must find ways
of discovering that a crime may have been committed before they
can even begin the process of gathering evidence that might lead to a
prosecution."

In 1969, former Manhattan district attorney Robert Morgenthau
warned that it was essential "that law enforcement agencies do not
follow the path of least resistance and concentrate their efforts only
on crimes which are readily discovered—crimes which are generally committed by the poor." But that is precisely what happened.
Financial predators had decimated neighborhoods across the United
States, demonstrating how destructive these crimes could be, but no
one ever launched a sustained effort to stop them. White-collar criminals have always had more influence and power to prevent investigation and arrest, and that power extends to whether there are laws
on the books that define their acts as crimes. As a result, no one was

investigating, arresting, and prosecuting white-collar criminals to the extent they were pursuing street criminals. The broken windows theory was not applied to financial crimes. New laws weren't being enacted. Agencies investigating white-collar crime did not receive additional funding, while federal programs to provide assistance and funding to local law enforcement had been ramping up beginning with the Law Enforcement Assistance Act in 1965. The act was the starting point of the federal government's involvement with local law enforcement and the "war on crime," which, more accurately, should have been called the "war on some crime." It was followed soon after by the 1968 Crime Control and Safe Streets Act. The 1994 Violent Crime Control and Law Enforcement Act led to more police and prisons for street criminals, but no one was suggesting beefing up any of the agencies investigating financial criminals. The budget for the SEC was slashed in 1994. (As was the FBI's budget, but the decrease was modest.) So while the crackdown on street crime accelerated, leading to a rise in complaints of police brutality in New York (and across the country), a corresponding crackdown on financial crimes had yet to be mounted. Fraud continued, but places like Rikers weren't filling up with bankers.

Instead, white-collar criminals enjoyed a largely unfettered crime spree, while people of color were being stopped on the street without cause, and if no other reason could be found to detain them, the police would fall back on the charge of disorderly conduct. The disorderly conduct statute is so broadly worded it can mean whatever the police and the courts want it to mean. As a result, for more than a century disorderly conduct arrests reflected the criminal justice biases of the time. In the nineteenth century there were more Irish men in prison under a disorderly conduct charge that any other group. In the twentieth century it was Black and Hispanic men.

The Commission to Combat Police Corruption (CCPC) was established in 1995, but it was created with officers like Michael Dowd in mind, and not those stopping and frisking innocent people, an act that was considered legitimate police work. The 1994 Crime Act ultimately led to locking up more Black men, and did not address the white-collar criminals who victimized them.

Murderers and other street criminals absolutely needed to be stopped and held accountable. But while the police were busy locking up street criminals, white-collar crime continued relatively unabated, and the subprime mortgage scandal of the 1970s would reemerge in a sophisticated and far-reaching form, involving so many more players and destroying exponentially more lives. Today only a small group of people even remember that it had all happened before and that little was done to stop it from happening again.

Every year featured new battles as East New York continual- ly strove to recover. After being turned down by the tony village of Southampton, NY, the Atlas Bio-Energy Corporation announced plans to build a wood-burning incinerator in East New York instead. The New York State Department of Environmental Conservation de- cided the company didn't have to file the usual Environmental Impact Statement, even though Atlas would be building in a residential area that included schools and day care and senior centers.

The East New York Community Against the Incinerator group quickly formed, chaired by Charles Barron, a community activist and former Black Panther who would later become a member of the New York City Council and New York State Assembly. A dogged East New York resident working with the group tracked down a city code prohibiting incinerators that ultimately saved the day.

The city initially ignored the letter bringing the code to their atten- tion. In response, hundreds of people attended a rally at the incinerator site on July 15, in 105-degree weather, joined by the reverend Johnny Ray Youngblood, members of the EBC, and other community groups. They followed up with letters and petitions and created a lot of bad press for the city. In August, the city reversed its earlier decision and informed Atlas it would have to prepare an Environmental Impact Statement. By November, the incinerator project was defeated. (The company would try again in 1996 and would be defeated once again.)

That same year, the Pratt Institute Center for Community and Environmental Development (PICCED) started meeting with East New York residents and community organizations like the East New York Urban Youth Corps and the United Community Centers, to develop plans for addressing issues like economic development, youth centers, and safety, paid for by a two-year grant from HUD. The group became known as the East New York Planning Group.

New maps of East New York were produced by Pratt depicting, among other things, the existing number of vacant lots, parks, community gardens, and recreational space. They found 220 lots being used as community gardens, some made up of adjacent lots to make a total of approximately eighty distinct gardens, including the New Visions Garden that Marlene Wilks, Eliza Butler, and others had started on Schenck Avenue in 1990. That is an "extraordinarily high number," the Planning Group wrote. East New York, it turned out, had more community gardens than any other neighborhood in New York.

"Some people who started those gardens remembered the buildings that were there and burnt down," said Sarita Daftary-Steel, a future director of the East New York Farms! project. Resurrecting those barren plots of earth to produce new life, color, fragrance and sustenance was invigorating and restorative. There's also "a lot of power and agency in being able to transform those spaces," Daftary-Steel continued. "People are really deciding what goes in there in every way, what's planted, and what activities happen. Having that much say over a space, it feels pretty rare. People get to express the neighborhood character a little bit, or build out their own little spaces that then get to be public spaces."

That fall the East New York Planning Group held "envisioning forums" in various parts of the neighborhood. They talked to East New Yorkers about their concerns and needs, and tried to come up with projects to address what was important to them.

The Pratt maps had revealed that there were 1,300 vacant lots in East New York that were owned by the city. They also highlighted the fact that there were only two supermarkets in central East New York supplementing the bodegas, which did not offer much in the way of produce. This gave them an idea.

Supporting the gardeners and establishing new gardens in these abandoned lots, they all realized, would speak to many of the issues raised in the forums. It would help decrease crime and provide much of what East New York needed: "employment, health, security, and recreation." The gardens could also supply fresh produce.

Around this time, UCC staff were making plans to bus the children from their day care center to Prospect Park to play because the playground in the park on Schenck Avenue was too dangerous. "We met with the parents," Mel Grizer remembered. "We discussed cleaning the park up instead and getting police surveillance." With their neighbors, they went in and, among other things, painted cheerful murals on the park house, restoring it to a place that was safe for children. The police cleared out the drug dealers from the vacant building that sat between the day care center and an abandoned lot. The city, who owned the building, fixed it up and families moved in. The UCC then turned their attention to the lot. They enlisted their neighbors to help them build boxes, and a trellis, and soon after they opened a farmers market. Teenagers and voluntary community farmers maintained plots in the early garden and tables at the farmers market to sell their produce. "We couldn't grow enough produce for a market," Grizer said, so they arranged for commercial farmers to participate.

Out of these early efforts, the organization East New York Farms! came into being and was officially established in 1998. Many others from the East New York Planning Group and people from outside the group were involved in addition to Mel Grizer and the UCC, and they included Perry Winston from Pratt, John Ameroso from Cornell University Cooperative Extension, and two of his trainees, Aley Schoonmaker and Georgine Yorgey. The East New York Farms! would continue what the early garden creators had started. Where there were once holes spreading throughout East New York, threatening to suck all the remaining homes into one gigantic mass grave of buildings, there would now be gardens. The former empty lot is now the UCC Community educational garden, which supplies produce for the East New York Farms Street Market on Schenck Avenue.

The EBC kept pushing forward. Construction of homes west of Pennsylvania Avenue finally began in 1996. The EBC still had their eye on the Spring Creek area along the southern perimeter of East New York. They were originally told the ground was too toxic for residential building, but the city would later change their position. The EBC was invited to submit a proposal, and in 1996 plans for five hundred homes for what would be part of a development called the Gateway Estates had begun.

The Mutual Housing Association of New York (MHANY) continued to rehabilitate buildings, and still more housing was made available through the Local Initiatives Support Corporation (LISC), a national organization that supported community development organizations. Carey Shea, the director of the East New York Urban Youth Corps, had been recruited by LISC. Reagan had "wiped out most of the HUD programs that East New York had relied on for years and years," said Shea. "But the one thing the Republicans kind of allowed to come forward was the Low-Income Housing Tax Credit (LIHTC). It was very experimental. No one knew how to make it work or how to use it. Andy Ditton, at LISC, figured a way that investors could partner with nonprofit organizations who had no use for a tax refund, but desperately needed the investment dollars." By 1996 the ENYUYC had bought and renovated thirty-three formerly abandoned buildings, and then started construction on seven more.

A complex web of political machinations ran underneath much of the housing efforts in East New York, with some groups siding with one politician or another, some of whom were as much interested in a patronage opportunity, or the good press, as helping East New York. "In East New York you have so many camps and so many people who are in so many folks' pockets, be they politicians or people who are connected to money, or have been given a job or a program," Charles

Barron told a writer for *City Limits*. Like community organizers everywhere, activists had to effectively manage conflicting agendas to get
anything done.

While housing efforts continued, the number of murders continued
to go down. In 1996 there were forty-three homicides in East New York.

There was other good news in 1996. It was the year the police finally
captured the New York Zodiac. On June 18 a call came in about a
fifteen-year-old girl who'd been shot at 2730 Pitkin Avenue. A shoot-
out with the police followed, which developed into a hostage situation. By this time Detective Sergeant Joe Herbert was now assigned to
Brooklyn North Homicide and was working as hostage negotiator. He
was brought in to assist. Herbert remembered his introduction to Pitkin
Avenue and the Seven-Five. He was a detective in the Seven-One
when an investigation in the mid-1980s took him to Pitkin Avenue.
"I had always heard about the Seven-Five. It was notorious." It was a
steamy summer night and they drove with the car windows down. "I
never heard so much gunfire in my life. I said to myself, 'Everything
that they say about this place is right.'" Over the police radio there were
more calls of "10-13, shots fired" then he'd ever heard before. "I said to
the guys I was with, 'This is unbelievable, this place.'" When he was assigned there later on, Herbert was honored by the transfer. "I felt like I
was walking into the most prestigious detective command, the busiest,
and I was very proud to be given this assignment."

Four blocks of Pitkin had been cordoned off, and snipers were
positioned on the roof while Herbert, sweating in his bulletproof
vest, talked to the shooter for three hours through a door. The shooter
agreed to surrender, but before he came out his arsenal of weapons was
lowered to the street in buckets. It took three buckets to empty the
apartment of thirteen zip guns and other items of destruction.

When twenty-eight-year-old Heriberto Seda came out, Herbert
arrested him and turned him over to Detective Danny Powers. Seda
didn't like his sister's boyfriend, they learned, so he had shot her and
held them both hostage. Back at the Seven-Five, Seda wrote out his

confession on a legal pad. At the bottom, before he signed his name, he wrote a symbol. Powers asked him what the symbol meant and Seda talked about Jesus and Faust. The Zodiac had signed his letters with the name Faust. Powers was very familiar with the Zodiac case and he put it all together. The symbol, all the zip guns, and the mention of Faust.

He took the written confession back to the crime scene and showed it to Herbert. "The handwriting jumped right out at me," Herbert said. He went through the rest of the confession. "This is the Zodiac," he said. Ballistics, DNA, and fingerprints would later confirm it.

As the carnage subsided throughout New York, people started to look back at the wreckage. From 1985 to 1996, there were officially 20,500 murders in New York. The actual total is likely significantly higher. When a medical examiner needs more information before classifying a death as a homicide, the ME temporarily classifies the death as a CUPPI (Circumstances Undetermined Pending Police Investigation)—and those are excluded from the homicide statistics. Homicides deemed "justifiable" are also not added to the list. Finally, a percentage of the thousands of people who go missing every year are actually homicides. But unless a body is found, their case remains on a separate list.

Of those 20,500 known homicides, 6,796 were never solved. Given that cases in which the suspect was freed or found not guilty are not returned to the total of open homicides, the number of cold cases is also likely higher in reality. Still, 6,796 is a lot of unsolved murders. Perhaps because they had a minute to breathe, Jack Maple, the deputy police commissioner of the NYPD, and Deputy Inspector Edward Norris, who was working in the office of the Chief of Department, floated the idea of establishing a Cold Case Squad.

The FHA Scandal

1974

In his summation, defense attorney Abraham Brodsky called the government's witnesses "liars," and "self-confessed wrongdoers out to save their own hides." But the jury had believed them. After one week of deliberations, they came back with guilty verdicts for the Eastern Service Corporation, Harry and Rose Bernstein, Eastern Service assistant vice president Florence Behar, and realtor and Eastern Service mortgage solicitor Melvin Cardona.

Years before, the first time Accetta won a case, the defense attorney asked to poll the jury to confirm the guilty verdicts that had just been announced. "I was all excited," Accetta said, "because I had won. Boy am I good." As each jury member was polled, Accetta inwardly cheered.

"Juror number 1, is that your verdict?"

"Yes."

("Yay!" Accetta yelled to himself.)

"Juror number 2?"

"Yes."

("Yay!")

"Juror number 3?"

Somewhere around the fourth or fifth juror, Accetta looked up and started watching the defendants, a young couple from Astoria who'd been passing counterfeit money. "Every time a juror said yes their heads drooped a little more, and a little bit more. I felt bad for them. You're going to jail and I'm putting you there. I grew up that day. After that I never gloated about getting a conviction again. As a prosecutor. This is your job. It's nothing to celebrate."

Until the Eastern Service case. When the jury found Harry and Rose guilty of sixty counts involving conspiracy, bribery, and making false statements, back at the U.S. Attorney's office, "I opened up a bottle of scotch. Harry and Rose were just evil people. They were corrupting the federal government as well as the mortgage people and the FHA programs they were taking advantage of." Someone was finally being held accountable for the financial and emotional cost to all those people who'd lost everything, to the neighborhoods where they lived, and to society as a whole. Accetta raised his glass believing Harry and Rose were the first of many who would finally answer for all that ruin.

The jury had yet to decide the fate of Dun & Bradstreet, the Dun & Bradstreet manager Arthur Prescott, and the former chief underwriter of the FHA's Hempstead office, Herbert Cronin.

On July 2, the jury foreman informed Judge Travia that they were hopelessly deadlocked on the charges for Herbert Cronin. Travia declared a mistrial. Accetta had made his peace with it when appraiser Joseph Jankowitz was ultimately acquitted, but he was deeply disappointed and angry about Cronin. "Because he was truly a bad guy, and at the center of the whole scheme. We never specifically proved he took money, only circumstances that put him in up to his neck. Very disappointing outcome."

The night before, twelve people in East New York became homeless when a fire in an abandoned building spread to the two buildings on either side.

A few days later, on July 5, mistrials were also called for Dun & Bradstreet and Arthur Prescott. To this day Accetta regrets that he didn't respond to Dun & Bradstreet's argument that Prescott's actions were essentially a drop in the bucket compared to the work of the entire company. "That's like a bank robber arguing, 'Look at all banks I didn't rob.'"

Edward R. Korman, U.S. Attorney David Trager's assistant and a future federal court judge in the Eastern District, told reporters that they hadn't made a decision yet about retrying the case.

Ten months before the trial, when Donald Carroll was sentenced, Judge Travia had said, "That whole scheme has cost the government upward of two or three hundred million dollars, and who's paying for that!"

"The public," one of the prosecutors answered.

Travia agreed, adding, "Joe Blow, the guy on the street, is paying for the high living of many."

Later, when the Bernsteins appealed their convictions, their lawyer would refer back to Travia's statement. "The Bernsteins live in a highly mortgaged and modest house. Both are physically impaired to the point where they could not indulge in high living if they could afford it."

Harry Bernstein was sentenced to five years in prison. His firm Eastern Service was fined $460,000, and he was fined $175,000. Rose got four years and a $50,000 fine. Melvin Cardona, who'd reached out to Agent Sniegocki in the hope of getting a more lenient sentence for cooperating, was given a concurrent sentence of two years and a $17,000 fine. Florence Behar was also given a two-year concurrent sentence and a $21,000 fine.

In July, Korman told reporters that twelve other cases were awaiting trial.

After sentencing had concluded in the Eastern Service, Inter-Island Mortgage Corporation, and United Institutional Servicing Corporation cases, the FBI approached the Eastern District about taking Springfield Equities to trial next. But the Eastern District "had enough of the FHA and VA mortgage fraud cases," FBI Agent Jeff Kay said.

"One thing you don't say to the FBI after they've spent all this time and money investigating a case is that you don't want to prosecute it.

We had the evidence and the witnesses. We couldn't go to the Southern District, it was a Brooklyn case."

Jeff Kay went to his boss at the FBI's New York office, who contacted FBI Headquarters in Washington to see if the Fraud Section of Main Justice might be interested in taking on the case. "The worst thing in the world for a local U.S. attorney," Kay explained, "is to have Washington call him and tell him, 'Hey, if you guys don't want to prosecute this case, we're going to send somebody from Washington to prosecute your case.'" The Eastern District decided they would prosecute the case after all.

Before the Eastern District was done during this crackdown on mortgage fraud, more than seventy criminals would be convicted and several mortgage banks closed.

Stanley Sirote's sentence reflected his cooperation and also the sympathy he'd managed to engender, even among members of the prosecution. "I always had the impression from Sirote that he was reluctant to get involved with these guys at the FHA and VA," said Jeff Kay. "But in his mind if he wanted to compete with Eastern and save his company he had to do what Eastern was doing and pay these people off. When Sirote became a cooperating defendant witness he came across with solid information and evidence. I don't recall Sirote ever giving us any false or misleading information." Sirote was sentenced to three years, suspended, and given a $40,000 fine.

Government witness Ortrud Kapraki cried before Travia sentenced her, in a desperate attempt for leniency. She was given a five-year suspended sentence and a $5,000 fine. Edward Goodwin got three years suspended, and a $5,000 fine.

During the summer, while everyone was waiting for sentencing, Nixon had lifted the moratorium he'd imposed on subsidized housing, and Congress passed the Housing and Community Development Act of 1974 under Ford. Sections 235 and 236 would resume, but funding was slashed.

■

When Romney resigned as the secretary of HUD in 1972, he wrote, "The experience has been a rewarding and invaluable one that, among other things, has deepened my understanding of our country's political processes." It is not difficult to read between the lines. It was not the system grounded in honor and integrity that the devout Mormon would have hoped to find.

Two months after the Eastern Service trial ended, on August 8, President Richard Nixon resigned as well. In his resignation speech he said, "I hope that I will have hastened the start of that process of healing which is so desperately needed in America," without referencing any wounds beyond those caused by Watergate. After listing his specific achievements in foreign affairs, he spoke only generally about what he had accomplished back home. "Here in America, we are fortunate that most of our people have not only the blessings of liberty but also the means to live full and good and, by the world's standards, even abundant lives." He failed to mention such fortune did not apply to people of color.

In another two months, and almost two weeks after sentencing for the Eastern Service case had concluded, Judge Travia joined the resignation procession. "I didn't think that might be my last big trial," he said of the Eastern Service case, while they were in court wrapping up post-trial motions. "I really took a lot of pains to do the best job I knew how on that case. So I paid very careful attention and listened to every witness and . . . Some of these witnesses were really something for the books." He did not name names, presumably because those listening knew exactly who he was talking about.

AUSA Ronald DePetris said, "I would certainly hope the length of the trial had nothing to do with your Honor's retirement."

"It did not. Let me put that to rest right now. I enjoyed that case, every day of it. Like everything else I have done all my life, I always enjoyed my job. When it came time to up and quit, I upped and quit. Wouldn't be the first time and it had nothing to do with the case. I have enjoyed every day I have been a judge in this court . . . I feel strongly about this case. I did participate with all my heart and mind."

Isaiah Montgomery had come home to East New York after having served in Vietnam just as Secretary of State John Lomenzo was uncovering evidence of housing crimes. Montgomery found a wasteland. "It was a lovely neighborhood" when he left, but "when I came back to East New York it was the biggest shock I ever had." The block where he lived was nothing but abandoned buildings and vacant lots. On some blocks, there was only one house left standing. "It could have been a great place for a lot of people, from a lot of different backgrounds, it could have been a marvelous place," said former resident Toni Richardson. "But somebody just threw a bomb in there and wrecked it."

The bomb throwers were now free on bail pending their appeals.

22

The Destruction of East New York

1996–2023

Five years after Julia Parker was murdered, despite a tremendous amount of resistance, the NYPD established a Cold Case Squad. There were a number of reasons why many within the NYPD fought against the formation of the squad. Until they merged in 1995, the New York Transit Police and the NYPD were separate police departments. At the time, there was a feeling in the NYPD that they were simply better cops than the Transit guys. The Cold Case Squad came about in part due to Jack Maple, a former Transit Police lieutenant. He filled the Cold Case Squad with a lot of former Transit detectives. If the Cold Case detectives, Transit guys no less, actually cleared some of the old homicides, it would make the NYPD detectives look bad.

As far as the Cold Case Squad commanders were concerned, if the precinct detectives weren't clearing any of the 6,796 unsolved murders, to hell with their fear of looking bad. The squad solved hundreds of cases in the first few years, but that initial run of success began to wane as the squad went from around fifty detectives in 1996 to fourteen in 2023. The number of unsolved murders has meanwhile increased from 6,796 in 1996 to an estimated 11,942 in 2023. (The reporting of clearance rates is chaotic and often conflicting. The unsolved murder total is based on an average clearance rate of 65 percent, and that percentage was calculated using NYPD printouts listing 8,977 open homicides from 1985 to 2009.) Fourteen detectives to solve nearly 12,000 homicides. With so many cases, how to even choose which to pursue? If anyone was going to object to the formation of the Cold Case Squad, it should have been the detectives assigned to it. They were facing an overwhelming number of cases, every one of which had defeated the detectives who had taken the first shot at solving them.

Of all the precincts in New York City, East New York has the highest number of unsolved murders. In 2021, Cold Case Detective William Simon agreed to take a look at Julia Parker's case.

Detective Simon joined the NYPD in 1999, after serving thirty years in the United States Army, where he was awarded a Bronze Star and a Purple Heart. In 2015 he transferred to the Cold Case Squad. He worked cases with the sometimes single-minded determination of an "army tank sergeant," another detective said. When the sister of a 1968 murder victim reached out to Simon just before the COVID lockdowns began, he picked up the case and had it solved before the year was out, despite the pandemic.

■

Julia Parker's case had initially gone to Detective Al Nesbot, with Detective David Carbone assisting. The detectives talked to everyone who had remained on the scene and came up with one viable witness. Mateo Alvarez was in front of his home with his wife and son when the gunfire began. According to Alvarez, after shooting Julia and Ashmat, the shooter fired four more times and then started running, "menacing people with this gun." Alvarez and his family took cover underneath a car, but he believed he got a good enough look to identify him. The detectives also spoke to Luis Garcia (not his real name), who had known Julia for years, and who ran into the street when the shooting began. But it was the DA's office who learned that Garcia not only got a good look at the shooter, who "pointed a big, black revolver at me" as he fled the scene, but that Garcia recognized him. On several occasions he'd seen him buying drugs in the lobby of a building across the street from Thomas Jefferson High School.

The detectives spoke with a number of people over the next few days. The most productive conversation was with one of Julia's relatives, Diego (not his real name). His information came from the people who worked for VSB, the drug dealer Julia was arrested with in North Carolina. Julia was going to testify against VSB, he said, and VSB had simply made sure that never happened. VSB gave a "crackhead a gun," drove him to the corner of Pennsylvania and Dumont Avenues, pointed out Julia, parked over on New Jersey Avenue, and waited. "The crackhead got out," Diego said, "walked down Dumont to Pennsylvania, came up behind her, and shot her."

This story didn't appear to be told by a victim's loving and sympathetic brother. Simon suspects Diego was somehow involved. Not necessarily in the killing of his sister, but, like Julia, he might have worked for VSB. According to the case files, after Julia died, someone yelled at Diego, "Why did you kill your sister?" He answered, "That's what happens when you fuck around." Why would they ask him that and not, "Why was your sister killed?" And why on earth would he answer the way he did?

Over the next few days Nesbot and Carbone got more versions of the same story. Julia was involved with drugs, she got caught, then she "snitched" on VSB. But what if this was nothing more than a rumor that had been going around? The detectives needed to find someone with firsthand knowledge of what had happened. They weren't about to bring VSB in until they'd built a solid case, and they didn't want to tip him off in the meantime. "They had one shot," Simon explained, "and if they brought him in and he said he wanted a lawyer, then that's it. It's over."

Julia's case file has very few DD5s, a follow-up form that is filled out every time something happens in a case. There are no DD5s indicating that the detectives tried to find out exactly who Diego had gotten his information from. No DD5s list the names of Julia's closest friends, or which of them they'd spoken to or tried to speak to. There's nothing about a possible connection to the Darryl Jenkins case, or any other murder in the neighborhood, and there are only a few DD5s describing what the detectives did to try to learn more about VSB, his associates, or the drug operation. Julia's mother, Nancy, told the detectives there was a birthday party for Julia's son coming up on September 21 and most of her closest friends were going to be there. Maybe if they came, they could find someone who knew more. But there's no DD5 indicating the detectives made an appearance.

The lack of DD5s doesn't necessarily mean they didn't do all of these things. It's likely they weren't quite as methodical about filling out DD5s as they would have been if there weren't over one hundred murders a year. Also, knowing that everything they write in a DD5 is going to be turned over to the defense if there's a trial, detectives will hold off writing about a lead they're following until they have solid information.

The DD5s did note that VSB was arrested for selling drugs on November 18, and that Mr. Fayetteville was in New York and had been arrested for criminal possession of a weapon the following day. Not long after that the detectives conducted a lineup, but only Mateo Alvarez was present, and not Luis Garcia, who said he actually recognized the shooter. Nothing came of it.

The last time a DD5 was added to the file was February 6, 1992. Nesbot had retired by then, and the detectives who took over the case attempted to speak to the person who allegedly drove the car that took the killer to where Julia and Ashmat Ali were hanging out, but he'd moved. Usually DD5s saying something along the lines of "no new developments" would be added periodically to a file, but no DD5s followed. For the next twenty-nine years no one opened Julia Parker's file.

■

When Detective Simon picked up Julia's case in 2021, he looked through everything the detectives in the Seven-Five had done and made a preliminary list of things he could do to follow up. He would reach out to the DEA to see where things stood with their case. He would track down VSB and Mr. Fayetteville, the men Julia was arrested with, to see what became of them. He would also locate Ashmat Ali, who was with Julia when she died. What did he remember? Was there anything he hadn't told the detectives because he was too afraid at the time? Simon would also try to find the original lead detective on the case, Al Nesbot. Was there anything he didn't record in the DD5s, a hunch he wasn't able to nail down, perhaps? Finally, he would contact Julia's family and friends. Julia's sister Milagros had supplied the names of the three people who knew Julia best. If she had confided in anyone, it would probably have been one of them.

A former cold case commanding officer once said, "If you don't have the God damn thing solved in a couple of days you've got a problem. In most cases, if you don't have viable leads within a couple of days, this thing isn't going to go. You're going to get stuck with a cold case." At the end of one year, the chance of solving a case that has gone cold has dwindled to 5 to 10 percent. After two years, that chance decreases to less than 1 percent.

With a thirty-two-year-old case, the odds were against Detective Simon. Every step he took led nowhere. The DEA couldn't help him. Without Julia they didn't have a case, and they had moved on. He learned that VSB had been deported to Jamaica twenty-five years ago after repeated drug arrests. Mr. Fayetteville's last arrest was in 2014 for drunk driving. If he'd learned that they were facing a trial, Simon could have tried working out a deal with them. "Help me with this case, and I'll see that the judge goes easy on you on this and the other charges." But there were no outstanding charges against either of them, and he was unable to learn anything from anyone else he contacted.

Julia's family wouldn't talk to him, her friends weren't talking to anyone, and no one would explain why. Perhaps they knew more about her involvement with drugs, and they wanted to protect her memory. Maybe they were just unwilling to reopen their wounds for strangers. Julia's father, who was initially angry when approached, softened and said, "You're doing a good thing, but I cannot help you." He agreed to reach out to his son, Julia's relative Diego, to see if he'd talk to Simon, but he didn't look hopeful. Diego was never heard from.

Simon was accustomed to the lack of cooperation. The neighborhood is understandably wary of the police. With unsolved murders he explained, "tragedies leave a scar so deep, that over time just gets worse. Some people have dealt with it and are reluctant to go back, especially if it leads to nowhere." He stopped for a minute, then added, "I hate calling families." Even if you have a solid lead, he explained, you have to convince a district attorney to take the case to trial. "You can't guarantee that anything you do will go anywhere." Simon is in many ways as hesitant to stir up terrible memories as the people he approaches.

Even those who wanted to help solve the case only led him to dead ends. Ashmat Ali hadn't held back all those years ago and couldn't offer anything new or useful. Al Nesbot, who still drives by the corner of Pennsylvania and Dumont and thinks of Julia and her murder, couldn't remember specific details about her case. He'd hoped that reviewing his notes from the case files would jog his memory, but it was a hope that would once again go nowhere.

Before Detective Simon retired in 2022, he arranged for another detective to take over Julia's case. Unfortunately, the detective who agreed to take the case did not do anything to move the investigation forward, and almost immediately went radio silent. After one meeting and a few texts, the next detective who said he would take the case was also never heard from again. The current Cold Case Squad, in its diminished state, lacked either the will or the manpower to do anything more, and the case files that Detective Simon had retrieved from the Seven-Five were returned to storage. That simple transfer removed the final hope of solving Julia's murder.

Now retired, Simon offered to continue working on Julia's case as a private investigator, but no new leads emerged. Former detectives and commanding officers and a DEA agent who was active in the Seven-Five were contacted. While some remembered Julia, none of them remembered having ever heard of the drug dealers she was involved with. Luis Garcia, who said he recognized the shooter, could not be found.

There was still one item in Julia's case files that offered a shred of hope: former detective Al Nesbot's handwritten notes. There was a possibility that they contained information that would help Nesbot remember something useful, a lead he wasn't able to follow all the way, a name he didn't want to write down on a DD5 until he had. But when Simon asked a former colleague still on the job to get the case files back from storage, he learned that detectives now need prior approval before requesting files, and for the most part, only cold cases where it was possible to conduct forensic genealogy were getting approved. Forensic genealogists use DNA analysis to find suspects by tracking them through relatives whose DNA is available in public databases. With thousands of unsolved murders, the NYPD was focusing on the ones they had a real chance of solving, and biological evidence that might provide DNA greatly increased their chances.

Biological evidence was never collected in Julia's case. This was not unusual. Using DNA to solve cases was still very new at the time of Julia's murder, and there wouldn't have been much biological evidence to collect in any case. The murderer didn't touch her. He shot her and ran, leaving no trace evidence. There were no records in the case files of any shells that had been collected at the scene. It was the end of the line. Julia's case files would remain in storage.

When Simon first read through Julia's case, he was optimistic about solving her murder. He'd even reached out to the FBI to form a joint investigation. He had two solid leads, VSB and Mr. Fayetteville. Surely he could find out enough to bring them in. Relationships change, and there was a chance that there was someone who'd been unwilling to talk then, who might be open to talking now. There wasn't. It was over.

Like every other cold case detective, Simon was not unfamiliar with the merciless reality of working in the Cold Case Squad. "85 percent of the cases I work on I can't solve. It's a horrible way to make a living.

Imagine that's your legacy," he said, "failing 85 percent of the time."

Unless the killer voluntarily steps forward, Julia Parker's murder will likely never be solved. With the squad in its current reduced state, neither will James Dyson's, who died so his neighbors could have a decent place to live, or Toya Gillard's, who was shot while reaching to save her little boy, or Frank Falleti's, the kindest man to ever operate a food cart. Solving the murder of eleven-year-old Eric Dean, who died at the beginning of it all in 1966, would take nothing less than a miracle.

The lack of answers for all those deaths has consequences. Mention Julia to her mother and she collapses into sobs that wrack her body so violently she struggles to breath. Multiply that by the mothers, fathers, brothers, sisters, and friends of nearly twelve thousand other victims, and you have an idea of the cataclysmic toll. Death is a fact of life, but murder, and particularly murders that lack even the semblance of closure, ruins the world for all those who are left behind. Even for those who didn't know the victims, in East New York, where squad cars are perpetually parked in the most dangerous projects and people still plan where they will walk and when, the neighborhood continues to struggle under the traumatic weight and unconscionable number of all those unanswered crimes.

The FHA Scandal

1974–1979

Perhaps because white-collar criminals have enjoyed a long history of committing crimes without any consequences, when the government occasionally has the audacity to hold them accountable, they have learned that responding as if they are the aggrieved party can be a winning strategy. But for the Eastern Service case it appeared, at first, that this strategy wasn't working. Louis Bernstein (Harry and Rose's son) sued the FHA when they'd stopped doing business with him following the March indictments. He lost. In 1975, Continental Management, formerly Inter-Island Mortgage Corporation, sued the FHA for money owed them from their mortgage insurance contracts. The government countersued for the money Inter-Island had paid in bribes, and won. Joseph Jankowitz, the FHA appraiser who was acquitted on June 18, 1974, reported to the FHA for duty, and sued for back pay. He lost.

In the meantime, the government and their victims were left with the aftermath. The damage was done and the prosecutions would not bring the city services back, renovate the neglected buildings, or fill the empty lots. The FHA now owned thousands of buildings that they'd insured for far more than they were worth. Every sale would be at a loss. East New York, which many compared to the bombed-out Berlin of WWII, was forced to recover in a city and country that even now was still not ready to fully acknowledge what had happened or summon the massive effort required to help them.

Before the year was out Accetta left his position at the Eastern District. Early on, Robert Morse had told him "hubris sets in after four years." Accetta was coming up on those four years and he was ready to move on. He did not have the relationship with U.S. Attorney Trager that he'd had with Morse, "So I moved to Colorado without a job, but with a couple of introductions." Soon after he got an interview with the incoming attorney general, who was in the process of hiring staff. Within two weeks, he became the first assistant attorney general. His legal assistant, Gale Drexler, had friends in Colorado and was planning a visit. Tony called her and said, "Bring clothes with you."

"Tony," she answered, "I'm really not going to come out without clothes."

"No, work clothes.'

"Why?"

"Because you have a job."

Accetta stayed in the position as long as he "was allowed to do my thing." When "politics decreed I couldn't," he quit and established a small firm doing general civil litigation. In 1998 he started The Accetta Group, LLC, conducting due diligence and fraud investigation for major investment banks, maintaining offices in New York, Denver, and London.

Assistant U.S. Attorney George Bashion was the next to leave, also in 1974. His father was ill and his family told him he was needed back home to help run the family carpet business. Bashion loved the law and was deeply disappointed to leave, but he couldn't turn his back on his family.

AUSA Ronald DePetris went on to become the chief of the Criminal Division. At one point he left the Eastern District to go into private practice, returning in 1982 to serve as the chief assistant U.S.

attorney. He left again in 1986, to specialize in white-collar criminal defense and civil fraud litigation.

HUD attorney John Kennedy did what he could to respond to the rampant fraud, including establishing the Mortgagee Review Board in 1975. HUD and FHA employees and others could refer cases to the board to make sure lenders were in compliance with all the housing program regulations. The Board had the power to withdraw HUD's approval to lenders to make FHA-insured loans, or to refer cases to the Department of Justice. The assistant secretary of Fair Housing had a seat on the board to review cases of discrimination, and the inspector general was advisor to the board. Critics would say the board never pursued fraud aggressively or often enough, and that is likely true, but it is also true of every other group pursuing financial crimes. And like every other group, they were never given the staff or the budget to do so.

Under Director Clarence Kelley, in 1975 the FBI reported that they'd increased their pursuit of white-collar criminals, which led to a 30 percent increase in convictions over the previous eighteen months. Critics would complain about them as well, including U.S. Attorney Trager, who in 1976 would tell the *New York Times*, "Most of the cases they bring to us are insignificant . . . I don't think they have the ability or the people to do the job in areas we consider priorities—official corruption and white-collar crime."

At the end of the year Kelley would continue to defend their white-collar efforts, saying that so far in 1976 there had been 4,600 convictions, an increase of 856 from the previous year, and that they now had more than 800 special agent accountants working white-collar investigations. This was, of course, nothing compared to the armies of police in every town and city across America going after street criminals. The Subcommittee on Civil and Constitutional Rights, of the Committee on the Judiciary, would conduct an inquiry in 1977 and find the FBI weak on white-collar investigation, focusing on welfare fraud and other small-scale crimes and noting the "reluctance on the part of FBI personnel, particularly at the supervisory level, to get involved in more complex investigations that may require significant allocation of manpower for long periods of time." The special agent accountants who investigated the Eastern Service case proved that they were more than capable.

The Justice Department kept pursuing cases. James Robinson, an attorney in their Criminal Division, testified in 1975 that "since October 1972 to today, [a Housing Fraud Task Force has] returned 594 indictments, against 752 defendants, resulting in 496 convictions, 85 acquittals . . . which leaves 171 defendants pending trial and a sizable number of investigations still in progress in the 17 target cities."

At the time Accetta left the Eastern District, there were other related mortgage fraud cases awaiting trial. The Eastern District pursued at least some of the cases that remained. Stephen Rosenbaum of Springfield Equities was found guilty in 1976 and sentenced to four months in prison and three years' probation. It was an incredibly light sentence, which exemplified another problem with white-collar prosecutions. Even when white-collar criminals are found guilty, judges are more lenient with them than they are with street criminals. As he imposed the sentence, Judge John Dooling said Rosenbaum, whose fraud had involved United States veterans, was a "fundamentally good man." AUSA David Gould took exception to the characterization. "No one was hit on the head," he responded, "but people suffered tremendously—communities were blighted." Dooling was not moved.

U.S. Attorney Robert Fiske Jr. complained that too many judges believe that being convicted is punishment enough for white-collar criminals, because "people won't talk to him at the bar in his country club." A businessman's fall "from grace with his peers" was a reasonable substitute for a prison sentence, and there was no need to pile on with incarceration.

After Springfield Equities, the Eastern District of New York declined to proceed with the remaining cases. It was possible that "the same attitude that delayed or prevented cases like this from proceeding back in 1970 prevailed again in 1975," Accetta theorized.

Walter Thabit returned to East New York at the end of 1975 to see what had happened since he left. Had the Eastern District prosecutions brought foreclosure and abandonment to a halt? Would he be able to see a difference now that housing rehabilitation had been proceeding for a few years? He conducted another vacant building survey. Since his last survey in 1971, another 450 buildings had been abandoned and 240 buildings were demolished. Twenty to twenty-five blocks in the Model Cities area may be "unrecoverable," he wrote, and another fifteen to twenty blocks between Van Siclen and Barbey were "all but destroyed." Business was not booming. "Shops along Sutter Avenue, the main shopping street, are still largely vacant," and two years after completion, the health center at Pennsylvania and Pitkin Avenues had yet to open. Houses "with poor wiring, bad plumbing, leaking roofs, rotted beams, and deteriorating plaster walls were still being sold at greatly inflated prices." It would take much longer to rebuild the neighborhood than it had to destroy it.

"Outside of Watergate and Vietnam, there is no greater scandal," said James M. Alter, chairman of Chicago's Governor's Commission on Mortgage Practices. "The cities are rotting and nobody seems to be responsible." Being snubbed at the country club was not enough to answer for this, and it wasn't going to bring the criminal activity to a halt.

In July 1976, U.S. Attorney David Trager filed a civil suit against Dun & Bradstreet, charging them with filing "false, fictitious, or fraudulent statements" on applications for FHA insurance for mortgages in Queens and Brooklyn. They hadn't succeeded in criminal court so they were going to try again in civil court. (Today the Eastern District is unable to locate the records for this suit.)

Harry and Rose Bernstein appealed their convictions and lost. The following year, even though they had yet to see a day in prison, Judge Weinstein, who was known as a great believer in rehabilitation and more lenient sentences, reduced their sentences. Harry's five years in jail became eighteen months in a community treatment center in the Bryant Hotel, but only at night, and he was "at liberty" on weekends.

Rose's four-year sentence was reduced to a year and a day, but she did go to actual prison. Once again, a judge decided that they'd suffered enough. "For all practical purposes," Judge Weinstein said, "they have been destroyed financially and in their status in society." AUSA Ronald DePetris was astounded. Accetta likes to tell the story that DePetris told Weinstein: "Your honor, this sentence is bullshit," and that Weinstein did not hold him in contempt. But DePetris said the story isn't true. He did, however, say that given "the serious nature of the crime . . . a community center sentence is a joke." Harry and Rose began serving their sentences in 1977.

Trager continued to go after Eastern Service, and that year a civil suit for $5 million was brought against the company. George Graff, the lawyer for Eastern Service, said Louis was running the day-to-day operations by this time. Harry and Rose were out of the picture.

In February 1978 Judge Weinstein extended Harry's probation, but he didn't need to go to the community treatment center anymore. He was, essentially, free. Two months later the FBI officially closed the Eastern Service investigation, and in May Eastern Service settled the Eastern District civil suit and agreed to pay $1 million.

Later that year, Weinstein extended his leniency to Ortrud Kapraki, and ended her probation. He did this, he said, because she couldn't practice real estate while on probation, apparently unaware that she no longer had a real estate license in New York. He also did not take into consideration she'd never shown a hint of remorse for what she'd done. She was the last person who should be selling anyone houses.

Ortrud Kapraki would continue to get into trouble for the rest of her life. In 1990 she filed for bankruptcy but was denied because the tax returns she submitted contained false information.

By 1978, except for Donald Carroll, the Bernsteins and everyone else who had pleaded guilty or been convicted were back on the streets.

The next year the *Washington Post* published an article about how mortgage defaults were still piling up. If things kept going the way they were, Milton Francis, a HUD deputy assistant secretary, explained,

"We are going to become the nation's biggest landlord," adding, "It's a rat's nest."

Over in East New York, which had become a literal rat's nest, and where the neighborhood continued to burn, Reverend Johnny Ray Youngblood had just bought a vacant synagogue amid the rubble and abandoned buildings on Hendrix Street. From this fortress he would grow his congregation, join the fledgling organization East Brooklyn Churches, and together with other men and women of faith, and many other community groups, fight to undo the damage that brought down East New York. The EBC would begin with the thousands of street signs that had been torn down and never replaced. It was the first of many battles, but they had little idea in 1979 the degree to which the slaughter would obliterate life and everything needed to maintain it while they struggled to turn it all around.

Julia Parker, who'd turned five that year, was just starting kindergarten.

Crisis in America's Cities

Excerpt from Martin Luther King Jr.'s speech, given in Atlanta, at the Southern Christian Leadership Conference, after the summer uprisings in 1967.

The policymakers of the white society have caused the darkness; they created discrimination; they created slums; they perpetuate unemployment, ignorance, and poverty. It is incontestable and deplorable that Negroes have committed crimes; but they are derivative crimes. They are born of the greater crimes of the white society. When we ask Negroes to abide by the law, let us also declare that the white man does not abide by law in the ghettos. Day in and day out he violates welfare laws to deprive the poor of their meager allotments; he flagrantly violates building codes and regulations; his police make a mockery of law; he violates laws on equal employment and education and the provisions for civic services. The slums are the handiwork of a vicious system of the white society; Negroes live in them but do not make them any more than a prisoner makes a prison.

Epilogue

In 1989, federal agents padlocked the Guardian Bank N.A. and seized its $7 billion portfolio of federally insured mortgages while they investigated Louis Bernstein, the president of the bank's mortgage-servicing affiliate, and others, for fraud. He pleaded guilty to bank embezzlement and one count of filing a false tax return. He was sentenced to five months in prison and fined $20,000. It was a light sentence from Judge Jacob Mishler, who was known for heavy sentencing, but a receivership was set up for the assets, and in this case, Mishler ordered Bernstein to pay $175 million, as a guarantor of a loan made as part of the scheme.

Walter Thabit went on to work as a senior planner for New York's Landmarks Preservation Commission until 1980, and from there he was an associate city planner in the city's Department of Transportation until 1988. Thabit also taught at the New School University, Hunter College, and Long Island University. In 1994, he received an Honor Award for Lifetime Achievement in Planning from the group Architects, Designers, and Planners for Social Responsibility. He received the Hall of Fame award from the Cooper Square Committee, where he was lead planner of An Alternate Plan for Cooper Square in 2004. He died in 2005.

In 2001, then Chief of Detectives William Allee reached out to Deputy Inspector Ray Ferrari, who was in charge of the Fugitive Enforcement Division. The unusually high number of exceptional clearances signed off on by Michael Race had not gone unnoticed, and Allee asked him to look into it. Ferrari gave the cases to the NYPD's Cold Case Squad to investigate. Around the office they came to be known as the "Race Cases." "There were over one hundred of them," said retired Detective Wendell Stradford. The detectives found a pattern of clearing cases based on one witness who pointed the finger at someone who'd recently been murdered themselves. This should not have been enough to close a case. "You have to lay out an indictment almost," Ferrari explained, "and prove that the person committed a crime." Which is not necessarily to say he didn't have the case right, "but he didn't gather enough compelling evidence, he was closing cases to get rid of them." The Race cases were not strong. "If these were high-profile cases, Manhattan cases," Ferrari said, "they never would have been closed with so little."

Vito Spano, who was the commanding officer of the Cold Case Squad at the time, said, "He never followed the protocols, I don't know how he got away with it." When contacted, Race said his commanding officer Captain John J. Finn and others had signed off on the clearances. After this brief initial contact, however, Race did not respond to further attempts to allow him to elaborate on his side of the story. Spano called Finn an unwitting accomplice, who trusted Race. Retired Lieutenant Commander Robert McHugh said, "He was smart enough to know that once he gets it signed off, blame can go elsewhere."

At least one member of the Cold Case Squad was sympathetic, and talked about how busy they were in the Seven-Five, and the enormous pressure to close cases. Derrick Parker, formerly a detective at the Seven-Five, agreed, saying, "The biggest thing with Michael Race back then was the clearance rates. The captain, the inspector, the chief, would always be on everybody's cases about solving these murders. They wanted these murders solved in a record amount of time."

In August of 2001 the Cold Case Squad gave an initial report of their findings for the Race cases. At least nineteen were cleared without sufficient evidence. Allee asked for the cases back, which he planned to turn over to the Field Internal Affairs Unit (FIAU). Then 9/11 happened and the investigation was put aside. Today, no one contacted at the NYPD knows what became of them. "He was saved by 9/11," said former cold case Lieutenant Commander Robert McHugh.

The EBC continued to build in East New York, constructing a total of 2,247 homes, which included 451 one-, two-, and three-family buildings in the Spring Creek area (which represent 681 housing units). Not everyone is in a position to own a home, or wants to, and the EBC has also built and renovated 1,406 apartments.

The East New York Farms! is still going strong and community gardens in East New York have flourished, with a pause in 1999, when then Mayor Giuliani tried to auction community gardens across New York City to developers. A battle commenced. Looking back, Perry Winston said, "People's energy and need for open space generated these community gardens . . . their existence is a demonstration of people's need for this resource." In East New York, the fact that the gardens "were part of the food supply system" became part of "the rationale for preserving the gardens." Many groups stepped in to help fight Giuliani's plan, including the New York Restoration Project, Green Guerillas, the New York City Community Garden Coalition, and Trust for Public Land. A string of lawsuits followed, including one from then New York State attorney general Eliot Spitzer. An agreement wasn't reached until 2002, and the agreement wasn't perfect. Some gardens were saved and some were lost. Today there are still more community gardens in East New York than any other neighborhood in New York City.

John Kennedy left HUD in 2005 and became the general counsel of the Federal Housing Finance Board. He retired in 2007.

Jeff Kay, who had left the FBI to become an AUSA in the Eastern District, left the Eastern District in 1979 and went on to have a long career working various positions in the United States Attorney's office in Fort Lauderdale, lastly as the deputy chief of the Organized Crime and Economic Crimes sections. He retired in 2012. After two years in St. Louis, special agent Jim Sniegocki was transferred to Louisville, Kentucky, where the cost of living and lifestyle suited his family best. He continued to investigate white-collar crimes and retired in 1987.

After serving as the assistant counsel, Antitrust Subcommittee, Committee on the Judiciary, United States Senate, Jack Blum went on to have a long career providing counsel in the areas of financial crime, money laundering, international tax evasion, and sanctions compliance. He worked twice as a consultant to the UN, ran the investigation into Lockheed Aircraft's overseas bribes, which led to the passage of the Foreign Corrupt Practices Act, and the investigation of the Bank of Credit and Commerce International, the biggest bank fraud case at the time. He retired in 2023.

Reverend Dr. Johnny Ray Youngblood was ordained and consecrated a Bishop on January 19, 2020, at the Pilgrim Baptist Church in Brooklyn.

■

Just before Christmas, in 2000, President Bill Clinton pardoned Stanley Sirote. The number of subprime mortgage loans, meanwhile, quadrupled.

The FBI warned in 2004 that mortgage fraud was "pervasive and growing."

In 2005 a Federal Reserve survey found that Black people were once again being targeted for subprime mortgages.

In 2007, it all started to implode. Much has been written about the subprime mortgage crisis of 2007–2008. Wall Street, banks, mortgage companies, mortgage brokers, and real estate investors discovered that they could make a lot of money bundling home mortgages into an investment vehicle called mortgage-backed securities. Later, in a page out of Harry and Rose Bernstein's playbook, they figured out that they could bundle and sell a lot more mortgage-backed securities by targeting low-income minorities and immigrants (and other low-income buyers), people who would do anything to own a home, and populating the securities with these high-risk loans, a.k.a. subprime mortgages. The growth of subprime mortgage origination during this period was unprecedented. Once again, no one was checking the loan applications to determine the homebuyer's ability to pay off a mortgage, or if the appraisals were valid, or if the information on the applications was even true. And, as in the 1970s, no one was checking the people who were supposed to check. All they cared about were the billions of dollars out there for the taking. If it all blew up, and everything came out, there was a long history of people getting away with it. It was worth the gamble.

When the loans failed, and it all began to unravel in 2007, many companies, like Bear Stearns and Lehman Brothers, went under and millions of people lost their homes, jobs, and pensions. Globally, the losses were in the trillions. Many, many trillions. Instead of prosecuting the people who committed these crimes, the government rewarded them with bailouts, paid for by the taxpayer, and used by the perpetrators to give themselves bonuses. The gamble had paid off. Only one person in the United States went to prison.

In his book, *You, the Jury: How Wall Street Cashed In On the American Dream and Nearly Killed It*, Accetta writes, "Despite a history of mortgage fraud since at least 1970, on balance nobody has ever really cared enough to put an end to it." As a result, "What began as simple mortgage fraud in and before 1970, has become, since at least 1999, the greatest organized criminal activity in history."

Only this time there was no AUSA like Anthony Accetta who was willing and able to prosecute.

In late 1972, months after Accetta's indictments, Jack Blum said, "We'll never know whether or not the 1968 housing program would have worked if properly administered, because it wasn't." Instead, the arc of justice bent toward greed. A world-changing opportunity wasn't just forever lost, future opportunities would be shot down based on what happened. Years later, having lost the last of his innocence about human nature, George Romney would say, "Whenever the federal government puts up a lot money for a program, there are people in this country who are going to find devious ways of getting it."

The foreclosure rate in East New York, which had gone up to 52 percent in the years following the 2007–2008 subprime mortgage crisis, was down to 16.6 percent in 2022. The city continues to grapple with how best to provide enough truly affordable housing to East New York. Alafia, a development planned for completion in 2030, will go up along Fountain Avenue, in an area that was once a mob burial ground. Critics say the rents are merely less than market rate and not truly affordable.

The demographics in East New York continued to change. The neighborhood went from 98.3 percent white in 1950, 63 percent in 1970, to 3.6 percent currently. Murders were down to 24 in 2023, a huge decrease, but still the highest total in New York City.

The Kerner Commission wrote that "inadequate sanitation services are viewed by many ghetto residents not merely as instances of poor public service but as manifestations of racial discrimination." In 2023, Mayor Adams announced the Jewel Streets Neighborhood Plan (a nicer name for The Hole) which would begin with $75 million in funding to address the flooding and sewage issues and build affordable housing. But residents have been promised help on and off for decades and they are skeptical. As of this writing, the city is still in the "learning phase" and an actual plan has not been drawn up.

The FHA, meanwhile, is insuring more mortgages for homeowners of color. According to their 2023 annual report, just under 20 percent of the mortgages they insured the year before were those of Black borrowers and just under 25 percent were for loans made to Hispanic borrowers.

For a time, Julia Parker's family struggled financially as they moved from place to place. At one point they moved to Killer Miller, into the same building where Julia's relative shot and killed David Winston, one month before Julia was murdered.

Today, Julia's surviving sister Milagros lives and works from home in a two-family building in Brighton Beach. Milagros, her three children, and her mother occupy the upstairs apartment, and her younger brother lives downstairs. Julia's son is doing well. Nancy Arlequin raised him as if he were her own child. He never called her grandma; he called her mama. "He is very lovable," Milagros says, and, "like his mother, very popular."

■

The cities that suffered the greatest abuse during the FHA scandal in the 1970s are still struggling. Helping them, and low-income families in general, remains a low priority. In a 2023 interview on NPR's *Fresh Air* program, Matthew Desmond, author of *Poverty, by America*, noted that "if you add up the amount that the government is dedicating to tax breaks, mortgage interest deduction, wealth transfer tax breaks, tax breaks we get on our retirement accounts, our health insurance, our college savings accounts, you learn that we are doing so much more to subsidize affluence than to alleviate poverty." Poverty persists, at least in part, because middle-income and wealthy families benefit from maintaining the status quo.

We also still don't know the full extent of white-collar crime. As of 2023, the FBI does not collect data, compile statistics, or regularly publish reports about mortgage fraud or corporate and financial institution fraud. Worse, unlike cold cases, which at the very least acknowledges that a crime has been committed, the number of undiscovered white-collar crimes likely surpasses the number of unsolved murders. A 2022 study conducted for the George J. Stigler Center for the Study of the Economy and the State estimated that only one-third of the corporate frauds committed every year are ever brought to light.

In 1972, Brian Boyer wrote, "Given the nature of men, money, and our government—our government, in this instance, and our society—I am not optimistic that disclosure of the FHA scandal will lead to a more virtuous future. It may only be a prelude of worse things to come."

He was right.

Coda

On July 19, 2023, I brought together Jack Blum, the assistant counsel to the Senate subcommittee investigating the subprime mortgage scandal of the 1970s, and Anthony Accetta, who prosecuted many of the perpetrators in New York, to see how they felt watching history repeat itself.

JACK: Here we are, fifty years and three financial crises later. At least three. But it's a process of repeat and repeat over and over, and how many times do you want to look at the same problem?

TONY: Well, back when we did the FHA thing, I thought we'd cleaned up the world.

JACK: I did too. And I thought we had also tagged a lot of the people, at least in the hearings, in the so-called honest world, the bankers and the backups. The people who gave the loans to the crooks, the people who financed it all, and the people who benefited from shifting all the risk from themselves to the government.

TONY: Well, the lesson was learned the hard way.

JACK: Tony went after the people at FHA and the other people who were involved in it peripherally, the people at Fannie Mae, which turned out later to be a massive problem, but all of that should have done something.

I'll tell you what happened. Louis Bernstein, about twenty years later, got control of a national bank on Long Island [Guardian Bank] and ran the same scam all over again. Only this time an order of magnitude higher than the original scam that the parents had been involved in.

TONY: Well, you got to remember that after I left, there was no appetite in the U.S. Attorney's office to continue those prosecutions. There were a number of indictments still outstanding, and most of those got dismissed for really simple lack of interest.

JACK: Really? Was this a problem of how complicated and expensive these prosecutions would be?

TONY: The actual cases themselves were not that complicated. Everybody makes out like prosecuting white-collar crime is impossible and actually it's quite easy. All you need to do is start at the bottom and work your way up, and it's human capital that makes those prosecutions.

STACY: When was your first inkling that all was not okay, that the crimes had not gone away? Was it the S&L crisis? Was it 2007–2008?

JACK: By 2008 it was screaming that it hadn't gone away, and 2008 was so similar with the liar loans and the false appraisals and all of the other things that went on it was almost a total replay. And I think, Tony, you and I talked on the phone at that time, and both of us were just cursing the fact that nobody was being prosecuted, that there were thousands of obvious cases. Nobody was touching them.

TONY: If you listen to Robert Mueller, there were thousands of prosecutions. But as I said in my book [*You, the Jury: How Wall Street Cashed In On the American Dream and Nearly Killed It*] that's totally irrelevant because they did not go after the real perpetrators and the real enablers, which were the investment banks, which had just begun to get into the mortgage business in 2000. That's what the real problem was. It wasn't a lack of prosecution of false statement cases and liar loans and brokers and appraisers.

Mueller bragged, "Oh, we did thousands of those." But Obama wouldn't touch the investment banks who were behind all of this securitizing the volume. What changed in 2000 was not the practice. What changed was the volume. The investment banks got into the business of originating loans through mortgage companies that they were scooping up by the dozens so that they could populate securities. That was the major, major difference between 2000 and March of 2007.

STACY: Did they own these mortgage banks in 2007 and 8?

JACK: In 2007 and 8, it was the mortgage banks, but then it was the other banks that were buying the mortgages in the secondary market. And they knew as they were doing it that the mortgages were no good, but they simply didn't care.

TONY: They weren't acting as middlemen. The investment banks were actually buying mortgage companies because they didn't want to just be funding mortgage banks and making money off the interest differentials. They wanted to process the mortgages and then package them.

JACK: They made use of the mortgage banks and the whole idea was packaging the securities. Securitizing the mortgages, and then selling off these securitized mortgages in bundles to buyers who had no idea that they were buying complete junk.

TONY: It was investment banks primarily.

JACK: There was not much difference between the investment banks and the regular banks because all of the walls had come crumbling down with deregulation.

STACY: Which deregulation, specifically?

JACK: Glass-Steagall, which separated banking from security dealing. By 2008, all of the big banks also were in the business of dealing in the markets, stock markets, and bond markets and whatever. And the consequence of that was this became another business for them, and a very profitable business.

STACY: Was anything put into place in the seventies to prevent this from happening again?

JACK: It's what shouldn't have been put into place, which was the deregulation and the tearing down of Glass-Steagall and the complete failure of supervision by the Federal Reserve. We had Alan Greenspan talking about how the markets would all take care of everything and you didn't have to worry about regulation. And the consequence of all of that was a perfect horror show, an absolute storm.

TONY: I think you're right. And the opportunity actually came about because the dot com bubble burst and there were trillions of dollars floating around waiting to be invested. That's when the investment banks said, "Oh, there's a market in mortgages. Let's create securities." And all those trillions of dollars then went into the mortgage business. So nobody could have foreseen that in the seventies.

STACY: Why do you think the banks weren't prosecuted?

JACK: In 1990, '91, I ran in a primary for the Democratic nomination for Congress in my congressional district. And I ran against a man named Tom McMillen, who was a former basketball player, big star, well-known, well entrenched. And the reason I ran was this:

He was on the House banking committee and as a member of the committee, he voted down the line with the bankers. He had raised close to $2 million from the banker's PACs in Washington. And I tried to bring that to public attention in the course of the campaign.

I discovered very quickly that the people who knew about what he did in Washington were not the people who were covering the race and trying to explain what it was that the bankers bought by buying a member of Congress.

STACY: That's the answer? That all our congressmen are bought off?

JACK: You can tell where the money is by the need of members of Congress to get to the right committees. They're looking for the committees that will bring in the most campaign contributions. Number one on the list is always Ways and Means, the top tax-writing committee. But in the period of the banking crises, everybody wanted to be on the banking committee because they knew that that was going to be the committee where the action was and where the money would flow. So this was a phenomenal problem.

TONY: I had about a twenty-minute session with a congressman from Colorado. I showed him a draft of my book on the mortgage crisis, I was with him for three and a half hours and he said over and over again, "You need to come and testify before my banking committee." And guess what? After that meeting, I never heard from him again. Ever.

JACK: My guess is he took that information into his head and immediately had some fundraisers with bankers where he talked about how much trouble they were in and how good it would be if we didn't hear from this attorney in Colorado who might have said something.

TONY: Stacy, you asked why there weren't any prosecutions. Why was there never one? Not a single prosecution of any major bank or banker growing out of the financial crisis of 2007–2008.

JACK: We wound up with all this talk about communism and social- ism and all the rest. We wound up with the entire banking system nationalized. And that was an amazing outcome, and that nobody went to jail for any of that is even more amazing, but not. That was one of the biggest mistakes of the Obama administration and it was a terrible mistake. It had to do with fear of the political power of these institutions. I think that there was a judgment made that this is a fight that we can't win, and the only way to go with it was to go with the flow and let it all happen and they did.

TONY: I don't think it was that, I think it was deliberate malfeasance.

JACK: Could have been.

TONY: If I were a prosecutor then I would've been trying to pros- ecute. People are not investigating, people are not going deep, and they're afraid of going to the top.

JACK: Well, it turns out that that is a major problem. And it leads me to another question, which I wonder what your views are on after all these years, which is the whole problem of the criminal justice system and what it takes to prosecute. I got involved with a bank called the Bank of Credit and Commerce International, and they were the big- gest bunch of crooks that ever came down the road in banking. And had it not been for Robert Morgenthau [the Manhattan district at- torney], there would've been no prosecution and no shutdown of the bank. The feds didn't want to touch it with a pole, and Morgenthau took it on, and really they were working that case and the people involved in the bank for the next ten years. But the problem was that how do you pin responsibility within the institution to individuals who are now going to be the ones who go to jail?

I watched prosecutors try to figure out, for example, Bank of New York, where they were doing the banking for all these Russian mob- sters. And the question was why didn't they prosecute bankers at the Bank of New York? And the answer was, every banker insulated himself from all the people down the line so that the only people who could easily be prosecuted were people who were sort of the designated fall guys. And the whole problem of we won't prosecute unless it's beyond a reasonable doubt, and we really can get a conviction coupled with the difficulty of proving that the people at the top knew, you've got a real problem with the system.

And I'll just talk about a case that I worked on, and it was for me, very instructional. It involved [a large accounting firm, name redacted] and I was helping represent an individual who had been caught up in selling bogus tax shelters. Well, there was a division in [the large accounting firm] that was actually in the business of creating bogus tax shelters. They had a lawyer who would churn out these letters that said the tax deal was fine, and this division was throwing off on the order of 70–75 million in profits for the accounting firm.

I had to review thousands of emails and text messages and God knows what, there wasn't a single text message that went from that group to anybody further up in the management. And the question was, how is that possible? Because here you've got a group that's giving the company a big chunk of its profits. How the hell can it be that the top people in the management don't know what's going on? Yet there were four partners down the line who go to jail, but the guys who obviously knew about it and condoned it were untouched. And it was how do you get the evidence on them? Apparently the retirement benefits and whatever else these guys who went to jail got outweighed whatever it was that they would've gotten if they'd cut a deal with prosecutors to go against the bosses. It's a real problem in the system.

TONY: It's always a problem.

JACK: These people at the top, it's like a mob case where the mob boss never says it directly, but the boys know what to do.

TONY: That's when you actually indict the institution and you bring the institution to its knees. And then those guys who went to jail either testify or they don't testify, but whatever evidence you had against them is enough to bring in the big guys and you shake down the big guys and sooner or later, one of those big guys is going to crack. Maybe he doesn't, but you do indict the institution.

JACK: Here's the real problem that you get. Defense counsel comes into the Department of Justice and says, "We've got 70,000 employees who will be out of work if you indict us, because if we're indicted, we can't audit anybody anymore. We're dead." And that's what happened with Arthur Andersen.

TONY: And guess what? All the Arthur Andersen innocent people went to other companies and the audits continued. So that's a bogus argument.

JACK: I agree with you.

TONY: It was like Dun & Bradstreet in my case, saying, "Oh, we have thousands of credit reports and here we're only dealing with a handful of them." That's like a bank robber saying, "Well, look how many banks I didn't rob." We never made that argument, which was a big mistake. We end up with a hung jury. But to me, if you keep digging, you are always going to find somebody that's going to get scared, that doesn't want to go to jail and is going to flip. It may not be the banker, it may be the banker's secretary, it may be the clerk who worked for the banker. Those people scare a lot easier. They don't have pensions. How deep did they go? I always start at the very, very, very bottom. Those people are scared shitless. They'll hand up their bosses in a heartbeat. And I did that over and over and over again.

JACK: I think you and I absolutely agree that the only solution to these problems in the end is criminal prosecution. That gives us some notion that people will obey the law from here on. And if there's no prosecution, it's hopeless.

STACY: As a layperson, what blew my mind the most was not only were people not going to jail, we were rewarding them. We were giving them piles of money. And then I learned later that there was no oversight. We didn't specify how they were going to spend this, and they just gave it to themselves in bonuses or at least some did. How can that happen?

TONY: Easy.

JACK: We just had Silicon Valley Bank go down and the owners of the bank, who perfectly well knew, or at least the officers of the bank who perfectly well knew the condition of the bank, had paid themselves an absolute fortune and bonuses. And now Congress is fishing around, "Well, maybe pass some clawback legislation." Well, clawback is exactly the word. The problem is the people who were involved in wrecking the economy and getting the bailouts walked off with enough money so that they could retire very comfortably to say the least. They were getting megabucks while everybody else was picking up the tab.

STACY: When I asked why didn't these prosecutions happen? What were the reasons? And fear was one of them that came up.

JACK: It's a pressure that comes through the system. Everybody's afraid. The politicians, in addition to getting all of the money that comes from campaign contributions, the politicians are afraid of the blowback that comes when, "Oh, yeah, you shut down my employer and this is really important." And then all sorts of people show up to tell the higher-ups at the political level, "Stand back because this is going to cause just total turmoil and you can't do it." And I've had that happen to me in the course of many investigations where it takes a pretty heroic politician to take the heat and go forward and fight the good fight. The pressure that's brought is unbelievable.

I can talk about it from another investigation I was involved in, which was the Lockheed aircraft bribery investigation. And we developed evidence that Lockheed had bribed the prime minister of

Japan, and the bribes were very substantial running into the many millions of dollars. And this was now stuff that we had to make public. Well, former secretary of state came in to see Senator Frank Church to tell him. "Oh, you can't do this because it will absolutely turn the Japanese upside down and it'll knock out all of the politicians who are allies in Japan and we're talking about national security, and boy, you can't touch this," and on and on and on. And it requires a politician who can say, "Look, I don't care about that. This is important. The hell with it. I'm going to go ahead." And indeed, the prime minister of Japan went to jail. And that was one of the rare times where in the course of my career I could see a politician taking the risky step, but the result being exactly what should have happened.

TONY: You use the word pressure, it's all about money. I love Frank Church. When I testified on the nursing home thing, I don't know if you know this, Jack, but he sent me a letter. And in my testimony I had said that the Colorado attorney general had lied, and Frank Church sent me a letter and he said, "I know somebody lied during those hearings and I know it wasn't you." Years later, his son was a minister in New York, and we got to know him really, really well. Those were people of real integrity. My big question is, where the hell are they today and why aren't they out there fighting?

JACK: You're asking exactly the right question. It's exactly the question I ask, and it's part of what's really eating at the heart of the country I would argue.

STACY: Who of integrity was around during the Obama years who didn't come forward to push for a prosecution?

JACK: There were people who I thought would be much more heroic, but I actually participated in a couple of meetings about the time when Congress was going to vote on bailing out the major banks in 2008 and what the members of the Senate confronted. And in this meeting we talked about exactly what had gone on. They said, "We really didn't have a choice." When the secretary of the treasury and the head of the Federal Reserve come in and say, "We're facing a financial crisis like 1929 where all the banks are going to fail, we've got to vote to bail them out. We've got to keep everything rolling. The entire world payment system will go down," and on and on and on about all the horrible things that were going to happen.

There were, I think four or five senators in this meeting. Nobody said, "Well, we might want to take that risk because it's the only way to clean it up." And nobody said, "We shouldn't go forward." Some of them were pretty straightforward guys. Byron Dorgan, North Dakota, pretty good character, but he simply got pushed into going along with things out of the horrible fears that were thrown at him.

TONY: So Jack, maybe you could help me close the loop then. Does that explain why Obama went ahead and imposed billion-dollar fines on people like Bank of America who they extorted into buying Mozilo's company [Angelo Mozilo and Countrywide Financial] and make it look like they were actually doing something? Billion-dollar fines look good, except when you consider that the profits were in the trillions.

JACK: Yes, of course. Those fines, and by the way, we've seen this time and again in the area particularly of an area that I worked a lot in, which is money laundering and offshore finance, the fines that were imposed on these banks, "Oh, the biggest fine in history." Well, it was like two weeks' profit and "Guys, knock it off. Don't try to buffalo the American public by saying, 'We've got a $500 million fine,' when it's two weeks' profit."

HSBC is my poster child for what's wrong with all of this. They were caught literally laundering a billion dollars worth of Mexican drug money. They had windows in their subsidiary in Mexico through which they received U.S. dollars. The bank took in U.S. dollars in specially designed boxes, and the bank laundered the drug dollars for these crooks and they were caught. It was just plain, straightforward caught. What should have happened was the banking license should have been revoked. Instead, they got a fine that was the equivalent of perhaps a month's profit. And you say, "Well, what happened here? Why did that go the way it did?" And it was, "Well, we have an institution that's central to the world's financial stability." "What the hell are you talking about? If that's the case, why are they dealing in Mexican drug money?"

STACY: I quit.

JACK: It's a real conundrum. We have to come up with ways of bringing some of these institutions in line and that will require holding the top, top management personally responsible and let them wear a different kind of pinstripe suit.

STACY: Was there anything either of you could have done differently? Jack, you in the Senate investigation and Tony, you in your investigation of these banks in New York, was there anything that you missed or that you could have done better or anything?

JACK: I think that what Tony did, what I did, the hearings we ran were as far as we could go at our level, and we didn't have the instruments of power. Tony wasn't attorney general. All I could do was lay it out for the public and hope there would be a response.

TONY: From 2000 to 2007, I'm sorry to say this, but my hands were tied because these were clients who I was advising not to do what they were doing. Jimmy Cayne asked me if I would look at their mortgage processes in 2000 and I did. I said, "Jimmy, you can't do this. This is not sustainable." Do you know what his answer was? "Fuck you. Do you have any idea how much money we're making?"

[Client's name withheld] were going to do a mortgage deal with the bank Santander in Spain. The country manager tells me, "You can't do it here. If you think you can get a foreclosure without paying bribes, it can't be done." I write a report, and the fifth-largest investment bank in the world tells me, "Tony, you got to scrub that report." I say, "No, I'm not scrubbing it." That report never sees the light of day. They do the deal, I'm sure, but I'm bound by confidentiality. I can't go to the *New York Times* or some TV station and say, "Here's what's going on," because then I'm in violation of my license.

JACK: You're talking now about another phenomenally important problem in all of this. When I was in law school, we talked a lot about legal ethics, and the line was supposed to be, when you're advising a client, you keep them out of trouble by making sure that they stay way over on the side of being honest. Of course, if they're caught and they're in court, you can defend them. You have to put the government to its proof. But counseling, your job, is to keep them out of even gray areas of law and keep them honest.

Well, it turns out that that's not advice that these guys want. What they want is how can I beat the system? So if you come in and you do what Tony did or what I did in a couple of cases, your client looks at you and says, "What am I paying you for? This is ridiculous. I can't follow this advice. Get out of here." And they'll find some compliant guy who will say, "Yeah, here's an opinion letter that says it's okay." And off to the race as they go and it's a race downhill. And the real problem is the money at the top of the legal system for doing this is absolutely remarkable.

It boggles the mind, if you're in my category or Tony's category, it's the kind of money we would only dream about. And it's really pernicious. It really is. It doesn't do the society any good. Our role as lawyers is to make the system work, to tell people what the law is and to have them obey it. And if you tell that to a group of lawyers, they look at you like, "Where did you come from?"

Well, the way they keep this crazy system going, and the way they keep it from being bright line ethics violations, is by dividing the task up into such tiny pieces that nobody gets to see the full picture and understand what it is that is the evil that is being perpetrated.

STACY: Do either of you see another big crisis?

JACK: It's a big tangled mess. It's very big money that takes people over the line. And the question is, how do we keep a society functioning in an environment where the only thing that counts is money? There has to be something.

STACY: Why do we hound these relatively insignificant street criminals to death while these huge monster criminals have essentially been on a hundred-year crime spree?

JACK: That's asked by every inmate and every jail in America, right? "How come they're coming after me?" Well, the guys who were there typically not only deserve it, but they probably deserve more than they got. But yes, it's a valid question. How come me and not them? And that's an issue that is a perpetual problem, and it's a problem that we have to find somewhere to address.

TONY: It's money and political privilege. The Bible says that there's nothing new under the sun. And Stephen Sondheim says, "Everything's different, nothing's changed, only slightly rearranged." And that is the history of mankind. There is nothing new here. You're really talking about the human condition and the power of money and politics.

JACK: Stacy, now let me ask a question. How long has it taken you to figure out what went on in the mortgage game when we were working on it back at the time? How much have you learned and how long has it taken you? So now for an average person to get worked up and decide, "Boy, this is something that we have to change and I'm going to push my political people to do it." What do you think the prospects are of someone who's not writing a book, figuring all of this out and acting on it?

STACY: I'm trying to write this book in a way that anyone could read it and understand it.

JACK: There's another problem, and this is a perennial problem with government programs. Somebody says, "Well, we've got to solve X by putting a program in place and giving these people money." Well, whenever there's free money, I can guarantee you that people line up to steal it. It's a guaranteed, it's a given. And we've yet to figure out how to do that in a way in which the money goes to the right place, to the right people and do it without creating some unbelievable bureaucracy that sucks up all of the money that's supposed to go to help someone. Maybe that's impossible to do, but putting that money out, it's like putting out honey and see if some flies will show up. You bet they will.

We can ask the questions, but the answer—what do you do about human nature and how do you make government work?—are two questions that I have struggled with my entire career, and I'm sure Tony has too.

TONY: Exactly. And it's exacerbated in America, because we have a failed education system. So that we have two or three generations of Americans who aren't going to be smart enough or sophisticated enough to even begin to ask the question, much less answer it. They're going to rely on talking heads and politicians telling them what to think because they don't understand or know how to think critically.

They can relate to a purse snatcher because it's direct and personal, but they can't possibly begin to understand how lying on a mortgage application or a car application or a loan application actually does directly impact them in the long run. But we don't have teaching that takes us down the direct line, which it really is. It's a direct line. It's not that convoluted. It's not that twisted. All you have to do is connect the dots, and the dots are in a pretty straight line.

Until we create a population that is curious and capable of critical thinking, I think we're in for a really, really bad turn. And I don't see any way around it with the education system that we have.

JACK: Well, I'll add something to what you've just said. The people who do have the mental wherewithal, and there are quite a number who are graduating from top law schools, from universities, too many of them are asking one question, which is, how do I get a slice of all the goodies that come out of this system? And they really don't ask other questions, which are, is it right, is it wrong? What are the long-term consequences of what I'm doing? How do I get a piece of the pie? How do I become a partner in the law firm? How do I become a partner in the accounting firm? How do I get to be a partner at Goldman Sachs? And you don't do it by saying, "Hey, that's not right." It turns out the people who say that's not right, don't have a marvelous career path. Am I wrong, Tony?

TONY: Tell me about it. Tell me about it.

JACK: Hey, what can I say? We're a couple of older guys who can say, we've accumulated a certain amount of wisdom along the way. And does anybody want to listen to us?

ACKNOWLEDGMENTS

There are so many people to thank. Where do I even begin? With Anthony Accetta, Jim Sniegocki, Jack Blum, Jeff Kay, William Simon, Michael Gecan, Milagros Martinez, and John Kennedy, who told me their stories. I begin with them because they put up with me all the way back to when I didn't know anything about mortgages, mortgage crimes, federal investigations, trials, or about the life of a young mother who lit up the world for her family and friends. There wouldn't be a book without their histories and their willingness to talk about them, but there are many others, listed further on.

Next, the people who helped me find information. Where are the trial records, property records, police and FBI records, and countless other materials from the sixties and seventies kept?? Thank you, Megan Dwyre (Special Access and FOIA Program, National Archives and Records Administration), Pamela J. Anderson (archivist, National Archives at Kansas City), Lucy Curci-Gonzalez, Brooke Raymond and Emily Moog (The New York Law Institute), Ken Cobb, Katie Ehrlich, Rossy Mendez, Julia Robbins, and Cristina Stubbe (New York City Municipal Archives), and Alan Singer (former editor of *The Link*).

What the hell is a collateralized debt obligation? A tranche? Thank you, my modest friends in the Midwest (you know who you are), John Arnold (rest in peace), and my brother Douglas Horn.

This was not an easy book to explain, initially. I owe my continued writing life to my agent, Julia Lord, who got it immediately, and then sent it to Quynh Do and Gillian Flynn, who read my proposal, saw the potential, and wrote me two of the most meaningful and life-changing letters I've ever received in my life.

My gifted editor Sarah Ried, and my friend/editor Howard Mittelmark, both of whom read the book over and over and over and helped shape it into something far better than it would have been (and did so without crushing my fragile writer's ego). Thank you for helping me write one of the most challenging stories I've ever faced. Thank you, Christopher Bonastia, who read through the final draft and offered invaluable and informed suggestions.

I kept the books of Brian Boyer, the late Walter Thabit, Keeanga-Yamahtta Taylor, Anthony Accetta, and Christoper Bonastia in a pile on my desk, where I referred to them repeatedly while writing this book. Thank you for your diligent research. I only hope my book is a useful addition to the history of this time and place.

And finally, the rest of the people who shared their stories and expertise and made that history come to life:

Ashmat Ali (friend of Julia Parker), Johnny Alite (former mob hitman), George Bashion (former AUSA Eastern District of New York), Vivian Bright (former chief executive officer of the LDCENY), Lucille Clark (East Brooklyn Congregations), Ira and Arthur Cutler, (who grew up in East New York), Sarita Daftary-Steel (East New York Farms!), Sid Davidoff (former administrative assistant to Mayor Lindsay), Ronald DePetris (former AUSA Eastern District of New York), Gale Drexler (legal assistant, Eastern District of New York), Jeff Eisenberg (grew up in East New York), Raymond Ferrari (former NYPD deputy inspector), Jan Goldberg (grew up in East New York), Mel Grizer (United Community Centers), Dr. Joyce Y. Hall (former project director for the Childbearing Center of East New York), Chuck Harrison (retired NYPD detective), Joe Herbert (retired NYPD detective sergeant), Barry Kestenberg (grew up in East New York), Larry Kolker (attorney), Judge Edward R. Korman (Eastern District of New York), Steven Lang (grew up in East New York),

John P. Lomenzo Jr. (son of Secretary of State John Lomenzo), Father
Edward Mason (East Brooklyn Congregations), Robert McHugh
(former lieutenant commander, NYPD Cold Case Squad), Ricardo
Nelson (father of Julia Parker's son), Al Nesbot (retired NYPD detective), Derrick Parker (retired NYPD detective), Sarah Plowden (East
Brooklyn Congregations), Richard Recny (former executive director
of the Local Development Corp. of East New York), Joe Sapienza
(retired FDNY captain), Maryanne Schretzman (former deputy com-
missioner for Policy and Planning at the Department of Homeless
Services), Carey Shea (former program director of the LDCENY),
Sister Margaret Smyth (former teacher at St. John Cantius, now de-
ceased), Vito Spano (former commanding officer, Cold Case Squad,
NYPD), Judith Stoloff (East New York Model Cities project), Wendell
Stradford (former Cold Case detective), Peter E. Tommaso (former
lawyer for Ortrud Kapraki), Alia Thabit (daughter of Walter Thabit),
Denise Thomas (retired NYPD detective), Robert Travia (grandson of
Judge Anthony J. Travia), Rodrick Wallace (author), Marlene Wilks
(East New York gardener), and Jennifer Wynn (real estate broker).

SOURCE NOTES

Murder Totals for East New York

The 1972 and 1973 numbers come from the Hearing before the Subcommittee on Crime of Committee on the Judiciary, First Session on Firearms Legislation, 1975.

1980–1991 are from the 75th precinct logbooks listing all homicides.

1985–2003 are from the NYPD CARS (Computer Assisted Robbery System) reports showing all open and closed homicides, citywide.

1990–2009 are from an NYPD Excel database listing all open homicides for East New York, accessed at the Cold Case Squad office.

2000–2023 homicide totals are from the NYPD website.

Books

Accetta, Anthony. *You, the Jury: How Wall Street Cashed In On the American Dream and Nearly Killed It*. Privately published, 2011.

Barer, Burl, Frank C. Girardot Jr., and Ken Eurell. *Betrayal in Blue: The Shocking Memoir of the Scandal That Rocked the NYPD*. Denver, WildBlue Press, 2016.

Biles, Roger. *The Fate of Cities: Urban America and the Federal Government, 1945–2000*. Lawrence, University Press of Kanas, 2011.

Bonastia, Christopher. *Knocking on the Door: The Federal Government's Attempt to Desegregate the Suburbs*. Princeton, Princeton University Press, 2006.

Boyer, Brian D. *Cities Destroyed for Cash: The FHA Scandal at HUD*. Chicago, Follett, 1973.

Cannato, Vincent. *The Ungovernable City: John Lindsay and His Struggle to Save New York*. New York, Basic Books, 2001.

Cobb, Jelani. *The Essential Kerner Commission Report*. New York, Liveright, 2021.

Danielson, Michael N. *The Politics of Exclusion*. New York, Columbia University Press, 1976.

Desmond, Matthew. *Evicted: Poverty and Profit in the American City*. New York, Crown, 2016.

Desmond, Matthew. *Poverty, by America*. New York, Crown, 2023.

Eisinger, Jesse. *The Chickenshit Club: Why the Justice Department Fails to Prosecute Executives*. New York, Simon & Schuster, 2017.

Ewing, Charles Patrick. *Insanity: Murder, Madness, and the Law*. Oxford, United Kingdom, Oxford University Press, 2008.

Fisher, Louis. *Presidential Spending Power*. Princeton, Princeton University Press, 1975.

Freeman, Samuel G. *Upon This Rock: The Miracles of a Black Church*. New York, HarperPerennial, 1994.

Fried, Joseph P. *Housing Crisis U.S.A*. Westport, Praeger, 1971.

Gecan, Michael. *Going Public: An Organizer's Guide to Citizen Action*. New York, Anchor Books, 2002.

Glueck, Grace, and Paul Gardner. *Brooklyn: People and Places, Past and Present*. New York, Harry N. Abrams, 1997.

Gottehrer, Barry. *The Mayor's Man*. Charleston, Booksurge, 2007.

Hauser, Thomas. *The Trial of Patrolman Thomas Shea*. New York, Seven Stories Press, 2017.

Heidenreich, Frederick J. *Old Days and Old Ways in East New York*. Privately published, 1948.

Hinton, Elizabeth. *America on Fire: The Untold History of Police Violence and Black Rebellion Since the 1960s*. New York, Liveright, 2021.

Hirsch, Arnold R. "Less Than *Plessy*: The Inner City, Suburbs, and State-Sanctioned Residential Segregation in the Age of *Brown*," in Kruse, Kevin M., and Thomas J. Sugrue, eds. *The New Suburban History*. Chicago, The University of Chicago Press, 2006.

Hunt, Jennifer C. *Seven Shots: An NYPD Raid on a Terrorist Cell and Its Aftermath*. Chicago, University of Chicago Press, 2010.

Perlstein, Rick. *Nixonland: The Rise of a President and the Fracturing of America*. New York, Scribner, 2009.

Lamb, Charles M. *Housing Segregation in Suburban America Since 1960: Presidential and Judicial Politics*. Cambridge, United Kingdom, Cambridge University Press, 2005.

Lardner, James, and Thomas Reppetto. *NYPD: A City and Its Police*. New York, Henry Holt and Co., 2000.

National Research Council, Division of Behavioral and Social Sciences and Education, Youth and Families Board on Children, Committee on Law and Justice, *Deadly Lessons: Understanding Lethal School Violence*. Lawrence, National Academies Press, 2002.

Ramsey, Donovan X. *When Crack Was King: A People's History of a Misunderstood Era*. New York, One World, 2023.

Satter, Beryl. *Family Properties: Race, Real Estate, and the Exploitation of Black Urban America*. New York, Metropolitan Books, 2009.

Starr, Roger. *Urban Choices: The City and Its Critics*. Baltimore, Penguin Books, 1967.

Taub, Jennifer. *Big Dirty Money: The Shocking Injustice and Unseen Cost of White-Collar Crime*. New York, Viking, 2020.

Taylor, Keeanga-Yamahtta. *Race for Profit: How Banks and the Real Estate Industry Undermined Black Homeownership*. Chapel Hill, The University of North Carolina Press, 2019.

Thabit, Walter. *How East New York Became a Ghetto*. New York, NYU Press, 2003.

Trump, Donald J., and Tony Schwartz. *Trump: The Art of the Deal*. New York, Random House, 2015.

Wallace, Rodrick, and Deborah Wallace. *A Plague on Your Houses: How New York Was Burned Down, and National Public Health Crumbled.* Brooklyn, Verso, 1999.

Podcasts

Heldman, Kevin. *What the Hell Happened in East New York?* Four-episode podcast co-produced with The Big Roundtable, 2016.

"Brooklyn, We Go Hard," March 16, 2016, and "East New York, Did It Work?," September 17, 2017. In *There Goes the Neighborhood.* Podcast. Produced by WNYC.

Archives

Shirley Chisholm Papers. Speeches 1971–1989. Rutgers Special Collections and University Archives, New Brunswick, NJ.

East New Yorker (1975–1981). Ronald Shiffman collection on the Pratt Center for Community Development, Center for Brooklyn History, Brooklyn Public Library, Brooklyn, NY.

Eastern Service Corporation FBI investigation records. National Archives and Records Administration, College Park, MD.

Industrial Areas Foundation records (1977–2011). Rare Book and Manuscript Library, Columbia University, New York.

John Vliet Lindsay papers (MS 592). Series XIV: Sidney Davidoff (Assistant to the Mayor), 1965–1973. Manuscripts and Archives, Yale University Library, New Haven, CT.

Maternity Center Association records (1907–2010). Sub-series 7.9. Childbearing Center of East New York (1985–1996). Augustus Long Health Sciences Library, Columbia University, New York.

Office of the Mayor of the City of New York, Subgroup Office of the Mayor, John V. Lindsay. The New York City Municipal Archives, New York City Department of Records and Information Services.

New York Police Department logbook documenting incidents and disturbances in New York City after the assassination of Martin Luther King Jr. The New York City Municipal Archives, New York City Department of Records and Information Services.

Police Department records on race riots, labor disputes, and other issues from 1964 to 1967. The New York City Municipal Archives, New York City Department of Records and Information Services.

Property cards for East New York blocks. The New York City Municipal Archives, New York City Department of Records and Information Services.

The New York City Municipal Archives.

New York City Department of Records and Information Services.

Records of the Pratt Center for Community Development Archives, Pratt Institute Library, Brooklyn, NY.

Walter Thabit Collection. Collection Number: 4215. Division of Rare and Manuscript Collections, Cornell University Library, Ithaca, NY.

Opening Quotes

President Lyndon B. Johnson's quote came from The President's Address to the Nation on Civil Disorders on July 27, 1967.

The Junius Henri Browne quote came from *The Great Metropolis, a Mirror of New York: A Complete History of Metropolitan Life and Society, with Sketches of Prominent Places, Persons, and Things in the City, as They Actually Exist,* Hartford,1869.

The Robert M. Morgenthau quote about white-collar crime came from "Equal Justice and the Problem of White-Collar Crime," The Conference Board, August 1969.

The Ann Fulmer quote came from *Burning Down the House: Mortgage Fraud and the Destruction of Residential Neighborhoods,* 2010.

Prologue

Marzulli, John. "Drug War Victim? Cops Probe Teen Mom's Slaying." July 20, 1991, *New York Daily News.*

1. The Destruction of East New York

Interviews with Milagros Martinez, Syd Davidoff, Mel Grizer, Vivian Bright, Barry Kestenberg, Jan Goldberg, Jeff Eisenberg, Steven Lang, and Ira Cutler.

Cannato. *The Ungovernable City: John Lindsay and His Struggle to Save New York.*

Glueck and Gardner. *Brooklyn: People and Places, Past and Present.*

Heidenreich. *Old Days and Old Ways in East New York.*

Perlstein. *Nixonland: The Rise of a President and the Fracturing of America.*

"SPONGE: A Society Keyed to Secrecy; Group That Picketed CORE at Fair Has No Office." April 28, 1965, *New York Times.*

Stern, Michael. "Mayor Pays Visit to Family of Boy, Offers Sympathy on Return to East New York Plea for Peace Made Earlier." July 22, 1966, *New York Times.*

Krebs, Albin. "Brooklyn Sniper Kills Negro Boy in Race Disorder." July 22, 1966, *New York Times.*

Stern, Albin. "Anti-Negro Group Loosely Formed; Sponge Members Are Whites in Interracial Areas." July 23, 1966, *New York Times.*

Kiernan, Joseph, and Henry Lee. "1,500 Cops Blanket East New York, Lindsay Urges Public to Keep Calm in Racially Tense Area." July 23, 1966, *New York Daily News.*

Mallon, Jack, and Anthony Burton, "A Changing District With Trouble in the Air." July 23, 1966, *New York Daily News.*

"East New York SPONGE Leader and 2 Face Burglary Charge." July 29, 1966,
    New York Times.
"A Cooler Is in Hot Water Again." August 13, 1966, *New York Daily News.*
Hofmann, Paul. "Opinions Differ on Gallo's Roll, He's Held Good or Dangerous
    as Flatbush Peacemaker." August 13, 1966, *New York Times.*
"Police Saturation Continues All Summer." August 13, 1966, *New York Amsterdam
    News.*
Lissner, Will. "P.B.A. Scores Use of Gallos by City, Police Spokesmen Call Role of
    Mobsters in Brooklyn Riots 'Civic Disgrace.'" August 15, 1966, *New York Times.*
"SPONGE Leader Accused." August 20, 1966, *New York Amsterdam News.*
Matthews, Les. "'My Son Is Not Guilty.'" August 20, 1966, *New York Amsterdam News.*
"Koota to See If Gallos Got Deal in Soothing of Racial Tensions." August 20,
    1966, *New York Times.*
"Conspiracy Case to Be Tried Again." June 14, 1970, *New York Times.*
"Mayor's Dove of Peace Held in Killing." April 27, 1969, *New York Daily News.*
Lizzi, Maria C. "We Only Done What Any Red-Blooded American Boys Would
    Do: The Making of Italian Americans in East New York, 1966." *Italian
    American Review* 1, no. 2 (Summer 2011).
NYPD Memorandum for the Police Commissioner, Unusual Disorder—75th
    Precinct, July 22, 1966.
Martin Luther King Jr. speech, "The Other America," 1967.
The ENY Projects Archives. http://www.astralgia.com/enyprojects/archives/.

1. The FHA Scandal

"New Rights Bill." April 20, 1968, *New York Amsterdam News.*
"Praise Rights Bill; See Need For More." April 20, 1968, *New York Amsterdam News.*
Zasloff, Jonathan. "The Secret History of the Fair Housing Act," *Harvard Journal
    on Legislation* 247 (2016).
Hon. Philip N. Brownstein, the Assistant Secretary of HUD and Commissioner
    of the FHA, speech at the Directors Conference, October 23, 1967, Real
    Estate Settlement Costs, printed in *FHA Mortgage Foreclosures, Housing
    Abandonment, and Site Selection Policies, Hearings before the Subcommittee on
    Housing, Committee on Banking and Currency,* February 22 and 24, 1972.
United States of America v. Bernstein et al. United States Court of Appeals, Second
    Circuit, 533 F.2d 775 (1976).
Criminal Docket 72-CR-587, The United States vs. Harry Bernstein, et al.,
    Eastern District of New York.
Criminal Docket 72-CR-349, The United States vs. Harry Bernstein, et al.,
    Eastern District of New York.
Hazel, Mycah. "The Kerner Commission's Last Living Member Says We Still
    Need to Talk about Racism." *All Things Considered,* Radio Diaries, NPR,
    September 2021.

2. The Destruction of East New York

Interview with Milagros Martinez.

Thabit. *How East New York Became a Ghetto.*

Pitkin, John R. "East New York." August 31, 1837, *Long Island Star.*

Bennett, Charles G. "Fast Start Urged for Slum Housing." September 23, 1967, *New York Times.*

Burks, Edward C. "Mayor Breaks Ground for Model Cities Project." July 31, 1969, *New York Times.*

Rabin, Bernard. "History Buff to Honor Founder of Woodhaven." May 11, 1978, *New York Daily News.*

Ferretti, Fred. "Where Have All the Breweries Gone?" August 9, 1978, *New York Times.*

Wilson, James Q. "The Changing FBI: The Road to Abscam." *The Public Interest* 59 (Spring 1980).

Martin E. Eisenberg, "Being Left in East New York: Tensions between Race and Class in Community Organizing, 1954–1980," City University of New York, 1999.

East New York Personal Surveys, 1966, Walter Thabit Collection, Cornell University Library.

Planning for the target area: East New York, Walter Thabit, planning consultant; David Stoloff, associate, 1967.

Interview of FHA on Its Vacant Buildings in East New York, Andrea Malester, April 7, 1969, Walter Thabit Collection, Cornell.

Peggy Gavan, "1921: The Pitkin Avenue Fire Cat and Her Lucky Halloween Kittens," October 31, 2019, https://hatchingcatnyc.com/2019/10/31/pitkin-avenue-fire-cat/.

"East New York, Brooklyn Facts for Kids," Kiddle Encyclopedia, October 2023. https://kids.kiddle.co/East_New_York,_Brooklyn.

2. The FHA Scandal

Interviews with Peter E. Tammaso and Christopher Bonastia.

"Lady Broker Accused in $600,000 Scandal." October 12, 1967, *Long Island Press.*

"Woman Held in Scheme to Fleece the Elderly." October 12, 1967, *New York Daily News.*

Clark, Alfred E. "Woman Accused of Cheating Aged." October 13, 1967, *New York Times.*

"Weaver Hails New Housing Bill." August 3, 1968, *New York Amsterdam News.*

"Broker and Aid Lose License in Loan Fraud." May 28, 1970, *New York Daily News.*

Tillotson, Amanda. "Race, Risk and Real Estate: The Federal Housing Administration and Black Homeownership in the Post World War II Home Ownership State." *The DePaul Journal for Social Justice* 8, no. 1 (2014).

Romney, George. "Accomplishments of HUD, 1969–1972." HUD Challenge, February, 1972.

3. The Destruction of East New York

Gottehrer. *The Mayor's Man.*
Thabit. *How East New York Became a Ghetto.*
Rogin, Richard. "'This Place Makes Bedford-Stuyvesant Look Beautiful.'" March 28, 1971, *New York Times.*
Todd, George. "East New York Could Be the Next to Blow Up." May 29, 1971, *New York Amsterdam News.*
Moor, Keith. "Youths Plug Along to Dry a Leaky City." September 20, 1971, *New York Daily News.*
Bonastia, Christopher. "Housing Desegregation in the Era of Deregulation." *Kalfou* 1, no. 2 (Fall 2014).
Materials related to the planning of the Ad Hoc Committee of East New York Housing Leaders; press conference about the housing conditions in East New York. Walter Thabit Collection, Cornell.
New York Fire Department 1971 Runs and Workers Engine and Ladder Companies, prepared by the Fire Bell Club of New York.

3. The FHA Scandal

Thabit. *How East New York Became a Ghetto.*
Gellman, Barton. "Dreams from His Mother." June 4, 2012, *New York Times Magazine.*
Biles, Roger. "A Mormon in Babylon: George Romney as Secretary of HUD, 1969–1973," *Michigan Historical Review* 38, no. 2 (Fall 2012).
Bonastia, Christopher. "Hedging His Bets: Why Nixon Killed HUD's Desegregation Efforts." *Social Science History* 28, no. 1 (Spring 2004).
1968 Annual Report of the U.S. Department of Housing and Urban Development.
Competition in Real Estate and Mortgage Lending Hearings, John P. Lomenzo's testimony, May 3, 1972.
Rabinowitz, Richard. Oral history interview conducted by Sarita Daftary-Steel, December 8, 2014, Sarita Daftary-Steel collection of East New York oral histories. Call number: 2015.011.17, Brooklyn Historical Society.
The Big Short. Movie based on *The Big Short* by Michael Lewis.
Delbert L. Stapley to George W. Romney, January 23, 1964. https://archive.org/details/DelbertStapleyLetter/mode/1up?view=theater.
Ferrari, Michelle, dir. "The Riot Report." *American Experience*, season 36, ep. 5, PBS, 2024.

4. The Destruction of East New York

Interviews with Joe Sapienza and Rodrick Wallace.

Thabit. *How East New York Became a Ghetto.*

Wallace and Wallace. *A Plague on Your Houses.*

"Rocks Hurled at Firemen." July 15, 1972, *The Evening Press*, Binghamton, NY.

Bird, David. "Union Fights Fire Department Cuts." December 22, 1972, *New York Times.*

Perlmutter, Emanuel. "City Held Unready for Emergencies." July 21, 1976, *New York Times.*

Stetson, Damon. "Firefighters Blame Cuts for Toll." March 31, 1977, *New York Times.*

Fried, Joseph P. "Fires in New York City Have Jumped 40% in Last 3 Years." June 16, 1977, *New York Times.*

Bonastia, "Housing Desegregation in the Era of Deregulation."

Kolesar, Peter, and Warren E. Walker. "An Algorithm for the Dynamic Relocation of Fire Companies." R-103-NYC, September 1972.

Sapienza, Joe. "Engine 236: A Personal History of Firefighting in East New York." Undated and unpublished essay.

Sternlieb, George. "Abandonment: Urban Housing Phenomenon," *HUD Challenge*, May 1972.

Tietz, M. B. "Toward a Theory of Urban Public Facility Location." *Proceedings of the Regional Science Association*, December 1968.

Wallace, Deborah, and Rodrick Wallace, "Letter to the Editor of Management Science re: Transfer of Emergency Service Deployment Models to Operating Agencies by Jan M. Chaiken, and the response from the Rand Corporation." *Management Science* 26, no. 4 (April 1980).

Wallace, Rodrick, and Deborah Wallace. "Origins of Public Health Collapse in New York City: The Dynamics of Planned Shrinkage, Contagious Urban Decay and Social Disintegration." *Bulletin of the New York Academy of Medicine* 66, no. 5 (September–October 1990).

East New York Revisited, March 1976, Walter Thabit Collection.

Report of the FLAME Committee (Fire Load and Manpower Emergency), Uniform Fire Department, City of New York, Fire Officers, Local 854, International Assn. of Firefighters, AFL-CIO Association, undated but approx. 1968, Wallace Collection on NYC Fires, Lloyd Sealy Library Special Collections, John Jay College of Criminal Justice, CUNY.

Wallace, Rodrick. "A Preliminary Study of the Brooklyn Fire / Abandonment Epidemic of 1971–1983: The Crisis That Was, the Disaster to Come." 1985 Wallace Collection, Special Collections, Lloyd Sealy Library, John Jay College of Criminal Justice, CUNY.

Fire Company Locations of New York City compiled by Mike Boucher. https://nyfd.com/cityhist.pdf.

New York Fire Department 1971 Runs and Workers Engine and Ladder
Companies, prepared by the Fire Bell Club of New York.
Runs and Workers. Data source: FDNY Bureau of Operations, proofread by The
Fire Bell Club of New York. http://www.fdnewyork.com/rnwindex.asp.
"The Riot Report," directed by Michelle Ferrari, 2024.

4. The FHA Scandal

Interviews with Otto Obermaier, Anthony Accetta, Ronald DePetris, George
Bashion, and Jeffrey Kay.
Biles. *The Fate of Cities.*
Bonastia. *Knocking on the Door.*
Danielson. *The Politics of Exclusion.*
Lamb. *Housing Desegregation in Suburban America Since 1960.*
Taylor. *Race for Profit.*
Flint, Jerry M. "Michigan Jeer Romney Over Suburbs' Integration." July 29, 1970,
New York Times.
Fowler, Glenn. "Operation Breakthrough Passes a Milestone." November 8, 1970,
New York Times.
Prial, Frank J. "The Forest Hills Co-Op, from Anger to Acceptance." April 21,
1976, *New York Times.*
Biles. "A Mormon in Babylon."
Szylvian, Kristin. "Operation Breakthrough's Forgotten Prototype Communities."
Oculus, a publication of the AIA New York chapter, vol. 84, no. 4, Fall 2002.
Schroeder, Milton R. "Land Use Planning for Assisted Housing—The President
Signals Retreat." *Law and Social Order,* 1971.
Letter from Wright Patman to George Romney, July 28, 1970, Committee on
Banking and Currency Report, Section 235 Housing Programs.
NASA Headquarters Oral History Project, Harold B. Finger, interviewed by
Kevin Rusnak, May 16, 2002.

5. The Destruction of East New York

Interview with Johnny Alite.
Fisher. *Presidential Spending Power.*
Hauser. *The Trial of Patrolman Thomas Shea.*
McQuiston, John T. "Suit Lays Blight to FHA Foreclosures." January 17, 1973,
New York Times.
Kline, Polly. "Suit Accuses FHA of 'Dumping' 100 Slum Structures." February 3,
1973, *New York Daily News.*
"The Budget: Nixon's Call to Counter-Revolution." February 5, 1973, *Time
Magazine.*

Kappstatter, Robert. "FHA Evictions OK, But U.S. Is Warned." March 2, 1973, *New York Daily News.*

Salpukas, Agis. "Moratorium on Housing Spells Hardship for Thousands." April 16, 1973, *New York Times.*

Brodey, Jesse. "Landlord Trump Retaliates, Sues U.S. for $100 Million." December 13, 1973, *New York Daily News.*

Yette, Samuel F. "Nixon's New Budget." April 1973, *Dawn Magazine.*

Warmbrand, Martin J. "E.N.Y. Health Centers Planned." November 1973, *East New Yorker.*

"No Housing, No Grants." June 25, 1977, *Washington Post.*

Bonastia, "Hedging His Bets."

Kramer, Douglas J. "Protecting the Urban Environment from the Federal Government." *Urban Affairs Quarterly* 3, March 1974.

"Resident's Suit Charges FHA Policy Harms Environment and Hastens Urban Decay." *Street Magazine,* no. 9, 1973.

Blockbusting in 1968 statute: "Equal Opportunity in Housing and Employment," *Annual Report of the U.S. Department of Housing and Urban Development, 1968.* Accessed via Hathitrust. Blockbusting in 1968 statute: https://law.justia.com /cases/federal/appellate-courts/F2/474/115/124860/.

Memorandum for the President, Daniel P. Moynihan, January 16, 1970.

Hearing before the Subcommittee on Crime of Committee on the Judiciary, First Session on Firearms Legislation, Appendix 4, 1975.

United States District Court for the Eastern District of New York, *United States of America v. Fred C. Trump, Donald Trump, and Trump Management, Inc.* Case No. 73-cv-01529.

Brotherhood Blocks Association of Sunset Park Inc., et al. v. Secretary of the Department of Housing and Urban Development, and Commissioner of the Federal Housing Administration. Civil Action No. 73 C76.

General Docket, United States Court of Appeals, Eastern District, Case 73- 1389, *Brotherhood Blocks Association of Sunset Park Inc., et al. v. Secretary of the Department of Housing and Urban Development, and Commissioner of the Federal Housing Administration.* March 7, 1973.

Sworn affidavit of Walter Thabit, United States District Court, Eastern District on New York, July 17, 1973.

"The Piel Brothers Build a Beer Empire in East New York," January 28, 2019. Brownstoner.com.

5. The FHA Scandal

Interviews with Anthony Accetta, Jim Sniegocki, and Dr. John Fox.

Memo SAC, New York to Director, FBI, re: Frank Sullivan, Eastern Service Corporation, FHAM, December 28, 1967, FBI Investigation Files 147-HQ- 17035, NY 147-2071.

Communication re: Eastern Service Corporation, February 28, 1969, FBI
Investigation Files.

6. The Destruction of East New York

Interviews with Mel Grizer and Chuck Harrison.
National Research Council. *Deadly Lessons: Understanding Lethal School Violence.*
Kaufman, Michael T. "Forest Hills Site Scored by Blacks." December 22, 1971,
New York Times.
Starr, Roger. "Point of View." January 28, 1973, *New York Times.*
Vanzi, Cass. "Bound and Dropped 4 Stories." January 24, 1975, *New York Daily
News.*
Bird, David. "Hospital in Brooklyn Open Despite Accreditation Loss." March 31,
1975, *New York Times.*
Fried, Joseph P. "City's Housing Administrator Proposes 'Planned Shrinkage' of
Some Slums." February 3, 1976, *New York Times.*
Warmbrand, Martin J. "Work Release Program Rejected by Community Planning
Board." March 1976, *East New Yorker.*
"ACT Block Association Protests Poor Sanitation." April 1976, *East New Yorker.*
Turso, Vito. "Abandoned Buildings: Cypress Hills Waits for City to Act." May
1976, *East New Yorker.*
Perlmutter, Emanuel. "City Held Unready for Emergencies." July 21, 1976, *New
York Times.*
O'Neill, William. "City Cutbacks Close Day Care Centers." September 1976, *East
New Yorker.*
Starr, Roger. "Making New York Smaller." November 14, 1976, *New York Times.*
Seigel, Max H. "Boy, 15, Shot to Death Point Blank; Officer Arrested in East New
York." November 27, 1976, *New York Times.*
Trachtenberg, Nancy. "E.N.Y. Leaders Meet Beame and Codd on Evans Killing."
December 1976, *East New Yorker.*
Merrifield, Andy. "Amateur Urbanism." *City* 19, no. 5 (2015).
Wallace, Deborah, and Rodrick Wallace. "Benign Neglect and Planned
Shrinkage." March 25, 2017, blog post, Verso Books. https://www.versobooks
.com/blogs/news/3145-benign-neglect-and-planned-shrinkage.

6. The FHA Scandal

Interviews with Anthony Accetta, George Bashion, and Jim Sniegocki.
"High Profit in Poor Housing." January 6, 1971, *Newsday.*
Rosenthal, Jack. "Romney, in Shift, Freezes Disputed Home Aid to Poor." January
15, 1971, *New York Times.*
Herbers, John. "Rights Panel Says U.S. Housing Plan Aids Segregation." June 11,
1971, *New York Times.*

Moritz, Owen. "Group Seizes Vacant Homes to Protest—and Repair." June 18, 1971, *New York Daily News*.

FBI Investigation Files 147-HQ-17035, NY 147-2071.

HUD Office of Audit, Summary of Findings in Interim Report Issued to Secretary Romney March 26, 1971, On Inspections of New and Used Single Family Housing, Insured Under the Section 235 Program.

The Federal Civil Rights Enforcement Effort Seven Months Later. A Report of the United States Commission on Civil Rights, May 1971.

Hearing before the United States Commission on Civil Rights, Held in Washington, D.C., June 14, 1971.

HUD Office of Audit, Audit Review of Section 235 Single Family Housing, 05-2-2001-4900, December 10, 1971.

DEFAULTS ON FHA-INSURED HOME MORTGAGES—DETROIT, MICH., Fifteenth Report by the Committee on Government Operations, June 20, 1972.

United States of America v. Bernstein et al. United States Court of Appeals, Second Circuit, 533 F.2d 775 (1976).

7. The Destruction of East New York

Interview with Chuck Harrison.

Ewing. *Insanity: Murder, Madness, and the Law.*

Hunt. *Seven Shots: An NYPD Raid on a Terrorist Cell and Its Aftermath.*

Starr. *Urban Choices: The City and its Critics.*

"Housing Patrolman Is Held for Murder." April 29, 1973, *New York Times.*

Rabin, Bernard, and Paul Meskil. "Charge Cop in Killing of Boy 10, Street." April 29, 1973, *New York Daily News.*

"Housing Cop Is Indicted in Youth Killing." May 5, 1973, *New York Daily News.*

"Major Owens' Statement on Patrolman's Acquittal." December 21, 1974, *New York Amsterdam News.*

Todd, George. "Brooklynites React with Shock and Anger." December 4, 1976, *New York Amsterdam News.*

Robinson, Major. "Brooklyn Coalition to Oust Erratic Cops." December 4, 1976, *New York Amsterdam News.*

Trachtenberg. "E.N.Y. Leaders Meet Beame and Codd on Evans Killing."

Siegel, Max H. "Boy, 15, Shot to Death Point-Blank." December 15, 1976, *East New Yorker.*

"A Safe Community." December 1976, *The Link.*

"Public's Help Sought in Murder Probe." September 9, 1977, *New York Daily News.*

"Residents Rally against Crime." October 1977, *East New Yorker.*

Dunning, Jennifer. "Two Officers Testify Colleague Killed Boy without Plain Cause." November 15, 1977, *New York Times.*

Seigel, Max H. "A Convicted Rapist Is Linked by Police to 2 Murder Cases."
    November 18, 1977, *New York Times*.
Dwyer, Jim. "A Police Shot to a Boy's Back in Queens, Echoing Since 1973." April
    16, 2015, *New York Times*.
"New York Zodiac Copycat: East New York, Then and Now." In *Break in the Case*,
    podcast, New York City Police Department.
ENY Projects Message Board. http://www.astralgia.com/enyprojects/forum/
    archives/archive1/archive.html.

7. The FHA Scandal

Interview with Anthony Accetta.
Accetta. *You, the Jury*.
Competition in Real Estate and Mortgage Lending Hearings, May 1972.
United States of America v. Bernstein et al. United States Court of Appeals, Second
    Circuit, 533 F.2d 775 (1976).
"Federal Compensation for Victims of the 'Homeownership for the Poor'
    Program." *The Yale Law Journal* 84, no. 2 (December 1974).
"Home Ownership for Lower Income Families: A Report on the Racial and
    Ethnic Impact of the Section 235 Program." June 1971, U.S. Commission on
    Civil Rights.

8. The Destruction of East New York

Interviews with Michael Gecan, Lucille Clark, and Sarah Plowden.
Gecan. *Going Public*.
Freeman. *Upon This Rock. Neighborhood Strategy Areas: A Guidebook for Local
    Government*. United States Department of Housing and Urban Development,
    1978.
"Sniper Slays B'klyn Girl, 15." May 23, 1978, *New York Daily News*.
McCarthy, Rose. "Who's Killing East New York?: The Crumbs We Didn't Get."
    September 1978, *East New Yorker*.
McCarthy, Rose. "Who's Killing East New York?: The Great Insurance Ripoff."
    October 1978, *East New Yorker*.
Hamill, Pete. "Pine Street Is Burning Again—with Pride and Ambition." June 11,
    1979, *New York Daily News*.
Leff, Laurel. "Community Spirit: Local Groups That Aid Poor Flourish by Using
    Confrontation Tactics." March 13, 1981, *Wall Street Journal*.
Hevesi, Dennis. "East New York: A Neighborhood Reborn." June 10, 2001, *New
    York Times*.
Freedman, Samuel G. "Edward Chambers, Community Organizing's Unforgiving
    Hero." May 6, 2015, *New Yorker*.

East Brooklyn Churches November 1980 Progress Report to Friends of East Brooklyn Churches, from Rev. John Heinemeier, Chairman, EBC Sponsoring Committee, Industrial Areas Foundation records, 1977–2011.

Undated document titled "Briefing Sheet on EBC House Meetings," Industrial Areas Foundation records, 1977–2011.

Undated memo from East Brooklyn Churches to the American Baptist Church, re: An Application for a 3-year Grant of $25,000, Industrial Areas Foundation records, 1977–2011.

Undated document titled "Background and History 1980 Founding," Industrial Areas Foundation records, 1977–2011.

8. The FHA Scandal

Interviews with Anthony Accetta, Jack Blum, Jim Sniegocki, Jeffrey Kay, and Gale Drexler.

Moritz. "Group Seizes Vacant Homes to Protest—and Repair."

Herbers, John. "Senate Panel to Study Effects of Mortgage Policies on Blacks." August 15, 1971, *New York Daily News*.

Kaplan, Morris. "U.S. Investigating 600 Realty Deals." September 24, 1971, *New York Times*.

Memo from SAC, New York (147-2071) to Director, FBI (147-17035) Subject: Eastern Service Corporation; Ortrud Kapraki, FHAM, August 27, 1971, FBI Investigation Files 147-HQ-17035, NY 147-2071.

Competition in Real Estate and Mortgage Lending Hearings, Boston, September 13, 14, 15, 1971.

George Romney's December 9, 1971, testimony at the Federal Government's Role in the Achievement of Equal Opportunity Housing hearing before the House of Representatives Subcommittee no. 4 of the Committee on the Judiciary.

United States of America v. Bernstein et al. United States Court of Appeals, 533 F.2d 775 (1976).

9. The Destruction of East New York

Interviews with Sarita Daftary-Steel, Lucille Clark, Sarah Plowden, and Michael Gecan.

Kaye, Danny. "My Life in a Watermelon." January 12, 1958, *The Sunday Parade Magazine*.

Witbeck, Charles. "Vegas Hit by Danny; Now T.V." August 16, 1960, *Bergen Evening Record*.

Caldwell, Earl. "In the Forgotten Land, Walk Softly and Carry a Big Stick." December 12, 1979, *New York Daily News*.

Tucker, Arnold. "East New York—the Arson Capitol?" March 27, 1980, *East New Yorker*.

McCarthy, Rose. "The Making of a Fire-Trap." March 27, 1980, *East New Yorker*.

McCarthy, Rose. "Eulogy to a Brave Woman." March 27, 1980, *East New Yorker*.

McCarthy, Rose. "Demolition Delay Contributes to Fireman's Death." March 27, 1980, *East New Yorker*.

McCarthy, Rose. "Fulton Street Blaze Rekindled." April 30, 1980, *East New Yorker*.

Vasquez, Susan. "Rat Explosion." July 28, 1980, *East New Yorker*.

McCarthy, Rose. "Hard Times at Ideal Corporation." July 28, 1980, *East New Yorker*.

Newkirk, Pamela. "East New York Fires Called Suspicious." August 2, 1980, *New York Amsterdam News*.

McCarthy, Rose. "Hilton Rivera Gunned Down in Effort to Save Girl." December 1980, *East New Yorker*.

"Bank's $7 Billion Mortgage Portfolio Seized in Fraud Probe." June 21, 1989, *UPI Archives*.

9. The FHA Scandal

Interviews with Anthony Accetta, Jack Blum, Jim Sniegocki, Jeff Kay, and John Kennedy.

Boyer. *Cities Destroyed for Cash*.

Hirsch. "Less Than *Plessy*: The Inner City, Suburbs, and State-Sanctioned Residential Segregation in the Age of *Brown*."

Taylor. *Race for Profit*.

Saunders, D. J. "1st Indictment Hits Broker in Home Grabbing Scandal." November 19, 1971, *New York Daily News*.

Graham, Dillon. "Romney Doesn't Think U.S. Ready for Forcible Integration Approach." December 10, 1971, *The San Bernardino County Sun*.

Thelen Jr., G. C., for Associated Press. "Speculators Exploit Inner City Home Program." May 1, 1972, *Arizona Republic*.

FBI Investigation Files 147-HQ-17035, NY 147-2071.

10. The Destruction of East New York

Interviews with Lucille Clark, Sarah Plowden, Father Ed Mason, Michael Gecan, Carey Shea, and Milagros Martinez.

Freeman. *Upon This Rock*.

Gecan. *Going Public*.

Kaliff, Joe. "Shirley Chisholm Speaks Out on Reagan's Budget Cuts." February 28, 1981, *East New Yorker*.

Hertzberg, Daniel. "New York's Finances Improve—but at Cost of a Decline in Services." March 19, 1981, *Wall Street Journal*.

"Food Prices Higher." April 18, 1981, *New York Amsterdam News*.

Enriquez, Carmen. "Civilian Patrol (Anti-Crime) Unit Searching for New Recruits." June 1981, *East New Yorker*.

Copage, Eric V. "Rap Services, Cleanliness at 4 Food Stores." June 9, 1981, *New York Daily News*.

"Church Power Shakes Up Supermarkets." September 12, 1981, *New York Amsterdam News*.

Tood, George. "Brownsville Man Held for Rape Attempt." September 26, 1981, *New York Amsterdam News*.

Bird, David. "Shelter for Men Opened by City at Brooklyn Site." October 22, 1981, *New York Times*.

"Owens Attacks Quotas." November 7, 1981, *New York Amsterdam News*.

Jones, Angela. "Angry East New Yorkers Want 400 Derelicts Out." November 7, 1981, *New York Amsterdam News*.

Brown, Frank Dexter. "Homeless Shelter Sparks Fear, Spite." January 2, 1982, *New York Amsterdam News*.

Giordano, Mary Ann, Mike Santangelo, and Murray Weiss. "Killer Bludgeoned, Assaulted Boy." May 26, 1982, *New York Daily News*.

Santangelo, Mike. "Ask Public to Help Find Killer of Boy, 9." May 27, 1982, *New York Daily News*.

Jones, Angela. "'Home' Blamed." June 12, 1982, *New York Amsterdam News*.

Eisenberg, Ariel. "A Shelter Can Tip the Scales Sometimes: Disinvestment, Gentrification, and the Neighborhood Politics of Homelessness in 1980s New York City." *Journal of Urban History* 43, no. 6.

Eisenberg, Martin E. "Being Left in East New York: Tensions between Race and Class in Community Organizing, 1954–1980." Dissertation, City University of New York, 1999.

Shirley Chisholm Papers, Speeches 1971–1989, Rutgers Special Collections and University Archives.

10. The FHA Scandal

Interviews with Jim Sniegocki, Anthony Accetta, John Kennedy, Jeff Kay, and Jack Blum.

Barlett, Donald L., and James B. Steele, "An Anatomy of Failure: The Poor as Homeowners." February 27, 1972, *Washington Post*.

Flint, Jerry M. "Romney Says His Agency Can't Solve Housing Problem; Concedes Errors." March 28, 1972, *New York Times*.

"Ghetto Shakedown." April 10, 1972, *Time Magazine*.

An FBI document dated February 10, 1972, containing a report by Ronald D. Hodges and James E. Sniegocki of information obtained from Edward Goodwin's meeting with the Bernsteins, FBI Investigation Files 147-HQ-17035, NY 147-2071.

Memo from SAC, New York to Director FBI, subject: Eastern Service Corporation; et al, FHAM; Bribery, February 23, 1972, FBI Investigation Files 147-HQ-17035, NY 147-2071.

United States v. Fayer. 573 F.2d 741 (2d Cir. 1978).

11. The Destruction of East New York

Interview with Michael Gecan.

Duddy, James, and Neal Hirschfeld. "Homicide Record Set in City." January 1, 1982, *New York Daily News*.

Gargan, Edward A. "Couple Charged in Death of Boy, 5." April 12, 1982, *New York Times*.

"Churches to Rebuild East New York Slums." July 3, 1982, *New York Amsterdam News*.

Lewis, Errol T. "Police Break Child Sex Ring in Brooklyn." August 7, 1982, *New York Amsterdam News*.

Major, Brian. "East Brooklyn Churches Accepting Applications." August 28, 1982, *New York Amsterdam News*.

Treaster, Joseph. "Students Protest Weapons Search at Their School." November 11, 1982, *New York Times*.

Jones, Angela. "Search for Reasons in Search of Students." November 20, 1982, *New York Amsterdam News*.

Sleeper, Jim. "East Brooklyn's Second Rising." December 1982, *City Limits*.

Hornblower, Margot. "Homes, Hope Rising from N.Y. Rubble: Brooklyn Rebuilds on Work and Faith." July 12, 1985, *Washington Post*.

Deslippe, Dennis. "As in a Civics Text Come to Life: The East Brooklyn Congregations' Nehemiah Housing Plan and 'Citizens Power' in the 1980s." *Journal of Urban History* 45, no. 5 (2019).

New York City Police Department Annual Report 1985.

Undated East Brooklyn Congregations report titled "Background and History: 1980 Founding," Industrial Areas Foundation records, 1977–2011.

Memo to: Mayor Edward I. Koch, From: Bishop Francis J. Mugavero and East Brooklyn Churches, June 2, 1982, Industrial Areas Foundation records, 1977–2011.

IAF Report, The Nehemiah Transformation, The Metro IAF Community Restoration Fund.

11. The FHA Scandal

Interviews with Jim Sniegocki, Anthony Accetta, Jeff Kay, and John Fox.

Asbury, Edith Evans. "Dun & Bradstreet among 50 Named in Housing Fraud." March 30, 1972, *New York Times*.

Saunders, D. J., and Owen Moritz, "Indict 50 in Wide Slum Home Frauds." March 30, 1972, *New York Daily News*.

Asbury, Edith Evans. "New Curbs on Housing Fraud Cited." March 31, 1972, *New York Times*.

"Romney Admits HUD Errors in Solving Housing Problems." April 1, 1972, *The Indianapolis Recorder*.

Andelman, David A. "Hempstead F.H.A. Works to Improve City Houses, Scene of Appraisal Abuses." April 4, 1972, *New York Times*.

Herbers, John. "F.H.A. Overhaul Urged by Percy." April 25, 1972, *New York Times*.

Asbury, Edith Evans. "U.S. Senate Calls 9 from New York to Testify about Housing Programs." April 26, 1972, *New York Times*.

"Certain Crime Convictions Up." March 3, 1975, *Asbury Park Press*.

"G-Men Take Aim on White-Collar Crime." November 18, 1976, *Daily Record*.

McClaughry, John, and Senator Charles H. Percy. "The Troubled Dream: The Life and Times of Section 235 of the National Housing Act." *Loyola University Chicago Law Journal* 6, no. 1 (Winter 1975).

FBI Recommendation for Incentive Award for James E. Sniegocki, April 7, 1972, detailing the FHA investigation.

12. The Destruction of East New York

Interviews with Milagros Martinez, Jennifer Wynn, Derrick Parker, and Richard Recny.

Glueck and Gardner. *Brooklyn: People and Places*.

Greer, William R. "Squatters and City Battle for Abandoned Buildings." August 2, 1985, *New York Times*.

"State Senator and 3 Others Arrested at Squatters' Site." August 23, 1985, *New York Times*.

"City to Turn Over 59 Buildings to Residents." October 10, 1987, *New York Amsterdam News*.

Erlanger, Steven. "New York Turns Squatters into Homeowners." October 12, 1987, *New York Times*.

"Toxic Waste Won't Go Away, Asbestos in the Air—PCB in the Water." September 1984, *The Link*.

McFadden, Robert D. "10 in Brooklyn Are Found Slain Inside a House." April 16, 1984, *New York Times*.

Associated Press. "4th Slaying Suspect Charged." April 11, 1985, *New York Times*.

Statistical Report, Complaints and Arrests, Police Department of the City of New York, Office of Management Analysis, Crime Analysis Section, 1983.

National Affordable Housing Act: Hearings before the Subcommittee on Housing and Urban Affairs of the Committee on Banking, Housing, and Urban Affairs, United States Senate, September 14, 21, 22, and 28, 1988. Statement of Charles Kamasaki, Director of Policy Analysis, National Council of La Raza.

Property records showing owners and the mortgage history for the buildings in East New York was accessed from the Automated City Register Information System (ACRIS) run by New York City's Department of Finance.

Heldman, Kevin. *What the Hell Happened in East New York?* Podcast. https://podcasts.apple.com/us/podcast/what-the-hell-happened-in-east-newyork/id1100289915.

12. The FHA Scandal

Interviews with Jeff Kay, Anthony Accetta, and Jack Blum.

Romney, George. Address to HUD, March 6, 1972. Referenced in David E. Vanderburg, review of *The Unheavenly City: The Nature and Future of Our Urban Crises* by Edward C. Banfield. *Interfaces* 2, no. 4 (1972).

Competition in Real Estate and Mortgage Lending Hearings, May 1972.

Defaults on FHA-Insured Mortgages (Part 2), Hearings before a Subcommittee of the Committee on Government Operations, Testimony of George Romney, May 3, 1972.

13. The Destruction of East New York

Interviews with Vito Spano, Derrick Parker, Robert McHugh, Dennis Bootle, Ray Ferrari, Rev. Edward Mason, Michael Gecan, Ashmat Ali, and Milagros Martinez.

Fein, Esther B. "Many Youths, Fearing for Safety, Carry Weapons at City's High Schools." February 25, 1985, *New York Times*.

Anekwe, Simon. "Nehemiah Plan Draws Fire at Bd. of Estimate Hearing." March 1, 1986, *New York Amsterdam News*.

Dallas, Gus. "Nehemiah Plan: 2 Sides Trading Charges." March 10, 1986, *New York Daily News*.

McCallister, Jared. "The Crack Heard 'Round the City." May 11, 1986, *New York Daily News*.

Kappstatter, Bob. "Delivered to Cops, Ma Was at Crack House." August 25, 1986, *New York Daily News*.

Seaton, Charles. "Wrong Tip, but Arrests Still Made." October 10, 1986, *York Daily News*.

Jeffries, Ira. "Squatters Battling Nehemiah Project for Right to Land." October 20, 1990, *New York Amsterdam News*.

Robbins, Tom. "Nehemiah-City Deal Near." October 5, 1992, *New York Daily News*.

Yzaguirre, Raul, Laura Arce, and Charles Kamasaki. "The Fair Housing Act: A Latino Perspective." *Cityscape: A Journal of Policy Development and Research* 4, no. 3 (1999).

The City of New York, Commission to Investigate Allegations of Police Corruption and the Anti-Corruption Procedures of the Police Department (a.k.a. Mollen Commission Report) Exhibit Eight, "The Failure to Apprehend Michael Dowd: The Dowd Case Revisited." July 7, 1994.

Bristol, Carlos. Oral history interview conducted by Sarita Daftary-Steel, July 29, 2014, East New York oral histories 2014–2015. Call number: 2015.011.02, Brooklyn Historical Society.

13. The FHA Scandal

Interviews with Jack Blum, Anthony Accetta, and Jeff Kay.

Antevil, Jeffrey. "Poor Being Cheated by FHA, Senate Unit Told." May 2, 1972, *New York Daily News*.

Asbury, Edith Evans. "S.E.C. Suspends the Trading in Stock of Mortgage Banker." May 6, 1972, *New York Times*.

Herbers, John. "Federal Agencies Press Inquiry on Housing Frauds in Big Cities." May 8, 1972, *New York Times*.

Reinhold, Robert. "Congress Is Asked for Power to Fight Housing Bias." March 22, 1979, *New York Times*.

"*United States v. Miselis*: Fourth Circuit Finds the Anti-Riot Act Partially Unconstitutional." *Harvard Law Review* 134, no. 7 (May 2021).

Competition in Real Estate and Mortgage Lending Hearings, May 1972.

Erin Blakemore, "How the Black Panthers' Breakfast Program Both Inspired and Threatened the Government." January 29, 2021, History Network.

14. The Destruction of East New York

Interviews with Richard Recny, Carey Shea, Father Edward Mason, Michael Gecan, Maryanne Schretzman, Milagros Martinez, Ricardo Nelson, and Jennifer Wynn.

Thabit. *How East New York Became a Ghetto*.

"New York's Poor Need Permanent Housing—Not Temporary Shelters." March 1986, *The Link*.

Barrett, Carlton. "What Causes Children's Anti-Social Behavior." September 12, 1987, *New York Amsterdam News*.

Depalma, Anthony. "The Nehemiah Plan: A Success, But . . ." September 27, 1987, *New York Times*.

Santangelo, Mike, and Franklin Fisher, "Crack Dens Raided, Cops Act Uptown and in B'klyn." October 2, 1987, *New York Daily News*.

McAlary, Mike. "Brooklyn Crime, the 75th's Passion for Murder, a Day in the Life of the Deadliest Pct." November 4, 1987, *Newsday*.

Fleming, Robert, and Ruth Landa. "Classmate Shoots Girl, 13." February 5, 1988, *New York Daily News*.

Kurtz, Howard. "Group Fights Long Odds to Build Low-Cost Housing." August 2, 1988, *Washington Post*.

"Shelter Plan for People with AIDS Hurts Homeless and E.N.Y." November–December 1998, *The Link*.

Buntin, John. "The East New York Urban Youth Corps and Community Policing: The Community Security Initiative Gets Underway, Case No. C14-99-1529.0." Kennedy School of Government Case Program, Harvard University, March 1, 1999.

Deslippe. "As in a Civics Text Come to Life."

"A Bank Jobs Program Continues—Despite Controversy." *Ethikos* 1, no. 6 (May–June 1988).

Bristol, Carlos. Oral history interview conducted by Sarita Daftary-Steel, July 29, 2014, East New York oral histories 2014–2015. Call number: 2015.011.02, Brooklyn Historical Society.

"Community District Fact-At-A-Glance," Brooklyn District 5, City of New York, Department of City Planning, 1987.

East New York Urban Youth Corps Year End Report. December 5, 1989, Municipal Archives, Mayor David N. Dinkins records, Box 2.2.12.5, Folder 182, Local Development Corporation of East New York, 1990–1992.

Memo from: BL, To: Files, ML, SDS, August 4, 1987, regarding East New York Urban Youth Corps, Municipal Archives, Mayor David N. Dinkins records, Box 2.2.12.5, Folder 182, Local Development Corporation of East New York, 1990–1992.

Letter from Reverend Johnny Ray Youngblood to Mayor Ed Koch. August 4, 1988, Industrial Areas Foundation records, 1977–2011.

Taking Back the Block: Stories of Community Renaissance. Documentary, APL-Anderson Productions Ltd NYC, 2004.

The Seven Five. Documentary directed by Tiller Russell, 2014.

14. The FHA Scandal

Interviews with Anthony Accetta, Jeff Kay, George Bashion, and Ron DePetris.

Boyer. *Cities Destroyed for Cash*.

Herbers, John. "Federal Agencies Press Inquiry on Housing Frauds in Big Cities." May 8, 1972, *New York Times*.

"Broker Guilty in Housing Fraud." June 9, 1972, *Newsday*.

"He Gets Year in Fraud." August 16, 1972, *New York Daily News*.

Curtis-Olsen, Zane. "The FHA Scandal in Philadelphia and the Lessons of Federal Intervention in the Inner-City Housing Market (1967–72)." *Poverty and Race* 25, no. 2 (April–June 2016).

Letter from Stanley Sirote to Donald Carroll dated May 8, 1972, Exhibit 5 in Hearings before the Subcommittee on Antitrust and Monopoly of the Committee on the Judiciary, May 1972, New York.

United States v. Milton Berlin. 472 F.2d 1002 (2d Cir. 1973). Court of Appeals for the Second Circuit.

15. The Destruction of East New York

Interviews with Michael Gecan, Carey Shea, and Ricardo Nelson.

"Granite Is Set to Acquire Mortgage Bank Company." September 12, 1972, *New York Times*.

Lee, Felicia R. "East New York, Haunted by Crime, Fights for Its Life." January 5, 1989, *New York Times*.

Pitt, David E. "Seized as a Shield in Street Gunfight, Boy, 3, Is Wounded." February 2, 1989, *New York Times*.

"Crack and Crime Plague ENY, 'TNT' Can't Turn Tide." March–April 1989, *The Link*.

"Held in Slaying." July 24, 1989, *New York Daily News*.

"ENY Shelter Now a Jail." September–October 1989, *The Link*.

Fleming, Robert. "Slaying Terrifies Tenants." December 22, 1989, *New York Daily News*.

Tyre, Peg. "Woman, 79, Murdered in B'klyn." December 22, 1989, *Newsday*.

Goldman, Ari L. "Boy, 11, Killed by Stray Bullet on Visit to Aunt." December 25, 1989, *New York Times*.

Sennott, Charles M. "A Courtyard of Death at City Project." September 25, 1990, *New York Daily News*.

Rosario, Ruben. "Not Killer, Says Jury." October 13, 1990, *New York Daily News*.

Dwyer, Jim. "Judge Mollen's Freak Show." October 6, 1993, *New York Newsday*.

Southall, Ashley. "Once the 'Killing Fields,' East New York Has No Murders in 2018." April 20, 2018, *New York Times*.

Weaver, Vesla M. "Frontlash: Race and the Development of Punitive Crime Policy." *Studies in American Political Development* (Fall 2007).

August 21, 2001, memo from the Brooklyn Cold Case Squad to the Commanding Officer regarding the homicide investigation of Toya Turner, and an August 23, 2001, memo regarding the homicide of Antonio Valesquez.

East New York Urban Youth Corps Year End Report. December 5, 1989, Municipal Archives.

15. The FHA Scandal

Interviews with Jeff Kay, Anthony Accetta, and John Kennedy.

Boyer. *Cities Destroyed for Cash*.

Fried. *Housing Crisis U.S.A.*

Thabit. *How East New York Became a Ghetto*.

"HUD Resumes D&B Contracts." May 5, 1972, *The Record*.

Kranish, Michael. "Nixon, Romney Relationship Came to Frosty End." June 27, 2007, *Boston Globe*.

Andelman, David A. "F.H.A. Barring All Mortgages in Sections of Brooklyn and L.I." June 28, 1972, *New York Times*.

Morgan, Jeffrey. "Mortgage Delay in Federal Funding." August 1, 1972, *New York Newsday*.

"Romney: Nobody Will Let George Do It." August 20, 1972, *New York Times*.

Bonastia. "Hedging His Bets."

Joshua P. Fried quote accessed in "The Housing Mess." July 20, 1972, *Congressional Record—Senate*.

16. The Destruction of East New York

Interviews with Sister Margaret Smyth, Marlene Wilks, Joseph Herbert, and
    Milagros Martinez.
Taylor. *Race for Profit.*
Raftery, Thomas, and Don Singleton. "She's Thrown to Death." February 11, 1990,
    New York Daily News.
Farrell, Bill. "Rapist Charged in Slay." March 16, 1990, *New York Daily News.*
"'Shield the Children' Campaign Joins Owens and National Guard in Tour." April
    1990, *The Link.*
"High School Health Clinics Are a Necessity." April 1990, *The Link.*
"East New York Rallies for Safe Libraries." April 1990, *The Link.*
"East New York Speaks Out to Mayor's Representatives." June 1990, *The Link.*
Curry, Jack. "3 Weeks Later, a Victim Shot by 'Zodiac' Dies." June 25, 1990, *New
    York Times.*
Fleming, Robert, and Joseph McNamara. "B'klyn Tot-Tosser Hunted." July 3,
    1990, *New York Daily News.*
Sims, Calvin. "Homeless Man Is Charged in Tossing Boy to His Death." July 7,
    1990, *New York Times.*
"Girl Hit by Stray Bullet Dies in NYC Hospital." July 25, 1990, *Democrat and
    Chronicle.*
Slagle, Alton. "3 Shots and Greed Add Up to 3 Lives." July 27, 1990, *New York
    Daily News.*
Gearty, Robert. "Farewell, Veronica." July 30, 1990, *New York Daily News.*
Herbert, Bob. "In 'Terror Dome.'" September 25, 1990, *New York Daily News.*
"New York City Must Shield the Children." September–October 1990, *The Link.*
Marzulli, John, and Dick Sheridan. "Kids in Crossfire of the Gun Battle." April 1,
    1991, *New York Daily News.*
Marzulli, John. "Homicide Rate Isn't Letting Up." May 8, 1991, *New York Daily
    News.*
"He Gets 25 Years in Roof Rape and Slay." June 20, 1991, *New York Daily News.*
Deslippe. "As in a Civics Text Come to Life."
Rabinowitz, Richard. Oral history interview conducted by Sarita Daftary-Steel,
    December 8, 2014, Sarita Daftary-Steel collection of East New York oral
    histories, 2015.011.17, Brooklyn Historical Society.
"The New York Zodiac Copycat." In *Break in the Case,* podcast, season 3, New
    York City Police Department.

16. The FHA Scandal

Interviews with Jeff Kay and Anthony Accetta.
Bonastia. *Knocking on the Door.*
Boyer. *Cities Destroyed for Cash.*
Taylor. *Race for Profit.*

Hurewitz, Mike, and Vincent O'Brien. "FHA Scandal: Director Pleads Guilty to Bribery." September 27, 1972, *Long Island Press*.

Moritz, Owen. "Silence Surrounds Realty Case." September 28, 1972, *New York Daily News*.

Friedman, Josh, and George Carpozi Jr. "L. I. GOP Plum Went to FHA Bribe Figure." September 28, 1972, *New York Post*.

Asbury, Edith Evans. "F.H.A. Reshuffles Indicted L. I. Staff." September 28, 1972, *New York Times*.

Friedman, Josh. "Millions for Bribe Suspect." September 29, 1972, *New York Post*.

Braestrup, Peter. "Housing Official Faults HUD Dispersal Efforts." November 22, 1972, *Washington Post*.

"White House Said to Plan Freeze on Public Housing." December 23, 1972, *New York Times*.

Hearings on the Priorities and Economy in Government before the Joint Economic Committee, Congress of the United States, Ninety-Second Congress, December 4, 5, 7, 1972.

United States of America v. Bernstein et al. United States Court of Appeals, Second Circuit, 533 F.2d 775 (1976).

Criminal Docket 72-CR-587.

United States v. Bernhard Fein. 504 F.2d 1170 (2d Cir. 1974). Court of Appeals for the Second Circuit, October 15, 1974. Docket Number: 1121, Docket 74-1446.

17. The Destruction of East New York

Interviews with Sister Margaret Smyth, Bill Simon, Father Edward Mason, and John Kennedy.

Cobb, *The Essential Kerner Commission Report*.

Browne, J. Zamgba. "Golden Seeks to Scrap Lease of 'Unsafe' Day Care Center." January 26, 1991, *New York Amsterdam News*.

Sclafani, Tony, and Michele McPhee. "Mother's Anguish as 3rd Son Slain." September 21, 2004, *New York Daily News*.

"Murder Stats Mean Little to Brooklyn Mom." December 26, 2004, *Asbury Park Press*.

Hevesi, "East New York: A Neighborhood Reborn."

Mollen Commission Report, Exhibit Eight. "The Failure to Apprehend Michael Dowd: The Dowd Case Revisited."

July 17, 1991, testimony of Edward Muir, director, School Safety Department, United Federation of Teachers, at the Hearings before the Subcommittee on Crime and Criminal Justice of the Committee on the Judiciary, House of Representatives, Selected Crime Issues: Prevention and Punishment, Safe Schools.

NYPD case files for the Julia Parker homicide, 61# 15420.

17. The FHA Scandal

Interviews with Anthony Accetta and Jeff Kay.

Bonastia. *Knocking on the Door*.

Boyer. *Cities Destroyed For Cash*.

"Ex-Aide Confesses Guilt in FHA Mortgage Bribe." March 10, 1973, *New York Daily News*.

Rudin, Joel. "Judge: U.S. May Stop Dealing with Defendant." July 31, 1973, *Newsday*.

Chapman, William. "FHA Scandal Spreads across Nation." March 10, 1974, *Washington Post*.

"Federal Compensation for Victims of the 'Homeownership for the Poor Program.'" *The Yale Law Journal* 84, no. 2 (December 1974).

Haynes, Charles G. "Keeping HUD's House in Order." HUD Challenge, November 1973.

Foote, Joseph. "As They Saw It: HUD's Secretaries Reminisce about Carrying Out the Mission." U.S. Department of Housing and Urban Development, Office of Policy Development and Research. *Cityscape: A Journal of Policy Development and Research* 1, no. 3 (September 1995).

Federal Register, Part III, Department of Housing and Urban Development, Debarment, Suspension, and Ineligibility of Contractors and Grantees, December 13, 1976.

"HUD Blamed as Detroit Homes Rot," *Congressional Record* 122, part 6 (March 15, 1976, to March 23, 1976).

Richard Nixon's Radio Address about the State of the Union Message on Community Development, March 4, 1973.

18. The Destruction of East New York

Interviews with Ashmat Ali, Father Edward Mason, Michael Gecan, and Milagros Martinez.

Morgan, Jerry. "Pulse of Activity Is Fading at FHA." June 1, 1974, *Newsday*.

Marzulli, John. "Slain Man's Pal Talks to Cops, Is Killed." July 19, 1991, *New York Daily News*.

Marzulli, John. "Drug War Victim? Cops Probe Teen Mom's Slaying." July 20, 1991, *New York Daily News*.

McFadden, Robert D. "16-Year-Old Is Shot to Death in a High School in Brooklyn." November 26, 1991, *New York Times*.

Fullilove, Mindy Thompson, et al. "What Did Ian Tell God? School Violence in East New York." In Mark H. Moore et al., eds. *Deadly Lessons: Understanding Lethal School Violence*. National Research Council, 2003.

Deslippe, "As in a Civics Text Come to Life."

"Morbidity and Mortality Weekly Report." *CDC* 42, no. 40 (October 15, 1993).

FDNY Safety Operating Battalion, Investigative Report, Firefighter Fatality,
    September 12, 1991, Brooklyn, Box 22-1919, Fire at 495 Atkins Avenue.
NYPD case files for the Julia Parker homicide, 61# 15420.
East New York Projects Bulletin Board, Lost and Found, The ENY Projects Sign-
    up Page, 2000 Archives.

18. The FHA Scandal

Trump and Schwartz. *Trump: The Art of the Deal.*
"21,000 New York Apartments Bar Blacks." August 15, 1970, *New Journal and
    Guide.*
Kaplan, Morris. "Major Landlord Accused of Antiblack Bias in City." October 16,
    1973, *New York Times.*
Brodey, Jess. "Landlord Trump Retaliates, Sues U.S. for $100 Million." December
    13, 1973, *New York Daily News.*
Kappstatter, Robert. "Trump's Suit against U.S. Is Thrown Out by Judge." January
    26, 1974, *New York Daily News.*
"Realty Outfit Loses Suit for 100-Million." January 26, 1974, *New York Times.*
Moritz, Owen. "Accord Ends Bias Suit against Big Landlord." June 11, 1975, *New
    York Daily News.*
"Minorities Win Housing Suit." July 9, 1975, *New York Amsterdam News.*
Kranish, Michael, and Robert O'Harrow Jr. "Inside the Government's Racial Bias
    Case against Donald Trump's Company, and How He Fought It." January 23,
    2016, *Washington Post.*
Mahler, Jonathan, and Steve Eder. "'No Vacancies' for Blacks: How Donald Trump
    Got His Start, and Was First Accused of Bias." August 27, 2016, *New York Times.*
United States v. Fred C. Trump, Donald Trump, and Trump Management, Inc. New
    York Eastern District Court, Case No. 73-cv-01529.
*United States District Court for the Eastern District of New York v. Fred C. Trump,
    Donald Trump, and Trump Management, Inc.* Complaint for Injunction
    Pursuant to Fair Housing Act of 1968, 42 U.S.C. 3601, et seq.
United States v. Fred C. Trump, Donald Trump, and Trump Management, Inc.
    Consent Order, No. 73 C 1529, June 10, 1975.

19. The Destruction of East New York

Interviews with Mark Brooks, Joe Herbert, Denise Thomas, Michael Gecan, and
    Father Edward Mason.
Desmond. *Evicted: Poverty and Profit in the American City.*
Marzulli. "Slain Man's Pal Talks to Cops, Is Killed."
Hacker, Tom. "NYC Girl's Death Hits Home in Vt." January 6, 1992, *The
    Burlington Free Press.*
"Apprehended in Shootings Tied to a Grudge. Security Had Been Heavy for
    Dinkins' Arrival." February 27, 1992, *Los Angeles Times.*

Myers, Steven Lee. "Robbers Slay Vendor, 78, a Neighborhood Institution." March 21, 1992, *New York Times*.

Rodriguez, Yolanda. "Vendor's Determination Proved Fatal, Family Had Urged Robbery Victim, 77, to Retire." March 22, 1992, *Newsday*.

Polner, Rob, and James Rosen, "Tot Is Shot in Her Crib." June 4, 1992, *New York Daily News*.

Wolff, Craig. "Officer Took Drug Payoffs, U.S. Charges." July 31, 1992, *New York Times*.

Baillou, Charles. "Brooklyn Community Artist Lauded in Death." August 1, 1992, *New York Amsterdam News*.

Baillou, Charles. "Roger Green Leads a Crusade to Save Our Youth." August 29, 1992, *New York Amsterdam News*.

Mitchell, Alison. "On a Frontier of Hope, Building Homes for the Poor Proves Perilous." October 4, 1992, *New York Times*.

Dwyer, Jim. "New Leads Explored in Teenager's Killing." December 3, 2013, *New York Times*.

Dwyer, Jim. "After Nearly 23 Years of Legal Struggle, a Conviction Is Reversed." September 17, 2014, *New York Times*.

Rummell, Nick. "Men Claim NYPD Framed Them for Teen's Murder." December 15, 2015, *Courthouse News Service*.

"2 Students Slain as School Awaits N.Y. Mayor's Visit: Crime: Schoolmate is apprehended in shootings tied to a grudge. Security had been heavy for Dinkins' arrival." February 27, 1992, *Los Angeles Times*.

Maldonado, Samantha. "Oft Overlooked on Brooklyn-Queens Border, the Hole Shows Risks of Ignoring Environment." April 4, 2022, *The City*.

Goodman, Sarah, and Kyle Schnitzer. "Brooklyn Man Exonerated after 14 Years in Prison in Another Case Investigated by Crooked NYPD Detective." January 18, 2024, *New York Post*.

Neighborhood Land Disposition Plan, East New York / New Lots, New York Department of City Planning, Fall 1992.

Mollen Commission Report, Exhibit Eight, "The Failure to Apprehend Michael Dowd: The Dowd Case Revisited."

First Year Report of the East New York Planning Group, Issues and Opportunities in East New York: A Report on the Envisioning Forums and Recent Developments in East New York, 1996, Walter Thabit Collection.

The Seven Five. Documentary directed by Tiller Russell, 2014.

19. The FHA Scandal

Interviews with Anthony Accetta, Gale Drexler, Jim Sniegocki, and Jeff Kay.

Breasted, Mary. "Dunn Bradstreet Mortgage-Fund Trial Proceeding Slowly, but Proceeding." November 18, 1973, *New York Times*.

Priai, Frank J. "Suicide Note Left by Morse Says He Considered Taking His Life Many Years Ago." December 6, 1973, *New York Times*.

"Congressional Investigators Suspect U.S. Has Only Skimmed Surface in Uncovering Major Housing Frauds." December 13, 1973, *New York Times*.

Bender, Judith. "Resounding Conclusion to FHA Case." July 10, 1974, *Newsday*.

United States of America v. Harry Bernstein, Rose Bernstein, Eastern Service Corporation. United States Court of Appeals, 74-2328, 74-2462, 74-2463, 74-2464 (1975).

United States Court of Appeals for the Second Circuit, Brief of Appellants Harry Bernstein, Rose Bernstein, and Eastern Corporation, Docket No. 64-2328, New York Law Institute.

20. The Destruction of East New York

Interviews with Michael Race, Mark Brooks, Joseph Herbert, Wendell Stradford, Dr. Joyce Y. Hall, and Milagros Martinez. The CompStat section was based in part from interviews with former NYPD Chief of Department Louis Anemone, former Deputy Commissioner of Operations Edward T. Norris, former Deputy Inspector Ray Ferrari, former Miami Police Commissioner John Timoney, and former Deputy Inspector Vito Spano, for my book *The Restless Sleep*.

Lardner and Reppetto. *NYPD: A City and Its Police*.

Ramsey. *When Crack Was King: A People's History of a Misunderstood Era*.

"Town Meeting Will Explore Health Care Proposals." February 1993, *The Link*.

Dwyer, "Judge Mollen's Freak Show."

Dugger, Celia W. "Youthful, Impressionable and Accused of Murder." May 17, 1994, *New York Times*.

Hevesi, Dennis. "Cuomo Recommends a Crime-Fighting Program for East New York." December 29, 1993, *New York Times*.

"Friend of Woman Set on Fire Sought." May 31, 1994, *Star-Gazette*.

Oliver, Chris. "Torched Mom Dies as Suspect Hunted." May 31, 1994, *New York Daily News*.

O'Shaugnessy, Patrice. "NYPD Eyes Dozens of 'Solved' Homicides, Police Say Ex-Cop's Cases Questionable." August 5, 2001, *New York Daily News*.

Sharkey, Patrick, Gerard Torrats-Espinosa, and Delaram Takyar. "Community and the Crime Decline: The Causal Effect of Local Non-Profits on Violent Crime." *Sociological Review* 82 no. 6 (October 2017).

Golub, Andrew Lang, and Bruce D. Johnson. "Crack's Decline: Some Surprises across U.S. Cities." National Institute of Justice, Research in Brief (July 1997).

Executive Director to East New York Urban Youth Corps Martin Dunn's February 22, 1996, testimony in the Crime and Community Opportunity hearing before the Subcommittee on Housing and Community Opportunity of the Committee on Banking and Financial Services.

September 29, 1993, letter to Chief Justice Milton Mollen from Father Brendan Buckley, Industrial Areas Foundation records, 1977–2011, Columbia University Rare Book and Manuscript Library.

Maternity Center Association records, 1907–2010. Columbia University, Augustus Long Health Sciences Library.

Professor Bernard E. Harcourt, in a March 30, 2015, talk at Columbia Law School.

"New York Zodiac Copycat: Return of the Zodiac." In *Break in the Case*, podcast, season 3, ep. 3, New York City Police Department.

20. The FHA Scandal

Interviews with Anthony Accetta and Gale Drexler.

Chapman, William. "FHA Scandals Spread across Nation." March 10, 1974, *Washington Post*.

"Looking Ahead: Improved Minimum Property Standards." April 1974, *HUD Challenge*.

Bernstein v. Travia. No. 1078, Docket 74-1456, decided April 15, 1974. Abraham H. Brodsky, New York City, for petitioner. Anthony T. Accetta, Asst. U.S. Atty. (Edward John Boyd, V, Acting U.S. Atty., D. N.Y., of counsel), for respondent. Petition from the United States District Judge for the Eastern District of New York before Kaufman, Chief Judge; Clark, Associate Justice; and Smith, Circuit Judge.

United States of America v. Harry Bernstein, Rose Bernstein, Eastern Service Corporation. United States Court of Appeals, 74-2328, 74-2462, 74-2463, 74-2464 (1975), Criminal Docket 72-CR-587.

21. The Destruction of East New York

Interviews with Mel Grizer, Sarita Daftary-Steel, Carey Shea, and Joe Herbert.

Bloomberg News, "S.E.C. Budget to be Trimmed." August 18, 1994, *New York Times*.

White, Andrew. "Spark the Fire." November 1995, *City Limits*.

Kershaw, Sarah. "Neighborhood Report: East New York; New Plan for Power / Old Unease." June 16, 1996, *New York Times*.

Kleinfield, N. R. "The Trail of 'The Zodiac': The Overview; Police Say Zodiac Suspect Admits Attacks That Killed 3 and Hurt 5." June 20, 1996, *New York Times*.

Sengupta, Somini. "Sparks Fly, and Plan for a Power Generator Fizzles out, Community Wins Incinerator Fight." September 29, 1996, *New York Times*.

Toy, Vivian S. "Man Said to Be Zodiac Killer Becomes Enraged at Trial." May 15, 1998, *New York Times*.

Godsil, Rachel. "The Streets, the Courts, the Legislature and the Press: Where Environmental Struggles Happen." *Poverty and Race Journal* 5, no. 3 (May–June 1996).

White-Collar Crime: The Problem and The Federal Response, Subcommittee on Crime of the Committee on the Judiciary, June 1978, quoting the American

Bar Association, Section of Criminal Justice. Committee on Economic Offenses, Washington, American Bar Association, March 1977.

Executive Director to East New York Urban Youth Corps Martin Dunn's February 22, 1996, testimony in the Crime and Community Opportunity hearing before the Subcommittee on Housing and Community Opportunity of the Committee on Banking and Financial Services.

Wilson. "The Changing FBI: The Road to Abscam."

Morgenthau, Robert M. "Equal Justice and the Problem of White-Collar Crime." The Conference Board, August 1969.

Federal Bureau of Investigation Budget, 1975–2003, from the Department of Justice Website.

"Rise in Negro Commitments N.Y.C.'s Correctional Institutions." Department of Correction of New York City Annual Report, 1941.

Howard Golden, Brooklyn Borough President, to Ms. Marilyn Gelber, Commissioner, Department of Environmental Protection, August 10, 1995, Industrial Areas Foundation records, 1977–2011.

East New York Planning Council General Meeting Minutes, Meeting of September 17, 1995, Walter Thabit Collection.

First Year Report of the East New York Planning Group, Issues and Opportunities in East New York: A Report on the Envision Forums and Recent Developments in East New York, 1996, Walter Thabit Collection.

Winston, Perry. Interview in "Asset Mapping," in *Urban Agriculture: East New York*, documentary. Produced by Urban Omnibus.

Hung, Yvonne. "East New York Farms: Youth Participation in Community Development and Urban Agriculture." *Children, Youth and Environments* 14, no. 1, Collected Papers (2004).

Letter from Mayor Ed Koch to Bishop Francis J. Mugavero, May 17, 1989. Industrial Areas Foundation records, 1977–2011.

"New York Zodiac Copycat: East New York Chaos." In *Break in the Case*, podcast, season 3, ep. 4, New York City Police Department.

"The Riot Report," directed by Michelle Ferrari, 2024.

21. The FHA Scandal

Interviews with Anthony Accetta and Jeff Kay.

Asbury, Edith Evans. "F.H.A. Fraud Trial Hears Summation." May 21, 1974, *New York Times*.

Kappstatter, Robert. "Jury Finds 4 Guilty in Mortgage Fraud Costing U.S. 200M." June 26, 1974, *New York Daily News*.

"Tenement Fire Displaces 12," July 2, 1974, *New York Times*.

Bender. "Resounding Conclusion to FHA Case."

Breasted, Mary. "Defendant Who Aided U.S. in F.H.A. Case Sentenced." September 28, 1974, *New York Times*.

Bonastia. "Hedging His Bets."

Criminal Docket 72-CR-587 (and related cases).

United States of America v. Harry Bernstein, Rose Bernstein, Eastern Service Corporation. United States Court of Appeals, 74-2328, 74-2462, 74-2463, 74-2464 (1975).

United States Court of Appeals for the Second Circuit, Appellants Appendix, Docket Nos. 74-2328 et al., *United States of America v. Harry Bernstein et al.*

Montgomery, Isaiah. Oral history interview conducted by Sarita Daftary-Steel, June 20, 2014, Sarita Daftary-Steel collection of East New York oral histories, 2015.011.15, Brooklyn Historical Society.

Richardson, Toni. Oral history interview conducted by Sarita Daftary-Steel, February 6, 2015, Sarita Daftary-Steel collection of East New York oral histories, 2015.011.18, Brooklyn Historical Society.

22. The Destruction of East New York

Interviews with William Simon, Al Nesbot, Joseph Hall, and Joe Herbert. The history of the Cold Case Squad is based on previous interviews with Louis Anemone, Edward T. Norris, Ray Ferrari, John Timoney, and Vito Spano, for my book *The Restless Sleep*.

Marzulli, John. "New Elite Unit Draws Fire." January 17, 1996, *New York Daily News*.

NYPD case files for the Julia Parker homicide, 61# 15420.

22. The FHA Scandal

Interviews with Anthony Accetta, Gale Drexler, John Kennedy, and George Graff.

"Defendant Denied the Presumption of Innocence Here." August 5, 1973, *New York Times*.

"Certain Crime Convictions Up." March 3, 1975, *Asbury Park Press*.

Ain, Stewart. "Gets 4 Months on Fraud Conspiracy." June 19, 1976, *New York Daily News*.

Bliss, George, and Chuck Neubauer. "FHA Wastes 4 Billion and Creates City Slums." June 22, 1975, *Chicago Tribune*.

Raab, Selwyn. "U.S. Attorney Calls F.B.I. 'Out of Step.'" July 4, 1976, *New York Times*.

Ingrassia, Michele. "Dun & Bradstreet Accused of Fraud." July 30, 1976, *Newsday*.

"G-Men Take Aim on White-Collar Crime." November 18, 1976, *Daily Record*, Morris County, NJ.

Seigel, Max H. "Judge Cuts Sentences of Couple in Housing Fraud of $200 Million." January 11, 1977, *New York Times*.

Marro, Anthony. "Suit on Alleged Housing Fraud Settled." May 17, 1978, *New York Times*.

Brown, Warren. "Defaulted Mortgages Piling Up at HUD." October 6, 1979, *Washington Post*.

Wilson, "The Changing FBI: The Road to Abscam."

Mortgage Servicing and HUD Property Management, Hearings before the Subcommittee of the Committee on Government Operations, statement of James Robinson, attorney, General Crimes Section, Criminal Division, Department of Justice, September 25, 1975, Manpower and Housing Subcommittee, Washington, DC.

Continental Management, Inc. v. United States. 527 F.2d 613 (Fed. Cir. 1975) Decided December 17, 1975.

Jankowitz v. United States. 533 F.2d 538 (Ct. Cl. 1976), April 14, 1976.

United States of America v. Harry Bernstein, Rose Bernstein, Eastern Service Corporation. United States Court of Appeals, 74-2328, 74-2462, 74-2463, 74-2464 (1975).

United States of America v. Bernstein et al. United States Court of Appeals, 533 F.2d 775 (1976).

Criminal Docket 72-CR-587.

Krohn v. Frommann (In re Frommann). 153 B.R. 113 (1993), April 12, 1993. United States Bankruptcy Court for the Eastern District of New York. Bankruptcy No. 190-11854-260; Adv. No. 191-1055-260.

153 B.R. 113, In "re Anne Frommann, a/k/a Ortrud Kapraki, a/k/a Ortrud Frommann, Debtor."

Crimes against Business, a Management Perspective, Proceeding of Seminars Held in New York, New York. September 14, 1976, Panel Discussion Moderated by Thomas C. Rooney, statements of Robert B. Fiske Jr., U.S. Attorney Southern District.

Thabit, Walter. "East New York Revisited (March 1976)." Walter Thabit Collection.

Epilogue

Interviews with Jeff Kay, Anthony Accetta, Alia Thabit, Derrick Parker, Robert McHugh, Dennis Bootle, Ray Ferrari, Wendell Stradford, Michael Gecan, and Milagros Martinez.

Desmond. *Poverty, by America*.

"Bank's $7 Billion Mortgage Portfolio Seized in Fraud Probe." June 21, 1989, *UPI Archives*.

Quint, Michael. "A Bank in Long Island Taken Over by F.D.I.C." June 22, 1989, *New York Times*.

Johnston, David. "Radical Rehab; There's Far to Go In Cleaning Up the H.U.D. Mess." August 13, 1989, *New York Times*.

Margolies, Jane. "Does This Brooklyn Housing Development Know the Secret to Long Life?" July 28, 2023, *New York Times*.

Howard, Hilary. "Snakes, Spores, and Sewage: Life in the Neighborhood Called 'The Hole.'" December 17, 2023, *New York Times*.

Urban Agriculture: East New York, documentary. Produced by Urban Omnibus.

Dyck, Alexander, Adair Morse, and Luigi Zingales. "How Pervasive Is Corporate Fraud?" George J. Stigler Center for the Study of the Economy and the State working paper no. 327, 2023.

Fulmer, Ann. "Burning Down the House: Mortgage Fraud and the Destruction of Residential Neighborhoods." U.S. Department of Justice, 2010.

FDIC v. Bernstein. Civil Docket for Case #: 9:89-CV-02080-JM, filed June 22, 1989, terminated September 19, 1997.

USA v. Bernstein. Criminal Docket for Case #: 9:92-CR-0318-JM-1, filed March 16, 1992, terminated November 23, 1993.

Federal Deposit Ins. Corp. v. Bernstein. 944 F.2d 101 (2d Cir. 1991), No. 1191, Docket 94-6315, Decided September 11, 1991.

East New York foreclosure rates from The NYU Furman Center for Real Estate and Urban Policy.

"Private Opulence, Public Squalor: How the U.S. Helps the Rich and Hurts the Poor." In *Fresh Air*, NPR, podcast. March 21, 2023.

FHA Annual Report to Congress Regarding the Financial Status of the Federal Housing Administration Mutual Mortgage Insurance Fund, Fiscal Year 2023.

INDEX

Prescott, Arthur, 4, 99, 130, 227, 251
Proce, Joseph, 192

Rabinowitz, Richard, 38, 190
Race, Michael, 2, 145, 218, 223, 273
Racket Squad, 64
Ramirez, Elizabeth, 144
Recny, Richard
  as LDCENY director, 160, 163
  replacement for, 178
redlining, 12–13, 22
  FHA's history of, 16, 31
  illegality of, 22
  of inner cities by FHA, 16
  by insurance companies, 91
  opposite of, 29–30
  return of, 181
Rivera, Frank, 2, 10, 22, 33
Rivera, Hilton, 104
Rivera, Lydia, 103
Rivera, Michael, 232
Robbins, I. D., 124, 213
Robinson, James, 267
Romney, George, 157, 207
  announcement of Operation
    Breakthrough by, 56
  attempt to halt Nixon's plans by, 199
  disillusionment of, 111
  as HUD secretary, 37
  Nixon's problem with, 54
  as secretary of Housing and Urban
    Development, 4
  speech to Economic Club of Detroit
    by, 121
  statement about the federal
    government by, 276
  tensions between Nixon and, 183
Rosenbaum, Stephen, as president,
  Springfield Equities, 4, 267
Rosenberg, Julius and Ethel, 216
Roth, Bernard, as president, United
  Institutional Servicing Corporation,
  4, 169
Rusnak, Kevin, 57

Santiago, Josephine, 99
SARs. *See* suspicious activity reports
Scarcella, Louis N., 222
Schoonmaker, Aley, 246

Schretzman, Maryanne, 178
Securities and Exchange Commission
  (SEC)
  budget of (slashing of), 243
  number of cases published by, 241
  suspension lifted by, 185
  suspension of trading of Inter-Island
    Mortgage Corporation stock, 155
Seidman, Irving, 64
Senate hearings
  Antitrust and Monopoly
    Subcommittee hearing, 133
  on Crime and Community
    Opportunity, 235
  expert testimony from (1970), 50
  Hart's announcement of hearings to be
    conducted, 121, 133
  Lomenzo's testimony during, 227
  usefulness to the FBI, 143
  Vogel's statement during, 156
  witnesses scheduled to testify during,
    151
Senate Subcommittee on Antitrust and
  Monopoly, 2
Seven-Five
  as A house, 234
  "catching team" of, 221
  claims of brutality from, 148
  clearance rates of, 177, 273
  crack house found by, 145–146
  crime within, 147–148
  as deadliest precinct in the country, 163
  Dowd as police officer at, 1
  Dunne as commanding officer of, 213
  Herbert's memory of, 248
  joke made at, 138–139
  letter received from New York Zodiac,
    192
  list of unsolved homicides, 114
  Maher as detective retired from, 83
  number of abandoned buildings
    according to, 32
  number of cops on patrol increased at,
    188
  Palm Sunday call to detective squad
    of, 138
  Parker as former detective from, 137
  pool taken at, 218
  Race as detective sergeant at, 2

ranking of, 137
statement allegedly made at, 230
transfer of Dowd to, 137
undermining of detectives' efforts at, 222
Shea, Carey, 2, 159–161, 165, 223, 247
Shearman & Sterling, 53
Simon, William, 2, 257, 261
Sirote, Stanley
bribery of Lama by, 184
FBI investigation of, 133
flipping of, 195
letter to Carroll written by, 168–169
meeting between Carroll and, 168
negotiations between Granite
Management Services Inc. and, 182
as president of Inter-Island Mortgage
Corporation, 4, 143, 195
refusal to testify by, 154, 168
60 Minutes, 75
Smyth, Sister Margaret, 2, 175, 186
Sniegocki, Jim
frustration of, 129
rage of, 89
as special agent, FBI, 4, 78, 80, 90, 97
transfer of, 170, 275
Southern Christian Leadership
Conference, 271
Southern District of New York, 253
comparison of Eastern District and, 52
Obermaier as United States attorney
for, 51, 195, 222
sibling rivalry between Eastern District
of New York and, 51
Spitzer, Eliot, 274
SPONGE, 7–9, 10, 127
Sporleder, James, 153
Springfield Equities Ltd., 36, 108
investigation of, 195
Rosenbaum as president of, 4, 267
Stanley-Van Siclen Merchants
Association, 189
Stapley, Delbert, 38
Starr, Roger, 71–73
State of the Cities, The, 48
Steedly, Michael, 187
Sternlieb, George, 112
St. John Cantius Church, 1, 2, 175, 178, 203

St. Michael's church, 73
St. Paul Community Baptist Church, 2, 93, 188
subprime mortgage crisis, America's first, 40–41
suspicious activity reports (SARs), 242

Tactical Narcotics Team (TNT) program, 178
tax evasion, 242, 275
Taylor, Laykama, 186, 188
Tenement Area South, 70
Thabit, Walter, 13, 84
background on, 272
as city planner, 2, 97
implementation of Vest Pocket
program by, 160
involvement with Model Cities
program, 43
number of abandoned buildings tallied
by, 32
as planner for New York's Landmarks
Preservation Commission, 272
Thomas, Denise, 222
Thomas Jefferson High School, 12, 24, 123, 144, 176, 203, 219, 258
Thurmond, Strom, 150
Timoney, John, 234
TNT program. *See* Tactical Narcotics
Team program
Torsney, Robert, 81–82, 126
Trager, David, as United States attorney,
Eastern District of New York, 4, 18, 228, 252, 265, 269
Travia, Anthony J.
as judge, Eastern District of New York, 4, 18, 208
retirement of, 226
statement of, 252
Trimboli, Joseph, 167, 222
Trump, Donald, 60, 215
Trump, Fred C., 60, 215
Trump Management, Inc., 60, 214–216
Turner, Paris, 114
Turner, Toya, 176

Underwood, Jacob, 114
United Community Centers (UCC), 92
director of, 1, 190